Volume 18

DIRECTORY OF
WORLD CINEMA
TURKEY

Edited by Eylem Atakav

intellect Bristol, UK / Chicago, USA

First Published in the UK in 2013 by Intellect, The Mill, Parnall Road, Fishponds, Bristol, BS16 3JG, UK

First published in the USA in 2013 by Intellect, The University of Chicago Press, 1427 E. 60th Street, Chicago, IL 60637, USA

A catalogue record for this book is available from the British Library.

Publisher: May Yao
Publishing Manager: Melanie Marshall

Cover image credit/caption: [Max Productions/The Kobal Collection]

Cover Design: Holly Rose
Copy Editor: Heather Owen
Typesetting: User design, UK

Directory of World Cinema ISSN 2040-7971
Directory of World Cinema eISSN 2040-798X

Directory of World Cinema: Turkey ISBN 978-1-84150-620-3
Directory of World Cinema: Turkey ePDF 978-1-78320-121-1
Directory of World Cinema: Turkey ePUB 978-1-78320-122-8

Printed and bound by Gomer, UK

DIRECTORY OF WORLD CINEMA
TURKEY

CONTENTS

ACKNOWLEDGEMENTS

a

Directory of World Cinema: Turkey is the outcome of the collective enthusiasm of scholars from around the world whose work is dedicated to the cinema of Turkey. It is also a volume that welcomes diversity, not only in terms of the array of genres, directors and films discussed but also as a result of the plurality of approaches, writing styles and insightful analysis of the contributors. I would therefore like to thank all the contributors who have generously and with great enthusiasm put their time and intellect into this project. I am indebted to Su Holmes (who now knows more Turkish words than ever before) for the amazing editorial support and her generosity. I am also particularly grateful to certain friends and colleagues whose conversations, suggestions and academic support have helped me more than they might have guessed. So, my heartfelt thanks to: Melanie Williams, Iain Robert Smith, Özlem Köksal, Ruken Öztürk and Murat Akser. A big thank you must go to Melanie Marshall, May Yao and Heather Owen for their amazing editorial support and patience. And, finally, the book would not have been possible without the understanding and encouragement of Kris Glover, Gülnihal Atakav and Nabi Atakav.

I would like to dedicate this volume to one film, *Sevmek Zamanı (Time to Love)*, and to the memories of two great artists: Metin Erksan (1929-2012) and Müşfik Kenter (1932-2012).

Eylem Atakav

INTRODUCTION

Scholarship on the cinema of Turkey has recently become a popular area of academic scrutiny. An increasing number of volumes (Akser, 2010; Arslan, 2011; Bayrakdar, 2009; Dönmez-Colin, 2008; Suner, 2010) in this field have been published in English. Although there are other volumes on Turkish cinema, these texts have not yet been translated from Turkish, and there remains much ground to be covered. What is known as 'Turkish' cinema or the cinema of Turkey outside Turkey is not, typically, identical to what is commercially successful *in* Turkey. This may well be the case, of course, for many national cinema cultures, given the often fraught relationship between commercial and critical success. The reviews demonstrate the plurality of cultures, religious and ethnic backgrounds in the history of cinema in Turkey. Some films do not travel well, as they pivot on culturally-specific topics and culturally-specific humour. As such, this volume seeks to bring together a wide range of films, which have enjoyed varying degrees of national and international visibility, and making them accessible to an international audience.

Directory of World Cinema: Turkey critically reflects on the industrial, social, cultural and political contexts within which film texts of Turkey are produced, exhibited and circulated. The volume is structured under different categories: the film of the year, festival focus, the cinematic city, directors, stars, industry spotlight, early cinema, fantasy and science fiction films, women's films, blockbusters, drama and transnational cinema. It is inevitable that these categories are slippery and porous, so the films discussed throughout these chapters can easily fit into more than one category. The volume provides an insight into the cinema of Turkey from early years to contemporary examples. It encompasses a range of different approaches including socio-political, industrial, aesthetic and contextual. Each section opens with an introductory essay, which aims to provide a context for the films/texts discussed. Each review provides a synopsis of the film as well as a critique, which offers the reader the reviewer's take on and value judgment of the film. Collectively, these evaluative summaries demonstrate a particular knowledge of the film's period, genre, director, narrative, characters, cultural significance and place in the cinema industry. Therefore, the volume analyses a range of the cinema of Turkey – through a discussion of a variety of political, social, cultural, and industrial aspects of films and genres. Of course, no volume can be exhaustive and there are, necessarily, many films, directors, stars and movements (including, for instance, the films of Zeki Demirkubuz, recent romantic comedies, horror, police dramas; Kemal Sunal and Adile Naşit) omitted here, some of which will appear in the next volume.

Films *represent* and *refract* aspects of reality with regard to the national culture from which they emerge. As these terms suggest, this is not a process of reflection, and nor is this image complete. Thus, the image of Turkish cinema that emerges from this volume can be conceptualized as a mosaic: each piece has its own story to tell which is significant in its own right. Whatever journey the reader takes through the volume, I hope that it is one structured by explorations, interconnections and new discoveries.

Eylem Atakav

Once Upon a Time in Anatolia, 2011, Nuri Bilge Ceylan © NBC Films.

FILM OF THE YEAR
ONCE UPON A TIME IN ANATOLIA

Once Upon a Time in Anatolia

Bir Zamanlar Anadolu'da

Studios:
Zeyno Film
Tiglon

Director:
Nuri Bilge Ceylan

Producers:
Zeynep Özbatur
Nuri Bilge Ceylan

Screenwriters:
Nuri Bilge Ceylan
Ercan Kesal
Ebru Ceylan

Cinematographer:
Gökhan Tiryaki

Art Director:
Dilek Yapkuöz Ayaztuna

Composer:
Erkan Altınok

Editors:
Nuri Bilge Ceylan
Bora Gökşingöl

Duration:
157 Minutes

Cast:
Muhammet Uzuner
Taner Birsel
Yılmaz Erdoğan
Fırat Tanış
Ahmet Mümtaz Taylan

Year:
2012

Nuri Bilge Ceylan's *Once Upon a Time in Anatolia* opens with a scene in which the truth is buried; it is there in front of us but hidden. The first thing we see is an image that is shot from outside a dirty window. The camera remains outside, but the faces behind the window slowly become visible: three men are having drinks inside a car-mechanic's workshop. We are left outside, the sound is distant, and the image is blurry. A truck passes by and wipes out the image. This was it; that is when it happened. Shortly after this scene, we learn that one of those men was killed by one of the other two. The following image is darkness in an open field: a ball of fire is coming towards us, one that burns the screen. Ever experienced being hypnotized while watching the flames? That is the fire approaching.

Co-winner of the Grand Prix award at the Cannes Film Festival this year (sharing the award with Dardenne Brothers' *Le Gamin au Vélo*), *Once Upon a Time* is a witty and poetic film, and possibly Ceylan's best yet. In addition to his breathtaking imagery and poetic sequences, the film has an immaculate sound design. It is also bolder and braver than his previous films, both aesthetically and narratively. This bold attitude extends to his casting choices as well, where one name in particular stands out: Yılmaz Erdoğan, who plays the police chief in the film. Casting Erdoğan, who is an established film-maker and a huge comedy star in Turkey, seemed like a brave move for Ceylan, but a worrying one as well. Considering Erdoğan's popularity in the country, his presence ran the risk of overtaking the film. However, within the first ten minutes, this fear proves to be unfounded. Every single performance, including Erdoğan's, is no less than brilliant.

The plot is simple: a murder takes place in a remote town in Anatolia and an investigation is underway. Loosely based on a true story, the film unfolds over a long night, going into the early hours of the next day, in a small town in the Kırıkkale province. The prosecutor, Nusret (Taner Birsel); the doctor, Cemal (Muhammet Uzuner); the police chief, Naci (Yılmaz Erdoğan); the driver, nicknamed Arap (Ahmet Mümtaz Taylan); the police officer, İzzet (Murat Kılıç); and the murder suspects, Kenan (Fırat Tanış) and his brother Ramazan (Burhan Yıldız), along with a few others, are travelling in three vehicles to locate the body of a young man (Erol Eraslan) who has been murdered. Kenan has apparently confessed to the murder and told the police that he can show them where he buried the body. But ironically, he fails to do so the first few times and is unable to find the exact location. 'These places all look similar', he says, adding that he had too much to drink that day and that the darkness does not help.

As the three cars travel, there are flashes of lightning, momentarily highlighting an aspect in each character's life, the scars they acquired, the pain they inflicted: the remains of the past do not remain in the past. It is during this journey that one of the most poetic scenes in the film takes place: an apple falls from a tree and the camera follows its journey. The apple, unhurriedly, rolls down, drops into the stream and, after a short journey in the water, joins other apples that apparently have been through the exact same journey, but are now rotting. Time in this scene becomes almost tactile. Death is inevitable, and life seems to be flowing, but what about everything else in between? The lies, the heart-breaks, the suppression, the ugliness? Why does even a mundane conversation about buffalo yogurt become a power struggle?

Many critics writing about the film have commented about its length: spreading over 157 minutes, the film is undoubtedly long. In a question and answer session after the film's screening at the London Film Festival this year, Ceylan said that he wanted his audience to be bored a little, like his characters were. I can safely say that he failed in that task. During this long gaze over a small town you are left with yourself – that is, you watch the film as yourself, since the director does not provide any of the mechanisms that would allow the audience to identify with one of the characters. Now, to be left alone with yourself for 157 minutes is very long for the faint-minded, for most of us in fact. But Ceylan's visual poetry, along with his affectionate attention to the mundane details of life, takes you on a journey.

Boredom is not necessarily the right word to describe this type of storytelling, at least not in the usual sense of the word, as used in order to describe uninteresting or unworthy activities/experiences. Perhaps it is the kind of boredom that Walter Benjamin defined as 'the apogee of mental relaxation'. Boredom, he said, is 'the dream bird that hatches the egg of experience'. Benjamin writes these words in relation to a particular (and rapidly disappearing) mode of storytelling and listening. In the same paragraph, he also says that, in that relaxed state, the listener (or in our case, the viewer) also needs to forget him/herself in order for the story to become memorable, to be turned into an experience. This might seem to contradict what I just said about being left with yourself; however, it is the self that goes through that experience and, hence, the self continues to be present. What is important here, I believe, is the rhythm of the self, which is replaced by the rhythm of the story. This is not an easy task, but it is one that Ceylan succeeds in achieving.

On the other hand, to those familiar with his work, a murder mystery might at first appear to be an odd addition to Ceylan's filmography. However, it seems to me that he finally found a way to do what he wanted to do in his 2002 film *Distant*, also awarded the Grand Prix at Cannes. Ceylan, when talking about *Distant*, described shooting a scene where the two main characters kill a neighbour and become partners in crime and guilt. But he later decided to cut the scene out, as he feared it would become the central story, something that he did not want. In *Once Upon A Time in Anatolia*, the murder is the centre of the story, but this, ironically, gives him a narrative space to gaze over the 'side' stories. It is not a coincidence that Ceylan's official web site contains the following in lieu of a synopsis of the film: 'Life in a small town is akin to journeying in the middle of the steppes: the sense that "something new and different" will spring up behind every hill, but always unerringly similar, tapering, vanishing or lingering monotonous roads...' This is pretty much what the film is about.

As the characters drive through the vast open fields of Anatolia with no buildings in sight, the land appears timeless and, coupled with Ceylan's use of space as well as his obsession with time, every single frame turns into a poetic utterance. However, the time-less appearance of the land does not mean it lacks time; rather, it compresses time in a different way. The journey, and the long takes of those vehicles approaching in darkness, appearing like balls of fire, almost unzips the land, what the land enfolds, transforming the space into (an aoristic) time.

This is a film about life and death, the ghosts of the past, the search for the truth, but perhaps more importantly, about power relations. In this respect it is very similar to Ceylan's previous film, *Three Monkeys* (2008), where he also dealt with secrets and ghosts and ways of exerting power over others. In *Three Monkeys* the characters were running away from the truth. In *Once Upon a Time in Anatolia* it appears, at first, that the characters are searching for the truth, but what they are chasing are the facts of the matter.

However, facts do not necessarily lead them (or us) to the truth. On the contrary, as long as they are good enough facts to narrate a story about an event (in this case a murder), the truth remains veiled, buried, possibly buried alive. It is in the characters' journey (the experience) to collect facts (as well as apples and melons and stories), which takes up an entire night, that the truth becomes visible to the senses. It is the experience, both the characters' as well as the audience's, that later becomes the truth.

When the corpse is finally found, we witness another detail of how the state apparatus works: it is what *they* say happened (in particular the prosecutor and the doctor) that will remain on the 'documents'. However, what they say happened is not necessarily what did happen; it is only having the authority to utter those words that makes them facts. The external examination of the body is done without touching it; questions are answered without being asked; and statements are written without witnesses ever talking. One cannot help but imagine these documents being read in the future, as the only accounts of what happened. The events will be judged based on these official documents. The facts spelled out in these reports will overwrite the truth. These official documents, and the obsession with them when it comes to narrating the 'truth,' resonate on many different levels with Turkey's recent history, particularly when thought together with the title. The story does not take place in the past (once upon a time). It takes place now, in the present.

Although the film is a journey into the dark emotional and material landscape, it is one that does not lack humour. On the contrary, the film is full of funny moments. One of the most memorable of these takes place towards the end: as the prosecutor is dictating his report to his assistant at the scene where the body is found, he jokes about the victim's resemblance to Clark Gable. The conversation, as he was expecting, turns quickly into how, in fact, he himself resembles Gable, to which he responds by brushing his moustache. These men share a moment of joy and laughter, which momentarily brings them equality. However, it is also an uncanny image: laughter by the side of a corpse. Life really is beautiful and ugly, funny and sad at the same time.

At the end of the film, the doctor, performing the autopsy (or rather, supervising the autopsy, as he never really touches the corpse), spells out the facts of the matter for the official report: 'no abnormalities were found', despite the evidence suggesting that the victim was buried alive. Why? That is left for us to think about. In this respect, Anton Chekov (for whom Ceylan has repeatedly declared his admiration) is not only present in quotations inserted in the dialogues, but also in Ceylan's interest in asking questions (and his disinterest in answering them). Sometimes, the truth is seen only when reflected, like our own faces, always with us but not always visible to us.[1]

Özlem Köksal

Notes

[1] This review was previously published on: http://www.jadaliyya.com/pages/index/3035/where-the-truth-lies

FESTIVAL FOCUS
ANKARA INTERNATIONAL
FILM FESTIVAL

Ankara International Film Festival was founded in 1988 under the leadership of Mahmut Tali Öngören and writer Aziz Nesin. In 1991, due to the Gulf War, it could not be organized but, in the same year, upon being incorporated into the structure of the organization which had been founded under the title of World Mass Media Research Foundation, it achieved an institutional identity and quickly became one of the four important international film festivals in Turkey. Together with the Flying Broom International Women's Film Festival and the Festival on Wheels, it is one of the three festivals organized annually in Ankara. The festival, which takes place in March every year, presents the audience with the year's most prominent films from Turkish and world cinema. The festival lasts ten days, and around two hundred films of different genres – from feature films to short-length films; from documentaries to videos – are screened for an audience of more than ten thousand cinema goers. During the festival, recent productions from around the world including US, Europe, Africa and Australia are screened. This offers an opportunity for the exhibition of films that would otherwise not have been screened in Turkey. Every year, important movie makers from various countries of the world participate in the festival with their productions, and also attend the activities as guests. Over recent years, among the guests of the festival were Harun Farocki, George Ovashvili, Aku Louhimies, Dominic Morisette, Siddiq Barmak, Jan Hřebejk, Krzysztof Zanussi, Yves Montmayeur, Jasmine Dellal, Jonathan Paz and Ari Sandel. During the festival, besides the film screenings, a number of panels, interviews, videoart performances and workshops have taken place. The festival is indeed significant in bringing together a variety of films and directors from different national contexts. It also creates a dialogue between the audiences, film-makers and films from different context. Whilst doing so, it creates a strong link between art circles and intellectual circles.

One of the aims of the festival is to support new and young film-makers. Indeed, the festival becomes a space where the debut films of a number of future movie directors are screened for the first time. Young movie directors who have already participated in the festival with short films, and won awards, take their chances once more with their feature films; for this reason the festival is considered as an 'ecole.' In addition, through what the festival refers to as collective screenings, film-makers from Turkey and diasporic film-makers get together. Already, the films of directors such as Fatih Akın, Ayşe Polat, Yüksel Yavuz, Nuray Şahin, Kutluğ Ataman and Hakan Şahin's works have been screened at the festival.

In addition to the exhibition of films from around the world, the festival offers a competition. The National Feature Film Competition offers awards in sixteen different categories, including the best movie director, the best actress and the best actor categories. There are also competitions for short films and documentaries during the course of the festival. The National Feature Film Competition has already awarded the works of prominent and internationally-acclaimed directors, including Zeki Demirkubuz, Nuri Bilge Ceylan, Semih Kaplanoğlu, Derviş Zaim, Ömer Kavur, Kutluğu Ataman, Fatih Akın, Barış Pirhasan, Yavuz Özkan, Yeşim Ustaoğlu, Yüksel Yavuz, Alper Özcan, Erden Kıral, Mahinur Ergun, Orhan Oğuz, Pelin Esmer and Tayfun Pirselimoğlu.

The festival also offers different thematic contexts each year for the films in the World Cinemas section. Power and rebellion, for instance, was a recent theme that formed a strand of the festival and it included films such as Reinhard Hauff's *Stammheim-Die Baader-Meinhof-Grupe vor Gericht*, Lindsay Anderson's ...If, Gillo Pontevorvo's Queimada, Miklos Jancso's Red Psalm, Koji Wakamatsu's United Red Army and Margarethe von Trotta's Rosa Luxemburg. In 2010, the festival focused on recent Brazilian cinema. Among the films from Brazil were productions such as The Year My Parents Went on Vacation, a film with various awards, directed by Cao Hamburger; Lais Bodanzky's Brainstorm which has also received several awards; Marcos Prado's Estamira which won awards in various festivals throughout the world; Marco Bechis's BirdWatchers; and the award winning Estomago: A Gastronomic Story. In the 'Masters' category of the festival exhibits work of some distinguished movie makers: Takeshi Kitano's Achilles and the Tortoise, Michael Haneke's The White Ribbon, Costa-Gavras's Eden is West, Peter Greenaway's Rambrant's J'accuse, Robert Guedigian's The Army of Crime and Theodoros Angelopoulos's The Dust of Time. Moreover, in 2010, part of the festival was dedicated to the memory of Eric Rohmer with the screening of his Pauline at the Beach and The Green Ray. Under the category of 'memory of the immortal movie directors Akira Kurosawa and Luis Buñuel's works have also been screened in the past.

One of the most popular and interesting activities of the festival is the 'Film Readings' workshops, during which the audiences are offered the opportunity to discuss films, at times in the presence of the crew of the films. This is significant in the creation of an intellectual environment during the festival.

The short films at the festival compete under the title of The National Short Film competition. This competition consists of categories including Experimental films, Fiction and Animation. There is another programme entitled 'Short without Limits' which presents a variety of short films from several countries around the world. In 2010, the short film category also contained the screening of an anthology from the Clermont-Ferrand Short Film Festival. This is illustrative of the international connections and interest. In 1993, a National Animation Films Competition was held within the framework of the festival; however, for financial constraints, this competition could not be carried on in following years. There is also the 'State of World' category, which consists of several documentaries from various countries of the world. In 2010, under title of the 'Afghan Dream', films about Afghanistan were screened to reflect critically upon 'the state of world'. The festival also gives room for the screening of video projections. Productions such as *Eyes of Memory* by Harun Farocki; *Collective Memory* by Antoni Muntadas; *Waters of Memory*, Genco Gülan and *Places of Memory*, Hakan Akçura, were projected within the framework of a video presentation which was performed under the title of Video: Space of Memory.

Starting from the first festival which was organized in 1988 until the twenty-first festival in 2010, there were numerous screenings, from the American independent cinema to the Italian comedies; the collective screenings of a number of film directors such as Ermanno

Olmi, John Schlesinger, Woody Allen, Leos Carax, Carlo Verdone and Andrei Mikhalkov Koncalovsky. During the twenty-first festival, there were films by W. F. Murnau, Costa-Gavras, Luis Buñuel, Fritz Lang, Jean-Luc Godard, John Waters, Spike Lee, Roman Polanski, Sergei Eisenstein, Jon Jost, Charles Chaplin, P. P. Pasolini, Mario Monicelli, Claude Berri, Andrzej Wajda, Krzystof Kieslowski, Dariush Mehrjui, Ettore Scola, Francesco Rossi, François Truffaut, Jean Renoir, Robert Bresson, Satyajit Ray, Sergei Parajanov, Alain Resnais, Wim Wenders, Jan Hrebejkand and Krzysztof Zanussi. As well as these important names from world cinema, collective screenings of Turkish directors such as Metin Erksan, Lütfi Ömer Akad, Atıf Yılmaz and Halit Refiğ were presented to the audience. The festival also presented several marginalized productions of Turkish cinema history; for instance, during the thirteenth festival, sci-fi/fantasy films made in Turkey were exhibited. Several productions of Turkish cinema which are considered as 'cult films' were also presented.

Overall, the festival has a significant place in the history of cinema in Turkey. Its international appeal makes it one of the most important exhibition and networking spaces in the world of films.

Ali Karadoğan

Flying Broom International Women's Film Festival.

FESTIVAL FOCUS
FLYING BROOM
INTERNATIONAL WOMEN'S
FILM FESTIVAL

The Flying Broom International Women's Film Festival has been successfully running since 1997 as an Ankara-based organization which celebrates women's contribution to and existence in the film industry. The festival gives out the Bilge Olgaç Honorary Award, the Lifelong Achievement Award as well as the prestigious International Federation of Film Critics Award. Flying Broom is the only event in Turkey where this award is given. Since 2009 the festival has been giving a new award entitled The Young Witch Award, which aims to encourage young actresses and to acknowledge young women's efforts in the cinema industry. By exhibiting a variety of films from all over the world, the festival intends to address women's issues whilst at the same time creating an environment in which discussions on gender, discrimination and violence against women take place. Making women film-makers and their work visible is the *raison d'être* of the festival. This issue around visibility is crucial as the cinema industry remains rather male dominated, not only in Turkey, but also across the world.

The festival has a different theme each year; for example, in 2009 the theme was 'the 1980s'; in 2010 it was 'love'; in 2011 it was 'power'. In 2009, for instance, in the festival programme there were 90 films by 81 female directors from 26 countries. Flying Broom helps film-makers and produces documentaries as well as publishing books about women's issues. The festival also offers competitions: a screenplay writing competition has been organized since 1999; also, since 2003 there is an international competition which recognizes excellence in film-making. The festival also gives the prestigious FIPRESCI (International Film Critics Federation) award in its competition open only to women directors. It also has strong links to the highly-esteemed, New York (US) based, women's films production and distribution institution Women Make Movies (WMM). Established in 1972 to address the under-representation and misrepresentation of women in the media industry, WMM is a multicultural, multiracial, non-profit media arts organization which facilitates the production, promotion, distribution and exhibition of independent films and videotapes by, about and for women. Representatives of WMM (including the Executive Director Debra Zimmerman) visit every year to screen their films at the same time as contributing to the discussions that take place during the festival.

It must be noted that the festival plays a crucial role in creating a cultural platform to discuss issues relating to gender through the use of filmic language; in introducing films by women directors from around the world to the festival audiences; in promoting national and transnational cinemas through allowing the works of women directors travel to Turkey; and last, but certainly not least, in improving the status and visibility of women in a rather masculine industry.

Eylem Atakav

Uzak/Distant, 2002, Nuri Bilge Ceylan © NBC Films.

FILM LOCATION
THE CAPITAL OF OUR 'IMAGINARY HOMELAND: TURKISH CINEMA'

İstanbul is one of the most cinematic cities of the world. In the history of the cinema of Turkey a large number of films either take place in İstanbul or refer to the city whilst others used it as a space for transition and transformation. İstanbul is like a magic light for the spectacle. Whatever the era or the genre, the core of all these films was to capture, to invade, to possess the city, as evidenced in the title of Aydın Arakon's 1951 film *İstanbul'un Fethi (The conquest of İstanbul)*. İstanbul, the old capital of the Byzantine and Ottoman Empires, has been the site of cultural archaeology since the 2000s. The city has been 'invaded' and 're-explored' by art historians, critics, curators and entrepreneurs of culture. The İstanbul Biennale, the İstanbul Film, Theatre and Music Festivals, museums, and İstanbul's recent designation as the European capital of culture, have increased the vitality of the art scene.

Cinema in particular has generated a series of discussions in Turkey and abroad after the release of *İstanbul Kanatlarımın Altında (İstanbul Under My Wings)* (Mustafa Altıoklar, 1996), a box-office hit in 1996. This film, about the attempt to fly over İstanbul by Hazerfan Ahmet Çelebi in the sixteenth century, served as a pioneer of what can be termed 'İstanbul films'. Followed by the success of *Eşkıya* (The Bandit) (Yavuz Turgul, 1996), film-making from the mid-1990s onwards has accelerated in quantity, variety and quality. Film-makers soon realized that the city offered and still offers a lot of new tales and stories and that these attract the new spectator of a globalized atmosphere in shopping malls and chain movie theatres. Another fact about this spectator is their being nourished for years by the transmission of Turkish films of the Yeşilçam period through private television channels. It can be argued that, more recently, audiences have become addicted to the television series produced in İstanbul that focus on the ideas of transformation of the cityscape and its inhabitants. Different *faces* of İstanbul can be traced back in a long tradition of literature on the city. Orhan Pamuk, for instance, crystallizes these faces and facades in his essays and novels, along with the works of authors, including Ahmet Hamdi Tanpınar and Reşat Ekrem Koçu. Writers like Umberto Eco, Jean Baudrillard and Edmondo de Amicis felt a drive to write, to tell about and to illustrate İstanbul.

Conferences and workshops on İstanbul, in Turkey and abroad, motivated social scientists, architects, city planners to question the changes in the city and its new social and cultural scene. İstanbul Studies centres were established to work on the basis of the intellectual capacity of the city. İstanbul has gained eminence over Ankara, the nominal capital of the Republic of Turkey, as the real capital of Turkey. One of the latest examples of cultural production is from the İstanbul Municipality and is a book series on İstanbul 2010 European Capital of Culture: *İstanbul's 100 films* (Kır 2010), a compilation about films made on and in İstanbul by Turkish and foreign directors. In his introduction to this book, Kır claims that the lost film, The demolition of the Monument in Ayestaphanos (Ayastefanos'taki Rus Abidesinin Yıkılışt, Fuat Uzkınay), as early as 1914, was also shot in İstanbul. The 100 films, selected from a wide range of İstanbul films, cover theatrical adaptations, the era of directors, social-realist films, women's films, new Turkish Cinema and cinema in Turkey in the 2000s, or genres that have been of great importance from the 1960s to the mid-1970s (family melodrama, comedy and musical).

İstanbul films have been a platform to represent, among other topics: decadence, betrayal and impotence: *Ebediyete Kadar (Till Eternity)* (Turgut Etingü, 1955); solidarity and friendship: *Üç Arkadaş* (Three Friends) (Memduh Ün, 1958); the liberation of women: *Şoför Nebahat (Nebahat, the Driver)* (Metin Erksan, 1960); the contrast between traditional and modern: *Küçük Hanımefendi* (Nejat Saydam, 1961); scenes for outsiders: *Ah Güzel İstanbul (Lovely İstanbul)* (Atıf Yılmaz, 1966); children on the street: *Yusuf ile Kenan*, (Ömer Kavur, 1979); road stories: *Çiçek Abbas* (Sinan Çetin, 1982), the gliding surface of the Bosphorus looking at the old city: *Teyzem (My Aunt)* (Halit Refiğ, 1987); fantasy, imagination and frustration: *İstanbul Kanatlarımın Altında (İstanbul Under My Wings)*

(Mustafa Altıoklar, 1996); and, last, but not least, dystopia: *Üç Maymun/Three Monkeys* (Nuri Bilge Ceylan, 2008).

From the Pension of the Civilizations (the brothel) in *Ah Güzel İstanbul* to the novel, *Museum of Innocence*, by Orhan Pamuk, there is a spectrum of memoirs, wounds, obsessions and ruptures. The creators, film-makers, authors and poets feel themselves urged to question this imaginary homeland in their films, novels, poems, and songs. The stories and the lyrics are mainly told by male voices with few exceptions (*Hamam*, 1997; *Harem suaré*, 1999, Ferzan Özpetek). Especially in the films of Yeşilçam a voice-over carries the message to the spectator as the master of the voice.

Historically, in many films, the city is framed horizontally, from the shores and fringes at the bottom of the picture and, at the top, the sea and the horizon in greyish to violet tones. However, a vertical framing of İstanbul in films is new and allows us to look at the city with an enriched gaze. In *Ah Güzel İstanbul* (1966) the shelters of the city are presented as the two sides of the coin: 'Kulübe-i Ahzan' (the cottage of the melancholy) and the old yalı (the heritage of the Ottoman Empire) are followed by the symbol of 1960s' modernity – the Hilton Hotel. A clash between the East and West is represented in *Medeniyet Pansiyonu* (*The Pension of Civilization* is a brothel in the film) where the protagonist exclaims 'I'm not going to stay here', pointing at the decadence brought in by modernity and false Western values.

The 1981 version of *Ah Güzel İstanbul* represents the city as the 'cul-de-sac' for antiheroes. The film is about a prostitute, who has migrated from Anatolia, and a truck driver who claim to be real İstanbullites: a claim that implies the importance of *belonging* to İstanbul rather than *being* İstanbullites. Open endings for both 'Lovely İstanbuls' leave a bitter sense of the city that deteriorates and becomes polluted as we are invited to gaze towards the sea from the Galata Bridge. This idea of a disintegrating city is also apparent in *Teyzem*. The paranoid-schizoid disease overwhelms not only the aunt's mind in the film but also ruins the city's provincial qualities, leading to an uncanny familial disintegration. Whereas, in *Ah Güzel İstanbul*, a nostalgia is still felt, *Teyzem* suffocates the audience with the damnation of incest.

Ferzan Özpetek's 1997 film *Hamam* shows images of fresh images of İstanbul as the old hamam reveals the multinational, multicultural and multilingual Orientalist discourse related to the concept of dislocation. A transnational attack against İstanbul also comes from Fatih Akın's attempt at the remapping of Europe by bringing its shores to İstanbul and to the Black Sea coast. This is another journey in search of the lost, hybrid and hyphenated identities. The city overcomes the quality of being a space for transition between the East and the West and becomes the centre of the chase after *les temps perdu*.

Some films, *Sevmek Zamanı* (*Time to Love*) (Metin Erksan, 1965) for example, do not offer a creative geography and the city of is fragmented into its centre, its outskirts and suburbs. This is also apparent in the films of Zeki Demirkubuz (*C Block*, 1994) and Çağan Irmak (*Mustafa Hakkında Herşey/All About Mustafa*, 2004). In some films, including *Beyoğlu'nun Arka Yakası* (*Beyoğlu's Back Side*) (Şerif Gören, 1987), *Gece, Melek ve Bizim Çocuklar* (*Night, Angel and Our Children*) (Atıf Yılmaz, 1993), the daylight in the city is revealed in the cold blue tones of outside spaces. Nuri Bilge Ceylan goes further into the core of the city and beyond the main and popular streets. His take on İstanbul is a dark one, which does not allow much room for hope. The city in his films creates a sense of nausea. Ceylan's *Three Monkeys*, Serdar Akar's *Gemide* (*On Board*) (1998) and Kudret Sabancı's *Laleli'de Bir Azize* (*A Saint in Laleli*) (1999) do not have the atmosphere of a refined city.

During the 1960s, İstanbul images and their representation of modernity filled in a gap for the female audience in the afternoon matinées in the provinces; in the 1970s, the city was represented as a space for the comedy genre and the migrants' stories, as in *Taşı*

Toprağı Altın. In the 1980s, İstanbul experienced the vague existentialist moods of the 'intellectuals', whereas, in the 1990s, the city revealed a new vitality through the works of some of the directors of the Yeşilçam period. Since the year 2000, İstanbul has become a city for national and transnational directors as well as the young generation of film-makers. Çağan Irmak, for instance, uses the city for his hip and 'gourmet' stories in *Issız Adam*. Yılmaz Erdoğan takes us into the big shopping malls situated near the poor areas of the city in *Neşeli Hayat*.

Overall, İstanbul is the capital of Turkey's imaginary homeland, and a resource for more films to come and more stories to write and tell.[1]

Deniz Bayrakdar

Notes

[1] For detailed analysis of more İstanbul films, see Köksal, Ö. (ed) *Word Film Locations: İstanbul*, Intellect 2012.

Üç Maymun, 2008, Nuri Bilge Ceylan © Zeynofilm.

DIRECTORS
NURİ BİLGE CEYLAN

The best way to introduce Nuri Bilge Ceylan to those not yet acquainted with his work is through one of his images. The picture is in black and white. A carnival ride sends people spinning across a cloudy sky. Their feet are blurred and they shriek high, excited squeals that thicken the fairground air. Below them, a young man drags on a cigarette. He looks up, his face blocked by shadow, at the swing passing high over his head. The shot is still and the camera is placed low. All the energy comes from the movement of the ride and the angle of the camera as it looks up into the sky, tilting the edges of the image toward each other. If you were to freeze the frame, the shot would make a striking photograph. This carefully balanced composition and the interplay of movement and stillness are central to Ceylan's style. His plots are spare, but his films abound with local detail, presenting everyday lives in surprising and unexpected ways.

Ceylan was born in Istanbul in 1959 and has spent most of his life there. He began to make films in the mid-1990s, after spending – much like some of his characters – several years adrift, taking photographs, travelling and wondering what to do with his life. By the time he made his first feature, A Small Town (1998), he was 39. For a first film, A Small Town is remarkably assured. It is a no-budget film, shot by a crew of only two. The sound was recorded after shooting, a process that turned out to be so painful that he resolved to shoot sync-sound on his next film, no matter what the cost. In fact, sound has since become a notable feature in Ceylan's films. Using very little music, he mixes the ambient sounds both to reflect the way we hear and to intensify moments of boredom and unease. As he explained to Ali Jaafar, 'every minor detail is created afterwards. You cannot create reality with real sound. The human ear is quite selective: when we talk we don't hear the waves' (Jafar 2007) A Small Town wears some of its influences heavily – Tarkovsky and Kiarostami have their prints all over it – but it also introduces images and ideas that become key motifs in his later work.

In addition to the silent short, Cocoon (Koza, 1995) Ceylan has made six features. They are: A Small Town (Kasaba, 1998), Clouds of May (Mayıs Sıkıntısı, 2000), Distant (Uzak, 2022), Climates (İklimer, 2006), Three Monkeys (Üç Maymun, 2008) and Once Upon a Time in Anatolia (Bir Zamanlar Anadolu'da, 2011). His films have had extraordinary festival success, with the four most recent all winning major prizes at Cannes as well as picking up a slew of other awards. Despite these accomplishments, Ceylan has continued to work with a small crew and frequently includes his family and friends in both on- and off-screen roles. He holds the production rights on all his pictures. These seven films share striking visual similarities. Motifs that appear in his photography – clouds, grassy fields, snow and rain – also punctuate the films. The same places and shots re-appear in different contexts, like a trace of each film left on the next. While some may argue that his visual vocabulary is limited, this way of making the same shot more than once strikes me as a distinctly photographic way of working. The repetition of certain shots – dry grass blowing toward the camera, people dashed by falling snow – is made with intent, as if with each repeated image something new might be revealed.

In 2006 Ceylan began shooting digitally, a move that has had an enormous impact on his style. His digital films feel freer than his celluloid ones, as if the new medium inspired him to take risks. In Climates, he kept the colour of the picture natural, but used the flatness of the digital image to explore scale and to allude to the shimmery surface of existence. In Three Monkeys he shifted the colour to reflect the unhappy family's emotional volatility. His editing in these two films is more experimental than it had been previously, time leaps and stalls, and the image and sound sometimes take divergent paths. One of the strangest moments in his work comes toward the end of Climates, when both narrative and image become abstract. Here, an interchangeable series of extreme close-ups take over the film, and the barely recognizable texture of hair and smoke become some of the film's most memorable images.

In part, Ceylan's success comes from the way he blends an art cinema aesthetic with the specificity of place, creating an image of Turkish life that resonates both in Turkey and abroad. Ceylan's films never seem overtly political, but keeping his productions small and continuing to work in Turkey is, as Asuman Suner reports, his way of resisting rampant consumerism (Suner 2010: 78). His films are filled with technology: phones, cameras, televisions, the Internet, products that both help and hinder his characters' progress. And, as in Turkish history, events often go missing. Pivotal plot points are elided, leaving his characters treading water in a murky aftermath of unreliable memories and dreams. His attention to local quirks suggest that Ceylan wants very much to share the everydayness of Turkish life as it is lived by the people he knows. In *Once Upon a Time in Anatolia*, a police officer argues with his superior over whether or not the store down the road from the police station sells buffalo cheese. In *Clouds of May*, an old man describes over and over how his forest will be cut down. We tire of hearing it, but on he goes. This is the stuff of real conversation, slow, banal and fascinating in turn. At times it is almost alienatingly specific but, through the quiet boredom of daily life, one gets a glimpse of what it might be like to be an ordinary person living an ordinary life, here, in this place.

Sarinah Masukor

DIRECTORS
ŞERİF GÖREN

Şerif Gören was born in 1944 in Xanthi. In 1956, he won a scholarship and moved to Turkey. In 1962, he started his career in cinematography as an assistant editor and, in 1974, upon the arrest of Yılmaz Güney he completed Endişe (Anxiety) and became a director. In 1975, at the twelfth Antalya Golden Orange Film Festival, Gören received the 'Best Director' and the 'Best Film' awards for this film and became known as the new representative of 'socialist cinema.'

Gören made films belonging to a variety of genres including comedies and melodramas. In general, his films are closely related to current events and they focus on country life and urbanization. Gören has directed commercial films as well as films with 'counter messages' (Kayali 2006: 184). His work can be studied in the context of three different periods, at times characterized by conflicting inclinations.

During the first period between 1974 and 1981, Gören developed his original cinematographic language by enriching it with Yeşilçam's codes and he established a place for his work within the Turkish film industry. This period, which started with Endişe (The Angst), a film treated with such a realistic approach that there was almost a taste of a documentary about it, and continued with other films which are considered to be important within the scope of his own filmography, such as Köprü (The Bridge), Derviş Bey and Almanya Acı Vatan; he also made more commercial films such as Deprem (Earthquake), İki Arkadaş (Two Friends), Taksi Şoförü (Taxi Driver), İstasyon, Nehir (The River) and Gelincik; and arabesque[1] films with a social perspective such as Derdim Dünyadan Büyük, Aşkı Ben mi Yarattım, Kır Gönlünün Zincirini; and Feryada Gücüm Yok and Evlidir Ne Yapsa Yeridir, which can be regarded as the first example of the comedies he has made. The main characteristics of his films made during this period are the positive emphasis on the 'community' and the belief in the inevitability of social upheaval. His 'populist' tendency supporting the social upheaval, which stands out both in Köprü and Derviş Bey and his arabesque films, gains an orientation with the passage from class difference to a point where these differences become less visible. The first period of Gören's filmography can be described as the period when most of the features of his identity as a director appear for the first time. The first examples of several themes which are repeatedly treated in Gören's subsequent films can be observed in this period.

The change in Gören's cinematographic style is the most prominent difference between these two periods. Starting in 1983, Gören has adopted a new cinematographic style which became significant in the films he made in 1984, such as Kurbağalar (*Frogs*), Firar (*The Escape*), Yılanların Öcü and Kan. He started using the vertical and horizontal pan shots, which he had previously loved, more rarely and preferred to create the action within the frame through the actions of the actors and focal changes, while creating the unity of time and place and motion through the editing; in the course of this period, adopting an understanding based on longer shots where the interactive relations between the people and the environment were shown in a continuity and the stage setting gained importance, he changed his cinematographic style. During this period, Gören's turn of phrase also changed in comparison with the previous period. In his previous films he usually preferred a chronological, literal and expressive style. In Firar, he used a turn of phrase woven with cutbacks; he started Kan with a cutback 45 minutes long and edited the film in two parts; and, in Beyoğlu'nun Arka Yakası, he adopted a multiple idiom, which he also used in Polizei. During his last period, which starts in 1988 in Berlin, he made feature-length films characterized by humorous social satire and urban documentaries. In 1990, following his film Feryada Gücüm Yok, he made Abuk Sabuk Bir Film, which criticized the media, and then took a three-year break. In 1993 he returned to the cinema with Amerikalı (The American) – a social satire which criticizes the 'Americanization' of Turkey and films containing violence and which makes references to certain scenes in films such as *Pretty Woman*, *Basic Instinct*, *Home Alone* and *Thelma and Louise*.

The main characteristic of Gören's films is the different orientations of the narrative. His human narratives also have two different orientations: those based on the male element in line with traditional popular cinematography; and those based on the female element, where the women are the main leaders, as in Derman, Kurbağalar and Firar. The second type of subject matter in Gören films is the narrative 'based on the story' (Onaran 1994: 30-34). His arabesque films and other films such as Deprem (*The Earthquake*), İstasyon, Alişan, Evlidir Ne Yapsa Yeridir, Adem ile Havva (*Adam and Eve*) and Güneş Doğarken (*While the Sun Rises*) are films which depict the characters uni-dimensionally and superficially. When the thematic structures of his films are examined, it is observed that three main subjects are evident: social and economic changes, socio-cultural transformation and conflict and man in the face of nature.

As a director who deals with social transformation and disintegration as a necessity and who believes that this can be assured by voluntary intervention, Gören subtly expresses his desire for a 'new order' in the films where the social and economic changes are treated alongside the main theme of the film. The second theme, which is treated within the scope of the main theme, is the problem created as a result of the social and economic changes: moving up the social ladder. Another theme is the discrimination of rich and poor which is generally expressed in the framework of judgments and ethical understandings of both social groups. Gören also treats the village (villager)/city (citizen) contrast in such a framework. In all Gören's films, the obligatory and determinative nature of the economic factors is particularly highlighted.

In some of the films based on the theme of socio-cultural transformation and conflict, Gören explores the conflicts between the intellectuals who are the generators of the social changes and the community which is against change. In other films within this framework (especially in Feryada Gücüm Yok), he criticizes a cultural industry which intertwines the media and state bureaucracy. Another theme which is treated in most of Gören films is the struggle between nature and man. Gören deals with nature as an environment which compels mankind to struggle for survival, but also represents 'freedom'.

Ali Karadoğan

Notes

[1] The term 'arabesque films' is named after arabesque music, which is a popular genre in Turkey influenced by Arab popular and Islamic folk music. These films have singers of arabesque music as their main characters and tell tragic life stories, particularly related to migration from Eastern to Western Turkey.

Yılmaz Güney, 1982 © Guney Film/Cactus Film.

DIRECTORS
YILMAZ GÜNEY

Born in 1931 to a lower-class Kurdish family in the South Anatolian city of Adana, Yılmaz Güney first encountered cinema as a bicycle delivery boy for a film company, distributing reels to the open-air cinema halls in town. In high school, he began writing short stories for his school journal and, when he moved to Istanbul to study Economics, Dar Films hired him as a screenwriter. His name became widely known after 1958 when he acted in a supporting role in Atif Yilmaz's *Bu Vatanin Cocuklari* (*This Country's Children*), which secured him two leading roles the following year. Between 1958 and 1966 when he made his directorial debut with *At, Avrat, Silah* (*Horse, Woman, Pistol*), he appeared in approximately fifty films and was the most popular actor in Yeşilçam.

In 1968 Güney made *Seyyit Han* (*The Bride of the Soil*) which he considered the first example of his signature directorial style. *Seyyit Han* is a product of his transitional period, following his experimentation with the western and the gangster genre (with which he became familiar as an actor). Güney, however, dismisses the western and gangster films as 'populist' attempts, which retrospectively came to occupy a peculiar place in his filmography. Though derided, these early experiences with the western and gangster genres would later influence his characters and themes. *Seyyit Han* blends the western genre, the village melodrama popular in Turkey from the 1940s, and *cinéma-vérité*. *Seyyit Han* plants a 'western saloon' in the middle of an Anatolian village. Film critics feted *Seyyit Han* as the most innovative film of the year and Güney was recognized as a successful director by the Turkish Cinematique Association, an institution run by leftist cinema writers and critics who were closely following the contemporary art cinema of Europe. A year later he made *Umut* (*Hope*, 1970) – considered to be the most successful example of Turkish 'social realism'. The film depicts a horse-cab driver who becomes a treasure hunter to support his family after one of his horses is run over by a luxury car. The disturbingly realist portrayal of the main character Cabbar within a highly-classed socio-economic context won him both fame and infamy: he was awarded best director at the national Golden Boll Film Festival in 1970, but the film caused tensions within the board of censors.

Güney is best known for the films he made in the 1970s. The period is marked by his engagement with leftist student and worker movements. In his 1971 films *Aci* (*Pain*) and *Agit* (*Requiem*), Güney continues to experiment with the western genre, but this time incorporating leftist discourse into the characters' dialogue. The song in *Agit* caused the film to be banned by the board of censors. In these films and others of the period, class-conflict and poverty are the main themes. *Zavallilar* (*The Poor Ones*, 1975), started by Güney in 1971 but interrupted by his imprisonment (for publishing a 'communist' novel), depicts a man who agrees to rent his body to diamond smugglers. Atif Yilmaz took up the film but changed the narrative to compensate for the absence of Yilmaz Güney as the lead character. In *Baba* (*The Father*, 1971) Güney tells the story of a man who goes to prison for the murder committed by his boss, in exchange for money. The film *Arkadas* (*The Friend*, 1974), made after his sixteen months in prison, shows two childhood friends who, after years apart, decide to visit their old neighborhood where they find that their class differences make their relationship impossible.

Arkadas proved to be the last directorial work that Güney completed in Turkey and his penultimate before *Duvar* (*The Wall*, 1983), which he finished in France in 1983. His attempt to direct *Endişe* (*The Angst*, 1974), a story about the cotton workers in Adana, was tragically cut short when he was imprisoned for a second time (for harbouring anarchist students). After Güney's imprisonment, his assistant Serif Gören completed the film. Güney wrote the scripts and supervised his next two films, *Sürü* (*The Herd*, 1977) and *Yol* (*The Road*, 1981) by way of correspondence and communication from his prison cell. He worked closely with his former assistants Zeki Ökten and Serif Gören, who actualized the films based on meticulously-detailed shooting scripts. Both *Sürü* and *Yol* represent a shift from the representation of class conflict and poverty that marked his earlier 1970s' films to a focus on the Kurdish issue that had been intensifying throughout the 1970s in south-eastern Anatolia. *Sürü* is a portrayal of the disintegration of a Kurdish tribe losing authority due to the incorporation of the Kurdish regions into the national capitalist economic system, and *Yol*, which shared the best picture award in 1982 Cannes International Film Festival, depicts the effect of militarization on everyday life within the Kurdish region. After his escape to France in 1981, his Turkish citizenship was revoked by the post-coup military order. His films were confiscated by the army because of their 'subversive' content and were not shown publicly in Turkey until the late 1990s.

Ali Fuat Şengül

Pandora'nın Kutusu, 2008, Yeşim Ustaoğlu © Film Yapim.

DIRECTORS
YEŞİM USTAOĞLU

Yeşim Ustaoğlu is one of the few female directors making films in Turkey. She became interested in photography while studying architecture at university and not long after made several award-winning short films. Her first feature film was İz (The Track, 1994). Then came Güneşe Yolculuk (Journey to the Sun, 1999), Bulutları Beklerken (Waiting for the Clouds, 2004), and Pandora'nın Kutusu (Pandora's Box, 2008). She also made a documentary film called Sırtlarındaki Hayat (Life on Their Shoulders, 2004).

The Track has traces of a thriller and detective story in a Kafkaesque setting, but it is not rated as highly as her other films. Inspired by a newspaper report about houses that were marked with an X and later burned to the ground because they were occupied by Kurds, Ustaoğlu and her ex-husband, director and author Tayfun Pirselimoğlu, wrote the story for Journey to the Sun. After their separation, Ustaoğlu continued working on the screenplay and subsequently received support from Eurimages to make the film, which gained international recognition and prestigious awards at European film festivals. The story revolves around two young men. Mehmet, a dark-skinned Turk working in Istanbul, is arrested and beaten for a crime he did not commit, largely because the police mistake him for a Kurdish man. Not long after, he discovers a red X by the door to his apartment. He is helped by Berzan, a Kurdish activist, and they become friends. Throughout the film, Mehmet experiences the discrimination directed at Kurdish people and eventually accepts a Kurdish identity to go along with the suffering. Having dark skin becomes a significant symbol in Journey to the Sun. His skin colour does not make Mehmet a Kurd but, treated like a Kurd, he learns to feel like a Kurd. In this regard, identities intersect, become critically significant, and are also slippery. It is noteworthy that Newroz Baz, who plays Mehmet, is himself Kurdish. Symbolically, to understand 'others' one has to be identified as an 'other.'

Although The Track and Journey to the Sun are different in form and genre, they share some common features: a bus stopped and searched at a checkpoint; women chatting about celebrities in the news; police interrogations. Ara Güler, the well-known photographer, appears in both films. Two characters, Cezmi in The Track and Mehmet in Journey to the Sun, have kara (meaning black or dark) in their surnames. Furthermore, both films offer a take on identity politics. One is about the relationship between torture and the torturer, yet it handles these elements in an abstract way. The other dwells directly on the Kurdish 'question', clearly intending to reveal the plight of Kurdish people who live in Turkey.

The concept of identity in the context of Turkey is also seen in Ustaoğlu's next film, in which she offers a female protagonist for the first time. In Waiting for the Clouds, based on George Andreadis' book Tamama, Eleni has kept her identity secret for 50 years. She was adopted by a Turkish family and given the name Ayşe when she lost her own family during the deportation of Pontus Greeks at the end of the First World War. Ever since she has lived with her Turkish identity. However, a visit from a compatriot impels her to remember her brother from whom she was separated during their forced migration. In the cloudy mountains of the Black Sea region where she lives, she broods on her previous identity and resolves to travel to Greece to find her brother. Her outward journey and her inward journey intersect; Ayşe travels to find her brother and herself. The documentary, Life on Their Shoulders, which Ustaoğlu made about the same time, is also a poetic film about the lives of women in the Black Sea region of Turkey. It shows that the men in this region do not do the hard work needed for survival; they only help the women, who work too hard. Throughout the film, the camera zooms in on the faces and hands of the women, revealing why they have grown old so soon.

Ustaoğlu's latest, internationally-acclaimed film, Pandora's Box, combines two of her personal quests: to find one's identity and to embrace the 'other'. Into this mix she adds alienation and lack of communication in a realistic story set in Istanbul. Among the several characters is an old and sickly woman in need of care who is taken to live with her three children and one grandson. The elder daughter, cold and rule-bound, tries to take responsibility but interferes with everyone else's life, especially her son's. Her brother lives an errant life and her sister is struggling to maintain her relationship with a partner outside of marriage. The grandson, like his unruly uncle, is in search of freedom. What make the film particularly interesting are the contrasts that occur when the rural mother joins her urban family. First the director takes the family to the countryside, then returns them with their mother to the city. Tsilla Chelton's performance as the mother, a fish deprived of water, is wonderful, even if her lines are sometimes hard to understand. Most notable in the film is the mother's relationship with the camera, which seems to share her moods. Like her, the camera looks for green among the tower blocks, so it turns hopefully around the bends of the roads and the highways, where the only escape is a glimpse of green or the sea.

In Ustaoğlu's earlier films (The Track, Journey to the Sun), the protagonists were male, but in her later films (Waiting for the Clouds, Life on Their Shoulders, Pandora's Box) one sees a shift to female characters in the central roles. In interviews, however, when asked about female sensitivity and her prominence as a female director, she has always stated that she does not believe in gender discrimination and has never said anything discriminatory about men. Ustaoğlu, however, already has an international appeal as one of the very few women film-makers in Turkey.

S Ruken Öztürk

Dervis Zaim.

DIRECTORS
DERVİŞ ZAIM

Derviş Zaim's is a cinema built on the cosmopolitan politics of memory and critical inheritance. He has produced political arthouse films about a cultural geography, where a vulgar politics of 'disinheritance' [redd-i miras] have prevailed for almost a century as part of the process of national identity building and modernization. As a Turkish Cypriot film-maker, his 'ambivalent situatedness' in the geographies and histories of Turkey and Cyprus has been the main motive for Zaim in his film-making: his 'split identity' depending on his nomadic comings and goings between Turkey and Cyprus, his exilic experience of having been forced to leave his homeland (Limassol, Cyprus) in his childhood, and his cultural exile from the Ottoman heritage through the Kemalist self-colonization, are the very groundless ground of his filmic reflections. For this reason, the cinematic specters of his politics of memory are likely to haunt both the boundaries of grand historical narratives and the geopolitical borders of divided territories, revolving around such traumatic topics as the biopolitics of intercommunal war, the cartography of ethnic violence, and the horrific conditions of disinheritance and cultural schizophrenia.

Zaim was born in 1964 in the southern Cypriot coastal town of Limassol. He was raised in a relatively peaceful environment although he spent a childhood between 1964 and 1974 in Turkish Cypriot ghettoes under the threat of being massacred by the Greek Cypriot nationalists. He studied economics at the University of Bosphorus, where he became involved in film. After graduating in 1988, he attended a course in independent film production in London and made an experimental video entitled Hang the Camera (1991). He subsequently wrote, produced and directed numerous television programmes between 1992 and 1994. His first experience in film-making was as director of the documentary Rock around the Mosque (1993), which addressed rock music and its conditions of possibility in Turkey. He completed his master's degree in Cultural Studies at the University of Warwick in 1994. His first novel, Ares in Wonderland (1995), won the prestigious Yunus Nadi Literary Prize in Turkey.

Zaim's feature debut Summersault in a Coffin (1996) was a tragicomic drama based on the modified life story of a real character and is widely regarded as a milestone in Turkish cinema. This neo-realistic film portrays the life of Mahsun Süpertitiz (Ahmet Uğurlu), who is a drifter, homeless and a petty criminal living out on the streets of the Rumelihisarı district in Istanbul and stealing cars at night to shelter from the cold winter. Zaim subsequently worked on another feature about the experience of his own exile from southern Cyprus, Via Beyrut, which has not been completed for political reasons. After having decided to postpone his aim of making a political film on the issue of Cyprus, Zaim made Elephants and Grass (2000), where he unfolds the secret memory of the corrupted Turkish state and its pathetic relations to what is usually called 'deep state', or a group of influential anti-democratic coalitions within the Turkish political system, composed of high-level elements within the domestic and foreign intelligence services, Turkish military, security, judiciary, and mafia.

Zaim's next project, Mud (2003), was based on the post-traumatic story of a Turkish Cypriot man, Ali, and his sister, Ayşe, who lost their family in a massacre after the 1974 fascist coup d'état, engineered by the Greek military junta, in Cyprus. The film emerges as a form of conjuring up the spectres of the past to develop a mode of counter-intelligibility in favour of never-tried political actions since 1974: it increases the intensity and power of ghosts to make both Greek and Turkish Cypriots able to reconsider their 'bordered' situation in a critical way. In one of the scenes Temel, as an individual haunted by the ghosts of his Greek Cypriot victims, tells his traumatic memoirs of the intercommunal war in Cyprus to an unknown spectator, running a simple hand camera. But he destroys the cassette just after finishing his 'cinematic confession'. Elsewhere in the film, pointing to the broken cassettes and dismantled film strips in his hands, he says, 'Sometimes I run my camera to tell all this, and then...'. These video séances of Temel not only situate the filmic medium as a kind of profane 'confession room', but also invite the spirits of the past to come back, to return to the present.

Mud was followed by the documentary Parallel Trips (co-directed with Greek Cypriot film-maker Panicos Chrysanthou, 2004), which explores the massacres commited by the Greek Cypriots and the Turkish Cypriots on both sides of the island during the war of 1974 and the traumatic legacy that remains today. Zaim holds his camera on the well-known slaughter of the Turkish Cypriot men, women and children of three villages on the central Cypriot plain, while Chrysanthou focuses on the killings of Greek Cypriots by their neighbours in Palaikythro. As a kind of 'minor' history, or an oral history, to deconstruct the political unconscious and the grand narratives of the nationalist imaginaries, the film is based on a series of lengthy and slow-paced anecdotes narrated by those who experienced the horror of the troubles in Cyprus, both Turkish and Greek. By means of encounters between film-makers, subjects and spectators and by unearthing the singular traumatic memories, Zaim and Chrysanthou consider the act of documentary film-making as a collective and performative writing of history: each moment of encounter might be a nexus to create a matrix of 'other' histories. These traumatic events are the key factors in the current organization and militarization of territory in Cyprus. Therefore, listening to the spectres and remembering the traumatic stories is not 'to know the enemy' but to examine the conditions which made the two sides enemies. As Zaim says,

> I wanted to drag their stories back from the hands of the nationalists, from those who have used these people for propaganda . . . We know we can live together, but we still have to ask why we did this to each other. If you leave things unsaid they will become the bad dreams that haunt us and will again be exploited by the nationalists. (cited in Gibbons 2004)

Zaim later became the producer of the Greek Cypriot director's fictional feature debut Akamas (2006), which revolves around a love affair between a Turkish Cypriot and Greek Cypriot. His last film on the Cyprus issue, Shadows and Faces (2011), which was seen by Cypriot viewers from both sides in a special screening on the Green Line that separates the city of Nicosia, examines the first serious conflict between Greek Cypriots and Turkish Cypriots in 1963, which resulted in the massacre of Turkish Cypriots by Greek Cypriots.

In his trilogy of Ottoman arts, Waiting for Heaven (2006), Dot (2008) and Shadows and Faces (2011), Zaim recontextualizes the Ottoman miniature, calligraphy and shadow play as 'philosophical diagrams' that make one able to produce new trajectories of thought regarding the multiple histories and heterogeneous cultural geographies of Turkey. He relocates the displaced aesthetic forms in favour of developing a new logic of editing and thereby redefines the filmic medium as a spatiotemporal openness through which editing 'divided spaces' and 'disjointed times' is possible. While he goes over the geopolitical borders and 'divided spaces' in his Shadows and Faces, the main theme of Waiting for Heaven is the 'disjointed time' in which the haunted subject, in a Derridean sense, is not present to itself.

Although on a cinematic level and in an indirect way, one of his main purposes of translating displaced aesthetic forms into cinema is to disrupt the homogeneity of the official discourse of history in Turkey, which has dominated the political and social atmosphere up until now. As Zaim says in an interview when he is asked whether his interest in the deconstruction of the tradition includes a critique of the 'official history', his answer insists on the possibility of 'other histories':

This film, *Waiting for Heaven*, is a gesture of awareness about these issues, I mean the monolithic discourse of the official history. For instance, Prince Danyal says with a faint sound to the painter Eflatun, 'People always support the winner. If I lose, let you paint my story.' Danyal's aim is to take precautions regarding being represented in a distorted way. Hence the film implies an awareness that although historical narratives are always written by winners, other narratives about history are possible. (Zaim, Sönmez and Tutumluer 2007: 80)

The cinematic ghosts in Derviş Zaim's films stress the traces of the 'unspoken', 'less-chronicled' or what is usually seen as 'insignificant'. Thus, his film-making practice enhances the potentials of 'critical archiving' and problematizes both the politics of forgetting and the current modes of archive production and destruction. As Akbal Süalp (2010) excellently puts it, Zaim's cinema seems to be 'the poetry of history in the simple present tense'.

Cihat Arınç

Ayhan Işik.

STARS
AYHAN IŞIK

Ayhan Işık (1929-79) was one of the biggest stars of Turkish popular cinema in the middle of the last century. Born Ayhan Işıyan in İzmir, he started his working life in a factory, while studying fine arts at university. In 1951 he won a 'search for a star' competition organized by the fanzine *Yıldız* (*Star*), and changed his name to Ayhan Işık. From then on he never looked back; in a 27-year screen career he made over 130 films, mostly playing the kind of heroic roles that eventually earned him the nickname *Kral* (The King). At the time of his death from a brain hemorrhage (aged only 50) he was due to star in a police series for Turkish State Television (TRT).

Throughout his career Işık played ordinary working people – mechanics, coach-drivers, architects – struggling to make a living in the country or the city (reflecting the social origins of the majority of his audiences). While some critics complained that Işık – like many of his contemporaries – played basically the same role in every film, film-goers enjoyed the fantasy of believing that they were in the presence of a man-of-the-people – someone whom they could trust. Işık never lost the common touch. Onscreen he was always willing to assist those in need (often at great personal cost), and his devotion towards his family members remained unshakeable – even when some of them broke the law. While the fanzines regularly wrote about his latest fancy acquisitions (cars, clothing, etc.), they likewise characterized Işık as a public-spirited soul, ever willing to give up his spare time to visit local hospitals or children's homes and perform spontaneous concerts – particularly in the latter part of his career.

Işık's public image changed little, even when he had established himself as Yeşilçam's principal male box-office attraction. In *Yaralı Aslan* (*The Wounded Lion*) (1963), he plays a factory worker who travels from Adana to İstanbul with three of his friends on the pretext of visiting his relatives. Realizing that they think of him as little more than a provincial bumpkin, Işık decides to have some fun at their expense by pretending to be a mincing effeminate with a penchant for flowery shirts and a perpetually runny nose. However he leads a double life, as he assumes the role of an avenger foiling plots to blackmail innocent factory-owners and their employees. The film contains an exciting climax where Işık kills off the villains in a prolonged gun-battle, removes his mask and thereby reveals his true identity. Unlike his outwardly-sophisticated relatives, his modest upbringing has given him a social conscience.

In films such as Zafer Davutoğlu's *Katilin Kızı* (*The Daughter of the Murderer*) (1964), Işık portrayed a family man fighting to retain custody of his daughter (Parla Şenol), after having brought her up as a single parent. His behaviour remains impeccable, as he refuses to go out with another woman (Hülya Koçyiğit) in case it would sully the memory of his late wife (who died in childbirth). The camera repeatedly zooms in on his wife's photograph, to emphasize how much her memory lives on in his conscience. The film ends with Işık understanding the importance of the nuclear family for his daughter's future well-being; hence he agrees to marry, while turning his late wife's photograph to the wall. A chapter in his life has come to an end. In two films dating from 1964-5, *Kral Arkadaşım* (*My Best Friend*), and *Sevinç Gözyaşları* (*Tears of Joy*), he plays a lawyer standing up for the old-fashioned virtues of friendship, loyalty and frugality. In the first film he triumphs over the villains; in the second, however, his virtues prove no match for Filiz the good-time girl (Ajda Pekkan). As in most Yeşilçam films, she meets a violent end; but not before she tried to shoot her sister Selma (Filiz Akın), who happens to be Işık's fiancée. The implication is clear – while all good people are vulnerable, it is important that they retain their integrity to avoid falling into corruption like Selma.

Religion – understood in this context as the need to recognize divine power, while being aware of one's community responsibilities – formed an important theme in Işık's films. *Bir Avuç Toprak* (*A Handful of Soil*, 1957) contained a scene in which an entire village is shown praying to God for the loss of one of their number. In *Aslan Pençesi* (*The Lion's Paw*, 1966) Işık plays İsmail, whose younger brother Yılmaz (Kuzey Vargın) departs from the moral straight and narrow to join local mobster Reşit (Turgut Özatay) in a life of crime. Yılmaz ultimately sees the error of his ways and marries his teenage sweetheart, but the two of them have to be punished for their crimes, as they are pursued by Reşit and his mob. Even though İsmail offers temporary shelter in his forest retreat, Yılmaz cannot escape his inevitable fate as Reşit shoots him in the back, while the thugs rape and kill Yılmaz's young wife. İsmail enacts some form of revenge by killing Reşit, but can do nothing else other than to drag Yılmaz and his wife's corpses out of the retreat and join their hands together in death. The film ends with İsmail sinking to his knees, offering a silent prayer. Happiness eludes him, in spite of pursuing a virtuous life; he seeks divine guidance to help him secure 'the key of freedom' from material and worldly affairs. In time he might become someone who could respect the divinity while setting an example of humility for others to follow.

If this is to be achieved, however, then Işık's characters had to be prepared to give up worldly pleasures and devote themselves to specific causes. In *Aşktan Da Üstün* (*Superior to Love*, 1962), he plays Binbaşı Kemal (Major Kemal), another Turkish spy infiltrating the Ottoman government to discover details of their latest campaigns. However he proves so convincing in the role that his fellow Turks believe that he has betrayed them – especially when he falls for rich countess Nilüfer (Peri Han), even though he has already pledged his troth to the honest village girl Perihan (Serpil Gül). Kemal's brother Captain Nazmi (Ahmet Mekin) is so incensed that he bribes Nilüfer to pass on information about Kemal's movements in the Ottoman corridors of power. The film's conclusion is predictable: Nilüfer is eventually killed for being untrustworthy, while Nazmi understands that the most effective means for his brother to prise secrets out of the Ottomans was to develop a close relationship with Nilüfer–something that the major was duty-bound to do, even if it put his family loyalties at risk. The two brothers are briefly reconciled, before Nazmi shoots the Ottoman leader Muallim Ismail Hakkı (Nubar Terziyan) and then perishes himself in battle. Kemal looks skywards and nods his head slightly, as if understanding the divine logic that decrees that sacrifices are necessary if the Turkish people are going to achieve their dream of freedom.

While such films strengthened Işık's image as a selfless personality, blessed with the common touch, they also confirmed his status as a national hero of the Turkish cinema. Işık captured the mood of increasing national self-confidence, as Yeşilçam put the Turkish film industry firmly on the cinematic map (it became the third largest in the world). At the same time, Işık's star image showed him dedicating himself to virtue, based on an understanding that belief in the divinity transcends distinctions between good and evil, rich and poor.

Laurence Raw

Hülya Koçyiğit.

STARS
HÜLYA KOÇYİĞİT

Hülya Koçyiğit's acting career on screen started when she was 16 years old, in the 1960s. She was famous for her portrayals of pure, virtuous, self-sacrificing young girls who were always on the good side of the sharp female duality of good versus evil. She was known typically for melodramas and the titles of her films indicate the kind of films she appeared in: Uzakta Kal Sevgilim (Stay Away, My Love, 1965, Ulku Erakalin), Bitmeyen Çile (The Endless Suffering, 1966, Arsevir Alyanak), Seni Affedemem (I Cannot Forgive You, 1967, Duygu Sagiroglu). She has appeared in more than 150 films, including some of the classic texts of the cinema in Turkey. Examples are Susuz Yaz (Dry Summer, 1963) directed by Metin Erksan; Gelin (The Bride, 1973), Düğün (The Wedding, 1973), and Diyet (The Blood Money,1974), directed by Lütfi Akad; Susuz Yaz (Dry Summer) directed by Metin Erksan and David Durston, which won the Golden Bear at the Berlin Film Festival in 1964; and Almanya Acı Vatan (Germany, the Bitter Homeland, 1979), Derman (The Remedy, 1983), Firar (The Escape, 1984), and Kurbağalar (Frogs, 1985), all directed by Şerif Gören.

Koçyiğit later became a self-assured woman who fought to resist the dominance of men while attending to her own sexual needs in the characters she performed. This transformation in her performances was neither unconscious nor spontaneous. Koçyiğit, working with her husband, Selim Soydan, and director Şerif Gören, has indeed had a significant effect on the transformation of her image on the screen. Their first collaboration was Almanya Acı Vatan (Germany, The Bitter Homeland, 1979). In this film, as in her previous films, her voice was dubbed.

This film has two main themes: alienation caused by mass production, and gender. Güldane, played by Koçyiğit, lives among Turkish immigrants in Germany. A scene in the factory where she works is representative of the treatment of women in the workplace. A supervisor stands by a machine and demands that she start to work. She yells, 'Nein! Enough is enough!' 'You are late.' 'Nein!' 'You went to the bathroom.' 'Nein!' One is reminded of Diyet (Blood Money, 1974), an earlier film with Koçyiğit, in which a woman takes a stand in solidarity with a union. At first she wants to destroy the machine that had severed her husband's arm, but she stops, and looks into the eyes of the audience, proclaiming: 'It is not the machine's fault … It is our fault. IT IS OUR FAULT!' As her eyes fill with tears, her voice is the voice of a common conscience. Güldane in Germany is miserable both at home and at work. She has met and married Mahmut, but he treats her cruelly. When she is impregnated by him, however, she is transformed. Unable to continue working and investing her earnings, she leaves Mahmut and returns to her homeland to give birth to her child. This film is illustrative of the ways in which her performances and characters have shifted and for this reason is a significant film in her career.

Koçyiğit received the Best Actress award at the Antalya Film Festival (1984) for Derman (The Remedy, Şerif Gören). The film is based on the struggle between nature and human beings in the context of work-related migration. Mürvet, a midwife, is appointed to work in a village in harsh working conditions in Eastern Turkey. She is courageous and helpful – again a new and different role for Koçyiğit. The local people call Mürvet by her surname, Derman, which in Turkish means 'remedy', 'cure', and also 'power'. This is the first film in which Koçyiğit uses her own voice. Surprisingly, in one short scene, she is seen naked, and the camera captures her body image from behind, in a bath – another bold departure from her earlier films.

In Firar (The Escape, Goren 1984) she plays the role of Ayşe, who has to leave her children and go to jail, her bundle in her arms, her head covered. Over time, she removes her headscarf and starts to smoke, which is a signifier of the change in her character from a conservative and religious woman to an independent woman. She develops a relationship with a prison guard and manages to escape the prison. Although she is reunited with her children, she knows that she will be caught again, and, sure enough, this soon occurs.

Koçyiğit received the Best Actress award at the Nantes Three Continents Film Festival for her performance as Elmas in Kurbağalar (Frogs, Goren, 1985). The setting is a Western village where one must struggle to make ends meet. At the outset, Elmas loses her husband and is left alone with her child. The men of the village make a living by collecting and selling frogs. Husbandless, Elmas resorts to collecting frogs as the men stare at her. For an actress, merely touching the slimy frogs in this film was praiseworthy. Like Mürvet in Derman (The Remedy), Elmas mesmerizes two men: Hüseyin, who has just returned from military service, and Ali, who has just been released from prison. She falls in love with Ali. In the end, it is not Elmas but Ali who suppresses his sexuality in accord with traditional values. This is noteworthy in a Turkish film: a man trapped by moral law and tradition and a woman who does not yield to him.

Koçyiğit received the best actress award at the Amiens Film Festival in 1988 for her role as Melek in Bez Bebek (The Rag Doll), directed by Engin Ayça. Melek's husband has been in prison for a long time, causing her anguish and sexual longing, which Koçyiğit captures subtly in one scene in which she lies alone on a double bed. Later, when Melek's husband is about to be released from prison, she hires a painter to decorate the house. She is strongly attracted to the painter and, although he seems at first to force her to sleep with him, she later reveals that she deliberately did not resist. Koçyiğit's performance is impressive and powerful, particularly when Melek is shaking in shock while the painter kills her husband. However, one realizes in retrospect that she had killed her husband in her mind before he was actually killed, so that she could sleep with the man she desired.

Family is not the focus in Koçyiğit's later films. In Almanya Acı Vatan (Germany, the Bitter Homeland), a woman leaves her husband and chooses to give birth to her child without her husband by her side. In Derman (The Remedy) there is neither a husband nor a child. The central character is a midwife who has an affair with a doctor while at the same time taking an interest in another man. In Firar (The Escape) two children are born out of wedlock. The central character kills her lover because he refuses to marry her and legitimize their children, and then she initiates a relationship with another man. In Kurbağalar (Frogs) a widow sleeps with a man who is not her husband. In Bez Bebek (The Rag Doll) a woman's adulterous lover kills her husband. In all these films the husband is either dead, or soon to be dead, or abandoned. Hülya Koçyiğit portrays women who struggle against the opposition of men in a man's world and a man's workplace, women who are both defiant and aware of their desires. In Firar (The Escape) sexuality is seen from a female perspective; it is not unusual that men look lustfully at women, but in this film, a woman is sufficiently self-assured to look lustfully back at them. As a star who has a special place in the cinema of Turkey, Koçyiğit has changed and developed as her characters have changed and developed. It is disappointing to note here, however, that today, as an older star, she is not cast for many films.

S Ruken Öztürk

Türkân Şoray.

STARS
TÜRKÂN ŞORAY

Türkân Şoray has been a star of the Turkish cinema for over half a century. Born in 1945, she graduated from Fatih Kız Lisesi in İstanbul. While living with her mother and sister Nazan (also an actress) in rented accommodation, she found out that the landlords were the parents of Emel Yıldız, one of the earliest stars of the Turkish cinema. This proved to be Şoray's passport to stardom: by 1960 she had made her film debut in the melodrama Aşk Rüzgarı (Love Wind), aged just 15, and was signed to a long-term contract.

In the next five years Şoray established herself as the principal female star in Turkish cinema (acquiring the popular soubriquet 'Sultana' in the process), making over sixty films in the process, and, while doing so, acquired more and more artistic influence over her material. By 1969 she had created what came to be known as the 'Şoray Rules', which gave her almost total artistic control over her film career. They gave her the right to be given a script at least one month before shooting began and make whatever changes she desired. She could choose her cast, as well as director; anyone contradicting her could be deemed surplus to requirements. Every film she made had to be shot only in İstanbul, and she would not work on Sundays.

In her early career Şoray appeared as the ingénue – a young girl invariably ruled by her parents, whose sole aim in life was to find the right man. In Gençlik Rüzgarı (The Wind of Youth, 1964), Şoray's Fatma has to cope with her father, who has been jailed for murdering his wife's lover, as well as two lovers competing for her hand in marriage – the ever-reliable Mehmet Ali (Ediz Hun), and American would-be tycoon Charlie (Süleyman Turan). Eventually her father is released and cleared of all charges, while Fatma opts for stability (as personified by Mehmet Ali). Although frustrated in his suit, Charlie generously wishes Fatma and Mehmet Ali future happiness.

From the mid-1960s onwards Şoray reinvented herself as a young woman trying to cope with the responsibilities of marriage. As Türkân in Elveda Sevgilim (Goodbye My Lover, 1965), Şoray is forced by her tyrannical father to spurn her lover Kemal (Ediz Hun) and marry Osman (İzzet Günay) instead. Osman is her distant relative; Kemal, on the other hand, is a member of a rival family, who has been feuding with Türkân's family for generations. However she refuses to comply with her father's wishes and elopes with Kemal. Enraged by this wanton show of disloyalty, her father pursues the lovers but accidentally falls into a quagmire. Kemal rescues him, and the three of them are reconciled as a result.

Sometimes Şoray's characters made the wrong choice of marriage partner – and suffered terribly as a result. In Seven Kadın Unutmaz (A Loving Woman Does Not Forget, 1965), Şoray plays Türkân, an office worker who falls in love with an attractive young man (Ediz Hun). However things do not work out between them; the young man marries an older woman (Çolpan İlhan) who turns out to be an alcoholic. Türkân enjoys her clandestine meetings with the young man, but realizes that she will always be 'the other woman', unable to marry her chosen lover. Eventually she takes the only course open to her in a society that, for all its apparent openness (with semi-naked women like the younger Şoray appearing scantily clad in the fanzines), still frowned upon adulterous relationships.

As the 1960s evolved into the 1970s, so Şoray rethought her screen image once more; now she played women who were strong and determined, posing a challenge to the constricting conventions of behaviour imposed on them in a patriarchal society. In Vesikalı Yarım (My Licensed Beloved,1968) she plays Sabiha, a prostitute working in a nightclub who meets honest artisan Halil (İzzet Günay). Although not interested in him at first, Sabiha is gradually won over by his innocent charm, and resolves to leave her profession and set up home with him. A few years earlier this kind of arrangement would be unthinkable on screen (witness Seven Kadın Unutmaz), but director Lütfi Ö. Akad allows them at least a few moments of mutual happiness. Sebiha eventually tires of life as a housewife and returns to her old ways, much to Halil's disappointment. Although she repents later on, she finds to her chagrin that Halil has moved away, leaving her isolated.

In some of her later melodramas, Şoray offers new possibilities for women. *Selvi Boylum Al Yazmalım* (1978) offers a good example, as Şoray's Asya forges a new life for herself and son Samet (Elif İnci) with the amiable middle-aged Cemşit (Ahmet Mekin). She is not in love with him, but he offers a reassuring presence for her son. Asya's husband İlyas (Kadir İnanır) unexpectedly returns, having previously abandoned her for a younger woman, but now professing eternal love for her. Asya is drawn towards İlyas – despite his behaviour she has always been in love with him – but her mind is made up for her when Samet runs away from İlyas and into Cemşit's arms. Marriage as an institution counts for little; what matters most for Asya is that she should create a stable and loving environment in which to bring up her son.

Şoray's preoccupation with female roles is nowhere more evident than in Şerif Goren's *On Kadın* (*Ten Women*, 1987), where she portrays multiple characters – a battered village housewife, a middle-aged woman raped by her close relative, a campaigning journalist, a gipsy, a high-society feminist. Some of these women are assertive, others downtrodden; but what unites them all is that they are victimized by a patriarchal society. Both the housewife and the middle-aged woman are arrested for killing their male assailants; the journalist is jailed for lewd behaviour in a hotel room (despite the fact that she is only working there with her male colleague); the feminist risks imprisonment for standing up to the police, despite the fact she is trying to protect a wife from being abused by her husband.

During the 1980s and 1990s Şoray reinvented herself yet again as a mature performer. *Hayatımın Kadınsın* (*You are the Woman of My Life*, 2006) contains a remarkable commentary on Şoray's previous career as an actress. Ostensibly she plays a singer called Asuman, who has retired from regular performance and is now doomed to a life of drudgery with violent second-husband Nejat (Yıldırım Memişoğlu). However, she encounters long-time fan Tayfur (Uğur Yücel), who reminds her about a brief romantic encounter they had enjoyed several years previously after one of her concerts. At first she pretends not to remember but she admits, later, that she had been attracted to Tayfur, but never taken the opportunity to tell him. She had spent time enjoying the superficial benefits of stardom – money, drink, and a limitless succession of casual yet meaningless affairs. Having left the bright lights behind, she can now understand the importance of close personal relationships as a way of coping with her (increasingly violent) life. The film ends with Tayfur killing Nejat and driving off into the sunset in his motor-launch to begin a new life cohabiting with Asuman and daughter Ahu. As in *Selvi Boylum Al Yazmalım*, the subject of marriage is discreetly avoided.

By reinventing herself according to different circumstances, Şoray has been able to occupy the public gaze for five decades now, and not retire into a fantasy world of her own creation.

Laurence Raw

INDUSTRY SPOTLIGHT
YEŞİLÇAM

Yeşilçam (literally meaning Green Pine) is a metonym similar to Hollywood, which is used by the film industry in Turkey to refer to popular cinema and distinctive films made in the period from the 1950s to the 1990s. Yeşilçam is one of the small streets in İstanbul, where many actors, directors and studios were based during the period. Auteur directors, including Ömer Lütfi Akad, Metin Erksan, Halit Refiğ and Atıf Yılmaz, made individual efforts to move the cinema of Turkey to a unique place –particularly with the melodramas, comedies and musicals they made. Their films as well as many others were mass-produced, which resulted in a considerable increase in production numbers: between 1960-1961, 81 films; 1961-1962, 115 films; 1962-1963, 130 films; 1963-1964, 127 films; 1964-1965, 181 films; 1965-1966, 214 films; 1966-1967, 209 films; 1967-1968, 179 films; 1969-1970, 231 films were made.[1] Yeşilçam cinema and films have distinctive qualities that give clues about the mode of production. The films have similar aesthetic and cinematographic qualities. They are recognized for being low-budget productions using little, or old, technological equipment; for having preferred locations for particular genres (luxurious estates in the city for melodramas; historical sites for historical or fantasy films, etc.); for their the dubbing methods used (all films were dubbed); for the use of non-professional actors and actresses; for more emphasis on the story and less care shown towards performance, for their shooting and editing quality; and last, but certainly not least, for one-dimensional (and at times unrealistic) characters. During the Yeşilçam period, melodrama was a popular genre; however, there were comedies, series films, films with child leads, adventure, action, fantasy and horror films. Particularly in the 1960s, social and ideological shifts also led to a social-realist approach in cinema. Yet, many of these films did not offer much criticism or any solutions to the issues they focus on and represent. The quality of films (in terms of their *mise-en-scène* and cinematography) was rather poor, a resultperhaps of the low-budget and mass production conditions they were made in. There was, therefore, no improvement in the quality of films despite the considerable increase in the number of films made by Yeşilçam producers. Yet, audience expectations were low as they were interested in the stories the films told, and the experience of going to the cinema was more interesting than the cinematographic and aesthetic qualities of a film. After the 1970s, Yeşilçam suffered with the arrival and spread of television in Turkey. Films that were made served the nation with their entertainment and particularly comedy values. These films could not travel outside Turkey as they offered culturally- and nationally- specific messages. Yeşilçam was a period in Turkish cinema which is remembered for its mass produced films, popular novel adaptations, comedy series, melodramas, and stars.

Dilek Tunalı

Notes

[1] For details see, Özgüç, A., *Türk Filmleri Sözlüğü 1-2* (Dictionary of Turkish Film 1-2) İstanbul: Sesam, 1994.

EARLY CINEMA

The mainstream film history in Turkey has a tendency to view and construct its subject within the Westernization paradigm of a 'Turkish' national cultural criticism. The intentions of this short essay is, firstly, to reconsider the Turkish film historiography and, secondly, to strive to reveal the global, cosmopolitan and the heterogeneous elements of the early stages of cinema life in the formerly Ottoman lands. This introduction reviews films all made before the foundation of the Turkish Republic in 1923, namely the films by Manaki Brothers and kept at Macedonian Cinematheque and the films that are kept at Mimar Sinan University's Centre of Cinema and Television's archive.

It may be tempting to perceive this topic, early cinema in the Ottoman lands, as transnational or international. However, it may also be an anachronism to do so, since the nation state (that formed the Turkish Republic) was not yet established when the following films were made. Thus, it is important to point out the question of an umbrella term to categorize these films: 'an Ottoman cinema', 'the cinemas of the Ottoman Empire' or 'the cosmopolitan Ottoman cinema'. As this question awaits an answer, another concern arises, namely the globalized characteristics of early cinema itself.[1] Hence, these films may actually go beyond any local categories, as we know and use such categories today.

The Westernization paradigm dominant in the cultural criticism of Turkey assumes Euro-centric modernity as a reference point and the Turkish modernization project as a belated one in relation to the European model. Considering 'cinema and modernity as points of reflection and convergence', the assumption of belatedness seems conveniently applicable to most of the aspects of early cinema in Turkey. According to the film historians, it was basically the inadequacies that defined the film industry in Turkey. Even as early as 1923, when the Turkish Republic was just founded, film criticism was dominated by the insufficiency of Turkish film production. Vedat Örf, in a reproachful tone, mentions the scarcity of Turkish (narrative) film productions and indicates that, until then, only two local productions were made (*Binnaz* and *Mürebbiye*, both made by Ahmet Fehim in 1919).[2] According to Örf, *Binnaz* (Ahmet Fehim, 1919) attracted a much bigger audience than it actually deserved. For him, *Binnaz* was much appreciated as the first national picture, even though it suffered greatly from technical inadequacies due to the low budget stemming from the conditions of the World War I.[3] Indeed, reading the memoirs of Cemil Filmer, who was the arts manager of the film, it appears that this film was made under grotesquely poor conditions:

> There was a clerk in charge of our budget, who would always warn us about the expenses. I can never forget this: in one scene the man would get angry with his wife and throw a glass jug into the mirror. The clerk objected to this, as both the mirror and the jug would be too expensive to break. Therefore Ahmet Fehim Efendi [the director] came up with a solution, we would use a non-glass jug and the man would throw it into the window instead of the mirror. Yet the clerk again objected 'someone should stand behind the window and catch the jug before it falls on the ground'.[4]

These insufficiencies certainly define the industry as a 'belated' one in relation to the Western European and Northern American models. It is noteworthy, however, that one needs to shy away from seeing these different periodizations emerging from cultural factors. Even if we were supposed to define it as 'belated', this occurs not out of a cultural interest in novelties but out of a certain level of wealth and technological advancement.

The unfortunate loss of the Ottoman/Turkish silent films may add another perspective in a consideration of the writing of film history. Printed on nitrate and kept in the National Film Archive in Ankara, these films were burned in the 1950s during a fire that destroyed the archive. Some of the surviving copies are now held in the Mimar Sinan University's Centre for Cinema and Television archive, in İstanbul, under rigid supervision. The film catalogue in this archive is not readily available. According to the archivists there are only two films kept from the silent period, and the locations of the rest of the films are still somewhat of a mystery.

Thinking about the mysteries that were influential in film history writing, it is necessary to underline once again the role of the construction of a national cinema narrative. Another reflection of this approach inspires the never-ending debates surrounding the 'first Turkish film', which is almost officially accepted as 'Ayestefanos Abidesinin Yıkılışı' (The Demolition of the Monument of St. Stephen), allegedly made in 1914 by a Turkish soldier and film-maker Fuat Uzkınay. This mythical film is described as having depicted the destruction of the Russian Monument, built by Russians as a symbolic result of a victory against the Ottomans near the city of Istanbul at the Russian-Ottoman War (1877-1878). No copies of the film can be found, nor are there any still photographs or official documents related to this 'first picture'. Perhaps ironically, this imaginary film, as the basis of a national film history narrative, can be read as an allegory of the nation as an imaginary community. A first national film that depicts the cleansing of foreign cultural traces in the construction of a national memory remains merely as a legend in the material plane. This allegory is made clearer if we also consider the dismissal of other foreign traces in Turkish film history: the traces left by Manaki Brothers, the earliest film-makers of the Balkans.

Films of the Manaki Brothers have scarcely been looked into, although their national identities have been a heated debate among Serbian, Greek, Romanian and Macedonian national cultural historians. Born as Ottoman citizens in a Vlach village on Macedonian grounds of today's Greek lands (Ianaki Manaki was born in 1878 and Milton Manaki in 1882, in Avdela near Grevena), the Manaki Brothers were the official photographers of both the Romanian king and the Ottoman sultan. They both went to a Romanian school and Ianaki died in Thessalonica (1954) as a Greek citizen, Milton in Bitola (1964) as a Yugoslav citizen. As pointed out earlier, Turkish film historiography seems to disregard these important figures due to national concerns, imbricated with religious identities and loyalties, despite the fact that Milton Manaki, older when his films were (re)discovered, was admittedly proud of having filmed the Ottoman bureaucrats and the sultan.[5] It should be noted that the Manaki brothers made more than 40 short films, carefully protected and kept at the Cinematheque of Macedonia in Skopje. According to some of the interviews with Milton Manaki, their films were never shown in public, and even the brothers did not view their own films.[6] Hardly convincing as this may seem as a categorical statement, some of the films remained undeveloped and some were kept away from the projector, as they were on nitrate and easily flammable. According to the archivist and filmologist Igor Stardelov of the Macedonian Cinematheque, the Manakis sold their films to the Macedonian State Archive in 1955, and only then did Milton see his films for the first time.[7] Another reason for the neglect of their own films could be that they were known as photographers and made their living as such rather than as cinematographers. This may also account for the subject matters of their films, some of which may be seen as souvenirs, such as wedding ceremonies and café openings. Not all of their films are 'lighthearted', of course, as the official photographers of the Ottoman Sultan and the Romanian King, the Manaki Brothers shot films of execution of the rebels, parades (sometimes by the armies of different countries), religious holidays and celebrations (such as Saint George's day, celebration of Epiphany and the like), the arrival of Sultan Resad in Thessalonica and in Bitola in 1919 (as two different short films), and a Romanian Delegation's visit of Bitola. These newsreels, although supposedly never displayed in public, were described by Milton Manaki as better records of history than most American and French films.[8] In addition to the records of public events taking place in Bitola and Thessaloniki, Milton and Ianaki also filmed the everyday life of the area such as folk dances, school children, butchers, laundresses, weaving women (including their own grandmother Despina), horses outside the veterinary station and the like. These 'everyday life films' all show some type of 'attraction', such as the teacher's punishment of the children who 'acted' like the teacher when the teacher was away but the camera was still there to shoot them, and a scene of an intercourse between horses along with a picture of the constant movement of a sewing machine somewhat resembling the apparatus of the cinematograph. In most of these films, we see the characters' aware-ness of the camera, either in the way they wave and look at the camera or in the way they virtually greet the camera operator. This self-awareness, common as it was in other early films, may also stem from the fact that Bitola was a small town and the Manaki brothers were well known there. We are still unsure whether this was because film-mak-ing was a rare practice in this town (and those who were filmed were unfamiliar with the apparatus, which is unlikely) or because the people in these pictures wanted to greet the Brothers who were well known as 'eccentrics' by the public of Bitola. In some of the films, it is possible to see Milton Manaki directing the crowds for the *mise-en-scène* or simply passing by in front of the camera, while Ianaki Manaki is operating it.

The Manaki Brothers embody an important part of the history of the cinema of the Balkans or 'the oriental periphery of Europe', in which most nations came under totalitar-ian regimes, fought with foreign occupiers and had an ambivalent relationship with their Ottoman legacy.[9] The Brothers may be posited as representing an intersection between various nations in the Balkans, while some other examples from the Ottoman cultural heritage can be read as being under the influence of the 'traditional' performing arts and the 'modern' cinema while displaying the 'global' early cinema trends on the issues of gender.

As mentioned earlier, Mimar Sinan University's archive allegedly holds only two of the silent films from Turkey; *Bican Efendi Vekilharç* (Sadi Fikret Karagözoğlu, 1921) and Binnaz (Ahmet Fehim, 1919). It would be a misleading attempt to do a textual analysis of these films based on their current versions in the archive. The copy of *Bican Efendi Vekilharç* is around four minutes shorter than the original version, while *Binnaz* is almost two thirds shorter than its original length.[10] The films were re-edited in the 1950s by film historians, since until then the pelicules were randomly kept together without any order until the moment they were found.[11] More importantly, one of them, *Binnaz*, is almost a third of its original length (the film was originally 45 minutes, but only 19 minutes of it is available at the archive).[12]

Bican Efendi Vekilharç is part of the slapstick series made about the adventures of an Ottoman gentleman named Bican Efendi. According to Giovanni Scognamillo, this character stems from a theatre play written by Ibnurrefik Ahmet Nuri Sekizinci.[13] Scognamillo argues that the success of the Bican Efendi films was due to their similarities with the stereotypical filmic tramp created by Charlie Chaplin. If more resemblances were to be found, this series may also be reminiscent of the Ottoman shadow-theatre Karagöz. Both narrations revolve around a character whose unpredictable nature leads to extraordinary ventures, and in both texts the main characters have unfixed identities along with a wide range of varying hobbies, professions and interests. *Binnaz*, on the other hand, is centred around a female character called Binnaz and a tragic story of a love triangle caused by this proto-femme fatale. Both *Bican Efendi Vekilharç* and Binnaz offer some of the significant characteristics of early cinema such as voyeurism and self-reflexivity. *Bican Efendi Vekilharç* has a key-hole shot and a belly-dance scene. The film also includes various scenes that function almost like a silent laugh-track. In order to emphasize the humour based on Bican Efendi's clumsiness, supporting actors are shown to laugh at him while holding their bellies. In *Binnaz*, it is the point-of-view shot that underlines the act of voyeurism. In one shot, the audience sees the eyes of an unknown person looking at the camera/projector hidden behind some clothes. In the next shot it appears that these eyes actually watch a party scene and two people kissing.

The cinema life that began in the Ottoman lands refers to a medium at the crossroads of ethnicities, dissolving and being constructed at the same time, in a period of transition from an empire to nation states in the case of the Manaki Brothers. In the case of *Bican Efendi*, it was a convergence point of different discourses with reference to an intermedial practice interconnecting the 'traditional' performing arts and the global silent film trends. In *Binnaz* and *Bican Efendi*, it also embodied a heterogeneous space, a space filled with gender roles, patriarchy and voyeurism, in a familiar blend for a modern audience of 'classical cinema'. These films may have come too early to be called transnational, yet they may form the base of a transnational film history, despite the inadequacies that somewhat determine our ways of seeing these films.

Canan Balan

Notes

1   See Tom Gunning (2008) 'Early Cinema as Global Cinema: The Encyclopedic Ambition', *Early Cinema and the 'National'*, eds: Richard Abel, Giorgio Bertellini and Rob King, pp. 11-17. London: John Libbey Publishing; Miriam Hansen (1999) 'The Mass Production of the Senses: Classical Cinema as Vernacular Modernism', *Modernism/Modernity* 6.2: 59-77.
2   Vedat Örf (1923) 'Milli Filmler', *Sinema Postasi*, 1 December, p. 3.
3   Ibid.
4   Cemil Filmer (1984) *Hatiralar: Turk Sinemasinda 65 Yil*. İstanbul: Emek Matbaacılık, p. 95.
5   Milenka Karanović (2004) 'Omnia Labor Vincit', in *Kod Najstari Snimatelja Balkanske Historije Ili Najstari Filmski Operator Na Balkanu*, ed. by Dejan Kosanovic and Milenka Karanović, Beograd,.
6   Ljuba Stojovic (1938) 'From the Archive, Newspapers and Recordings with Ljuba Stojovic', *Politika*, 22 March.
7   From a private interview with Igor Stardelov in 2006.
8   Milenka Karanović.
9   See Dina Iordanova (1998) The *Cinema of the Balkans*, London: Wallflower Press, (2006), pp. 6-9.

10 For the original length of Binnaz I rely on the information provided by Giovanni Scognamillo (2003). See *Türk Sinema Tarihi* Istanbul: Kabalcı, p. 47.
11 Personal interview with Giovanni Scognamillo.
12 Scognamillo, *Türk Sinema Tarihi*, p. 47.
13 Ibid. The theatre play itself was considered to be an adaptation of another play entitled *Le Pretexte* by Daniel Riche.

A Nation is Awakening

Bir Millet Uyanıyor

Studio:
İpek Film

Director:
Muhsin Ertuğrul

Assistant Directors:
Kemal Necati Çakuş
Nazım Hikmet Ran

Producer:
İhsan İpekçi

Screenwriters:
Nizamettin Nazif
Tepedelenlioğlu

Cinematographer:
Cezmi Ar

Duration:
82 Minutes

Cast:
Ercüment Behzat Lav
Emel Rıza
Atıf Kaptan
Ferdi Tayfur
Emin Beliğ Belli
Palmira

Year:
1932

Synopsis

This epic film is the tale of the Turkish National Struggle (1919-1922) against the Allied Powers after the Great War (1914-1918). It tells the story of a number of different characters. Three characters represent the Turkish national forces (Kuvayı Milliye); they are Lieutenant Davut, Captain Yahya and a teacher named Nesrin. Three other characters attempt to stop the resistance movement; they are Said Molla, Priest Frew and Ottoman officer Feridun. The film starts during the initial occupation of Istanbul by the Allied Powers in 1918. The Ottoman officer Feridun lures Nesrin into the forest where he forces himself upon her. Lieutenant Davut, who is in the forest on a secret mission for the resistance movement, saves Nesrin from Feridun's forceful embrace. Nesrin is indebted to Lieutenant Davut for his heroics and thus begins their love affair. Feridun learns of Lieutenant Davut's participation in the resistance and aims to kill him. After a series of events Captain Yahya saves Lieutenant Davut's life. During a fight with the Allied Powers, Captain Yahya is mortally wounded. The film ends with actual footage of the heroic marching soldiers along with Mustafa Kemal Atatürk and other national leaders.

Critique

As the first film with recorded sound in Turkey, A Nation is Awaking is a blend of two different narrative forms. The first one is the fictional part in which characters play the true personas of the time and the second is a documentary that is narrated with a voice-over with factual subjects such as images of the Turkish army and President Mustafa Kemal Atatürk (1881-1938). Therefore, the film is a powerful representation of 'hybrid film', sharing the characteristics of both fiction and documentary. Yet the structure of the film, especially during the transition between two parts is not well-formulated and aesthetically the juxtaposition of the images is flawed.

A Nation is Awaking begins after the occupation of İstanbul by the British and French troops in 1918. Some of the fight scenes may seem hostile to the French and British troops and their soldiers are portrayed crudely as they attack the local forces. There is no harsh criticism against the Greek forces although the local forces also fought against them during this time. Unfortunately, the black and white film makes it difficult to differentiate troops during the occupation scenes. The portrayal of the infantry is ambiguous and unclear, as the costumes are badly designed and do not distinguish one side's soldiers from the other's. Interestingly, the occupation forces were partly performed by amateur black actors to show the different armies and probably due to stereotyping. Some characters were performed by the actors from The City Theatre of İstanbul (Dar'ül bedayi) who did not have any previous experience in cinema. Thus, the acting is occasionally theatrical and expressive. The popularity of the film among the audience led some male actors such as Atıf Kaptan, who played Captain Yahya, to take roles in some other films in the following years (Zahir Güvemli, 1960: 244).

The documentary part of the film offers various facts about the National Struggle and the establishment of Turkey in 1923 and, thus, it is very patriotic and nationalistic. Indeed, the use of a narrator and the introduction of actual images onto the screen emphasize this notion. The didactic and informative tone of the narrator, intermingled with a symphonic orchestra and folk songs, accentuates the second part's style. This propaganda element is used with the symbols of the nation such as Atatürk, the Turkish flag, the national army with canons, weapons and planes to manifest the significance and pride of the new nation. In fact, the film fully celebrates the victory of the Turkish army and Atatürk. This is shown throughout the second part, such as in the last scene where the soldiers sing the heroic folk song with the following lyrics: 'March glorious Warrior, the bloody-sworded warrior, the River Meriç awaits you, the great warrior sovereign'.

Acclaimed director and theatre actor Muhsin Ertuğrul's *A Nation is Awaking* was supported by the government and based on a striking scenario written by Nizamettin Nazif Tepedelenlioğlu. The film is partially based on a true story and refers to Atatürk's memories and Tepedelenlioğlu's acquaintances who were prominent politicians and leaders of the National Struggle at the time. The film contains various references to Atatürk's famous *Nutuk* (*Great Speech*, 1927) and his reading of it is included in the second part. In fact another film of Ertuğrul, *Ateşten Gömlek* (*The Shirt of Fire*, 1923), also chronicles the National Struggle from the viewpoint of a soldier but it was not as well-received as was *A Nation is Awaking*. Director Ertuğrul was considerably influenced by Soviet filmmaking of the time, particularly the theories of montage. In 1924, Ertuğrul was trained in the USSR and made two films there, *Tamilla* (1925) and *Spartacus* (1926), and, for instance, in *A Nation is Awaking* Ertuğrul attempts to invoke the emotions of the audience using methods similar to Sergei Eisenstein's montage techniques through a dynamic juxtaposition of images.

When *A Nation is Awaking* was screened in 1932, Turkey was nurturing good foreign relations with neighbouring countries, especially with Greece. At the end of the film, the factual voiceover proclaims Atatürk's slogan 'Peace at home peace in the world.' In fact the young nation-state was pursuing the goal of neutrality during these years before the Second World War (1939-1945). Throughout the film bold statements help the audience to absorb the patriotic meaning of the story; overall this heroic film celebrates the birth of a new nation while breaking with Ottoman heritage.

Özde Çeliktemel-Thomen

Bican Efendi the Butler

Bican Efendi Vekilharç

Studio:
Society of Disabled Veterans'
Studio
(Malul Gaziler Heyeti Stüdyosu)

Director:
Şadi Fikret Karagözoğlu

Producer:
The Society of Disabled Veterans Film Factory
(Malul Gaziler Heyeti Sinema Film Fabrikası)

Screenwriter:
Şadi Fikret Karagözoğlu

Cinematographer:
Fuat Uzkınay

Duration:
22 Minutes
(the version held by the Mimar Sinan University runs for 11 minutes)

Cast:
Şadi Fikret Karagözoğlu
İsmail Galip
Şehper Karagözoğlu
Behzat Haki Butak
Nurettin Şefkati

Year:
1921

Synopsis

Bican Efendi is a butler who is charged with arranging a soirée. He oversees the preparations for it, makes the food arrangements and takes care of the mansion and guests. During the preparations, a set of accidents happens due to his clumsiness. While the guests enjoy the music and dance show, the police arrive at the scene of the party. At the end, Bican Efendi becomes hoisted with his own petard.

Critique

This funny and well-received comedy is the first of a three part series by director and actor Şadi Fikret Karagözoğlu featuring the leading character, Bican Efendi. The series include *Bican Efendi Vekilharç* (*Bican Efendi the Butler*, 1921), *Bican Efendi Mektep Hocası* (*Bican Efendi the School Master*, 1921) and *Bican Efendi'nin Rüyası* (*Bican Efendi's Dream*, 1921). The story is inspired by a popular play of the time by İbnürrefik Ahmet Nuri Sekizinci, called *Hisse-i Şayia*, which was first staged in 1914 (And 2001:98). The character Bican Efendi is an example of slapstick comedy, using tricks and other funny actions. Karagözoğlu successfully performed the character of Bican Efendi on stage for many years and later became synonymous with the role, similar to that of Charlie Chaplin and the character Charlot. As with other Ottoman films, actors with theatrical backgrounds were tapped to perform the lead roles and they employ many theatrical and expressive gestures in the film.

The 11-minute version of the film has been restored and is available today, owing to the efforts of Mimar Sinan University's Centre of Cinema and Television. Undeniably, the original structure of the film was subject to various changes in the arrangement of the narrative. Although the order of the scenes might have been altered, *Bican Efendi the Butler* in its restored form has a chronological structure. It begins with an introduction of the setting, the grand mansion of an upper-class Ottoman man. Then the main characters of the story are presented. They are Bican Efendi, the staff of the household, the owner of the mansion with his friends. The film finishes with an unexpected end due to Bican Efendi's unsuccessful attempts to turn events in his favour.

The key attraction of *Bican Efendi the Butler* is the absurd and funny situations caused by the clumsy Bican Efendi punctuated by his effective performance that helps keep the viewer involved in the story. Karagözoğlu uses slapstick elements of vigorous physical actions and accidents in the role of Bican Efendi. The film's appeal does not stem merely from the actions of a funny leading character but also from supporting actors such as female dancers in chic costumes and the servant who performs an amusing dance. The scene depicting the entertainment of the guests with live music is spectacular due to the dance show and Karagözoğlu's theatrics.

Bican Efendi the Butler is remarkably engaging and humorous not only because of its story and acting but also due to the cinematographer Fuat Uzkınay. His increasingly professional experience in handling the camera throughout the years shows his development of a new aesthetic style. In this film Uzkınay combines a mix of shots from close-ups to different camera distances. In particular, the last scene, featuring Bican Efendi's surprisingly direct gaze into the camera, suggests that Uzkınay is searching for a much fresher cinematography compared to his earlier films.

This comedy, a first in Ottoman cinema history, introduces the memorable character of Bican Efendi and it generated widespread interest among the audience at the time. *Bican Efendi the Butler* is an accomplished example of a well-developed narrative and cinematography enriched by the performers' charming acting and thus far remains a widely-esteemed film. Thanks to the restored version of this film, cinephiles today can have a glimpse of the earliest comedy of the Ottoman cinema.

Özde Çeliktemel-Thomen

Binnaz

Binnaz

Studio:
Society of Disabled Veterans' Studio
(Malul Gaziler Heyeti Stüdyosu)

Director:
Ahmet Fehim

Producer:
Society of Disabled Veterans

Screenwriter:
Münif Fehim

Cinematographer:
Fuat Uzkınay

Art Director:
Münif Fehim

Duration:
45 Minutes
(the version held by the Mimar Sinan University runs for 19 minutes)

Cast:
Mademoiselle Blanche
Ahmet Fehim
Rana Dilberyan

Synopsis

Binnaz is the name of a young and beautiful woman who is in love with a janissary named Efe Ahmet and is the eponymous heroine of this 1919 film by director Ahmet Fehim. Binnaz is a prominent courtesan in imperial Istanbul whose fame is also well known throughout the Balkans. Unsurprisingly, a young man from the Danube, Hamza Bey, learns about the beauty of Binnaz and becomes determined to find her. He successfully meets Binnaz after travelling to Istanbul, only to learn that she is in love with another man. The two men meet when Efe Ahmet saves Hamza Bey's life during a street fight. Hamza Bey gives Efe Ahmet his precious dagger as a gift to thank him. Eventually, their mutual interest in lovely Binnaz is revealed when they later meet at a coffee house. After a series of quarrels and jealous fits, Efe Ahmet injures Hamza Bey with the dagger. At the end, only one lover captures Binnaz's heart after some troublesome events. The film includes magnificent views from Topkapı Palace and scenes of Istanbul, particularly the Golden Horn.

Critique

Binnaz is the earliest fiction film made in Istanbul that has survived to the present. Hence, it provides a glimpse of silent film-making in the Ottoman Empire. Thanks to the efforts of Mimar Sinan University's Centre of Cinema and TV, *Binnaz* was restored from a nitrate print into video format. The 1919 film was originally 1338 metres and 45 minutes long; this version only runs for 19 minutes. Therefore, the only available version of the film has gaps in the story due to the new format and it does not provide as many sequences as it might have originally contained.

Based on Yusuf Ziya Ortaç's play of the same name, the story was allegedly inspired by Victor Hugo's play *Marion de Lorme* (1831).

Hüseyin Kemal
Ekrem Oran

Year:

1919

One gets a sense that the film targeted a high-society audience who would have been familiar with the play. The Society of Disabled Veterans's manager and experienced cinematographer, Fuat Uzkınay, handled the camera as stage performer *Mademoiselle* Blanche played the lead role of Binnaz. After the highly praised success of Ahmet Fehim's *Mürebbiye* (*The Governess*, 1919), *Binnaz* did not earn as much acclaim when it was released in Istanbul.

Set in the eighteenth-century Tulip Period of the Ottoman Empire, the story portrays the pursuit of sensual pleasure and self-indulgence that allegedly characterized the climate of the era. As the Tulip Period poet Ahmet Nedim's lines suggest, 'Let us laugh, let us play, let us enjoy the delights of the world', this period revelled in worldly delights such as feasts, ceremonies, dance shows, shadow play performances, and poetry readings. According to the mainstream historical perspective, the period is known for a highly-materialized consumption culture among the higher classes, yet it also witnessed the flowering of arts and culture. During the party scene in Binnaz, women belly dancing before the audience and Binnaz's lute playing portray some examples of arts and pleasure-seeking tendencies during the Tulip Period. Typical depictions of dance shows can also be observed in other silent films such as Şadi Fikret Karagözoğlu's *Bican Efendi the Butler* (1921). Although the film does not claim to embody actual personas from the time, the realistic settings at the mansion and other well-chosen *mise-en-scène* at Topkapı Palace evoke the eighteenth-century atmosphere. For instance, *Binnaz* opens with a scene portraying a parade of pashas, janissaries and other Ottoman administrators in the palace in order to capture the context of the time.

Binnaz's artistic endeavour can be especially appreciated in one of the most striking scenes depicting Hamza Bey's voyeuristic intrigue while Binnaz dances in the mansion. Hamza Bey's wide-open, dark eyes behind the curtains follow Binnaz's sensual moves and rhythmic dance. Additionally, Binnaz's moderately-revealing and elegant costume enhances her beauty and vitality. This short, but engaging scene also emphasizes her life as a courtesan. Her characterization as an attractive and worldly woman becomes noticeably more visible to the viewer after this scene.

The row between Hamza Bey and Binnaz is another crucial scene which is well preserved in this copy. This is the first scene in which the characters are shown together and is notable due to several close-up shots. Here Binnaz shows a mix of emotions because of Hamza Bey's unexpected visit; after all he is a stranger to her and she is in love with Efe Ahmet. During this conflict among major characters, the viewer gets the chance to observe other aspects of Binnaz while her internal struggles are revealed within a highly expressive performance. Scared, puzzled and anxious, Binnaz nevertheless manages to persuade Hamza Bey to leave by giving him a small kiss. In this partially still-camera setting, characters stand as if they are before a live audience which is a little reminiscent of a stage performance. Cinematographer Uzkınay's use of close-up shots enriches the scene by giving more importance to the major characters, specifically revealing the complexities of Binnaz's feelings. These delightful and meticulous shots express Binnaz's mood and, soon, her relief can be observed as she plays her lute.

As an object of desire for men, Binnaz is similar to the common representation of women characters as *femme fatales* among other films of the time (i.e., the French governess, Angèle, in *the Governess*). Although now only in bits and pieces of available copy, *Binnaz* still catches the viewers' attention with its provocative love story, elaborate costumes and well-chosen location shots, and stands as an important silent film reflecting the cinema heritage of the Ottoman Empire. In the film, Binnaz is living in happy times, in relatively-war-free days; entertaining men, capturing the hearts of strangers, yet this historical romance is and has been much more. *Binnaz* still offers other implicit meanings waiting to be explored by other viewers.

Özde Çeliktemel-Thomen

Hürriyet films

Hürriyet filmleri

Directors:
Ianaki Manaki
Milton Manaki

Producers:
Ianaki Manaki
Milton Manaki

Cinematographers:
Ianaki Manaki
Milton Manaki

Editor:
Igor Stardelov

Duration:
12 Minutes

Year:
1908 – 1912

Synopsis

The Manaki Brothers' *Hürriyet* footage now preserved in the Cinematheque of Macedonia covers six titles related to the Young Turk uprising in Manastır (today Bitola, Republic of Macedonia) in 1908. They present various phases of the new era up until 1912, the day when Bitola ceased to be a part of the Ottoman Empire. The Manaki Brothers documented the parades performed in Bitola at the 10 July festivals – the commemoration of the uprising – ('Manifestations on the Occasion of Young Turks' Revolution'; 'Parade on the Occasion of the *Hürriyet*'), ceremonies held for official announcements ('Turks Having Speech on the Hürriyet'), and Sultan Mehmed V Reşad's visit in 1911 ('Procession on the Occasion of Hürriyet'). The setting for the ceremonies features the new use of urban space and the ceremonial order through the revolutionary rhetoric: Shirok Sokak, the main street as the backbone of the parade and, at the end, the space dominated by military barracks as the official ceremonial area. The recurrent figures highlighted with close-ups seem to underline a pro-rebellion motivation of the cameramen: Niyazi Bey of Resen, the 'hero' of Hürriyet, the 'freedom coach' carrying five girls with dark ribbons inscribed with the main motto of Hürriyet (literally the freedom): justice, equality, freedom, brotherhood and unity.

Critique

The visual legacy of the Manaki Brothers gainsays in many ways the current patronizing historiographical frames on the history of motion pictures in the Balkans. Except a few studies that focused on the cinematographic idiosyncrasies of their work, or their position in the Balkanic film network – like 'Manaki' by Igor Stardelov (2003), or 'Orient Express' by Marian Tutui (2011) – the debate on the Brothers is largely filtered through nationalistic claims. They would be the Greek, Roman, Albanian and Ottoman pioneers of the Balkan cinema and the bearer of a myriad of ennobling titles: official photographers or cameramen both for the Romanian king and the Ottoman sultan. However, these historically- and socially-specific discourses, mostly underlined by a territorial and cultural defensiveness, fail in the analytical dissection of the Brothers' intricate socio-cultural allegiances and their protean creative strategies in concert with the turbulent transition of the Balkans throughout the twentieth century. The denomination 'Ottoman photographers and filmmakers', for instance, would hardly embody their diverse array of political ties, national affiliations, and the representational strategies they embraced under Ottoman rule. As Ottoman subjects from the Vlach community, they turned their camera to life, fairs, wedding ceremonies, religious rituals of various communities, and to Sultan Mehmed V Reşad as well. This plethora of variants urge for a more nuanced approach to the impetus behind their work, to begin with their ties with the Ottoman palace as the so-called cameramen of the Ottoman sultan: this is what their *Hürriyet* footage hints at.

Hürriyet was one motto of the Young Turk Revolution of 1908, and a generic denomination of the revolutionary era. The uprising against Sultan Abdul Hamid (r.1876 – 1909) reached its peak in 23 July 1908, when young officers in Bitola announced the restoration of the Ottoman constitution suspended in 1877 by the very sultan Abdul Hamid. The following day Istanbul newspapers made public this restoration, however, as an imperial decree by the sultan himself: The Young Turks led by the Committee of Union and Progress (hereafter CUP) and the Palace would subtly dispute the honour of the revolution.

Bitola was the town where Manaki Brothers opened their photo studio in 1905. From 1908 onwards, they played the part of revolutionary memorabilia collector: they photographed the leaders of the uprising – especially Niyazi Bey of Resen – and multiethnic, multinational celebrations of townsmen. Those images, reproduced soon after through newspapers, postcards and albums, circulated a visual narrative of the revolution all over the Empire. Their movie camera, the famous British produced Bioscope 300, was in charge too, yet the films, unlike the photographs, would have never been circulated: apparently, the Brothers did not or were not able to print their films on positive stock for projection, even if they probably intended to at the outset. The *Hürriyet* footage has been a part of the filmic corpus delivered to the Yugoslavian state by Milton Manaki in 1955. They have been restored, in 1996, in Hungary, and assembled and titled in the Cinematheque of Macedonia, under the supervision of Igor Stardelov, mainly based on the list made by Milton Manaki and available archival documents. However, an analysis through the sources in Turkish indicates that the films represent various phases of the Young Turk revolution between 1908 and 1912, which means a revision of the admitted current chronology relating most of the titles to 1908.

The Brothers' camera is selective. A general plan is often followed by a close-up to recurrent figures: the 'coach of freedom', the CUP banner and blazon, and Niyazi Bey. Actually, they recorded the festivals as an epic reminiscence of the uprising. In the early days of Hürriyet, the townsmen in Bitola are said to have attended the celebrations organized by the Palace too, but neither in their films nor in their pictures of *Hürriyet* have we seen any placard inscribed with pro-palace or pro-sultan watchwords, such as 'Long live our sultan!' Simply put, the Manakis, under Sultan Abdul Hamid II, apparently have not been the proud photographers/cameramen of the sultan. The new era witnessed the dethronement of Abdul Hamid in 1909, replaced by Sultan Mehmed V Reşad and the increasing power of the CUP on the state mechanism. This is when they established steady connections with palace authorities by filming Sultan Mehmed V Reşat in 1911, as was also suggested by documents from the State Archive of Macedonia. However, the debate still remains: What was the impetus behind the camera moves? A sense of 'revolutionary duty'? Or, because they were dedicated pro-Romania Vlach nationalists and the leaders of this community were in close cooperation with the CUP? Commercial expectations? Or, friendship with Niyazi Bey? Apparently, the camera does not show more than it has seen but, what it historically tells, reminds and inspires far beyond it.

Saadet Özen

The Governess

Mürebbiye

Studio:
Society of Disabled Veterans' Studio
(Malul Gaziler Heyeti Stüdyosu)

Director:
Ahmet Fehim

Assistant Director:
Cemil Filmer

Producer:
The Society of Disabled Veterans Cinema Film Factory
(Malul Gaziler Heyeti Sinema Film Fabrikası)

Screenwriter:
Ahmet Fehim

Cinematographer:
Fuat Uzkınay

Synopsis

The protagonist of the film, Angèle, is an attractive French governess who tutors the two children of a wealthy Ottoman family, lead by patriarch Dehri Efendi. Eventually, Angèle becomes an object of desire for the men at the family's mansion and she begins trysts with all of them. Amca Bey, Şemi and Sadri Bey, all attempt to attract her affection. As the lovesick Şemi learns the bitter truth he goes to Angèle's room, but he cannot believe his eyes upon seeing who is hidden in Angèle's wardrobe.

Critique

The Governess is the first fiction film of the Society of Disabled Veterans Cinema Film Factory and was directed by the famous theatre actor Ahmet Fehim in 1919. Unfortunately, there is no available copy of the film, but some visual materials can be found at the Turkish Land Forces Photo-Film Centre in Ankara. The film was based on author Hüseyin Rahmi Gürpınar's well-known novel of the same name which was also adapted into a play and staged several times. However, there is no hard evidence to determine how closely the film followed the original literary source. Aside from director Fehim, actors from Armenian, Greek and Turkish origins starred in the film, while Fuat Uzkınay handled the camera. Most of the location shots, including various scenes from Angèle's life in Paris, were completed in Gülhane Park in Istanbul.

Duration:

90 Minutes

Cast:

Madame Kalitea
Bayzar Fasulyeciyan
Ahmet Fehim
İsmail Zahit
Raşit Rıza

Year:

1919

Temaşa magazine describes the premier of *The Governess* in 1919 and claims that the audience greatly appreciated the film (İ. G., *Temaşa*, 17, 1919: 1). The first screening in Istanbul was attended by fifty to sixty people, including the Secretary for Ministry of War, the author Gürpınar, members of the Ottoman Red Crescent (Hilal-i Ahmer), journalists, a number of prominent women figures and the film crew. It is reported that the audience was happy to see their true 'national life and morals' projected onto the screen. The acting of Fehim and Madame Kalitea were highly developed and strong, yet some actors' performances were found very theatrical and were described as being like that of a pantomime. The setting was considered to be the biggest problem of the film. The shots depicting Paris and the mansion were poorly decorated and did not properly reflect the surroundings of a wealthy family (İ. G., *Temaşa*, 17, 1919: 2).

The Governess introduces a foreign governess which was a stereotypical subject and characterization found in the literature of the time. In fact, Gürpınar's novel was a criticism against the Ottoman Turkish families who had an 'alla Franca' life style, of mores modelled upon those of Western Europe at the time. This binary opposition between 'alla Franca' and 'alla Turca' was a common theme and shows the clashing socio-cultural atmosphere of Ottoman society. Angèle is portrayed as 'morally corrupt', whereas the Turkish men are depicted as unknowing victims caught in a trap woven by a 'foreign woman'. This relationship between 'good' and 'bad' and 'us' versus 'them' propels the audience to identify with the characters while the film shows conflicts and sharply formulates major characters and their actions. Angèle is confronted by the 'upstanding morals' of the Muslim family and this portrayal encourages the audience to judge behaviours of each character. Indeed, the subject of *the Governess* offers various alternative readings of moralizing class and gender roles within Ottoman society.

When the film was released in 1919, the Ottomans had been defeated during the Great War (1914-1918); consequently the Allied Powers were in the process of occupying Ottoman territories. Within this political climate, some contemporary film scholars today believe that *The Governess* is an example of 'passive national resistance' taken against the Allied Powers. Scholars assume that the film was not screened in other parts of the country because of the censorship exercised by the Allied Powers. During the period of occupation, the Allied Powers implemented visible control mechanisms and they took measures against resistance movements. For instance, regulations about going to theatres and movie-theatres were severely strict in Istanbul. Additionally, it was forbidden to screen German, Austrian-Hungarian and Bulgarian films during these years, as their films could have been manipulative in reflecting the ideology of the Central Powers (Prime Ministry Ottoman Archives, DH.EUM.AYŞ, 2/2, 21 C 1337, 1919).

The Allied Powers' regulations, which also affected the release of *The Governess*, do not necessarily mean that the film crew aimed at protesting against them by making this film. Moreover, today there is no copy of the film and even the intertitles were not preserved. Undoubtedly, the national consciousness was more visible after the defeat, and reviews also prove the film's success within the criteria of 'national life and morals', which were gradually changing in the empire at this time. The assumptions about 'passive national resistance' in relation to *The Governess* are currently difficult to confirm. Thus, the film should be re-evaluated within the larger socio-political circumstances and war-time policies during the late Ottoman era.

Fictions of the Ottoman cinema are mostly based on plays and literary sources and *The Governess* clearly exemplifies this tendency. The film still remains as one of the first acclaimed fictions in the filmography of Ottoman cinema, as it depicts the widespread situation of the urbanized Ottoman society between conflicts and transformations in blurred identity struggles and some groups' devotion to changing 'national morals'. If it survived today, *The Governess* would deserve a more nuanced credit for its underestimated accomplishments.

Özde Çeliktemel-Thomen

The Sword-girding Ceremony of Sultan Vahdettin

Sultan Vahdettin

Duration:
4 Mins 25 Secs

Year:
1918

Synopsis

The sword-girding ceremony of Sultan Vahdettin, in three sequences, presents highlights of the consecration ceremony of the newly-enthroned Sultan, performed in 1918. The first sequence opens with the outstanding figures of the Committee of Union and Progress (CUP hereafter): Enver Paşa, the Minister of War and Talat Paşa, the Grand Vizier. The setting moves to the district of Eyüp where the ceremony reaches its peak. Army officers parade in the 'alley of enthronement' between the Golden Horn shore and the Eyüp Mosque. The Sultan appears surrounded by the imperial guard regiment. The camera omitted the ceremony in the mosque and caught the story where the Sultan gets in the imperial carriage, with Cemal Paşa, the Naval Minister, behind him. In line with the tradition of visiting the tombs of ancestors on the way back to the palace, a high-angle shot exposes a parade in a cobblestoned alley with a mausoleum on the opposite side. The following sequence, as clarified with an intertitle in Ottoman Turkish, is to present the triumphal arc bearing the watchword 'Long live our sultan!.' A final intertitle presents the townsmen paying respects to the new ruler. The Sultan in his carriage listens to the speech of their mouthpiece.

Critique

'[A major harm to the Turkish cinema] was the alphabetic revolution. This one night decision has completely destroyed the value of the films with old-letter inscriptions. I brought all films in my possession to the Mount of Hürriyet [in İstanbul] and stroke a match over them' (Cemil Filmer). In 1928, the day when the young Republic of Turkey replaced Arabic characters with the letters of the Latin alphabet, the film dealer Cemil Filmer was surely not alone in losing his films. This crucial step in the Republican project of Eurocentric modernization, would send into oblivion an idiosyncrasy of the filmic 'Ottoman-ness': the inscriptions in Ottoman Turkish with Arabic letters were common among various kinds of motion pictures released in the Empire and during the early Republic, be it imported or locally produced by the Army Central Cinema Unit, The Society of National Defense, Society of Disabled Veterans, or individual initiatives.

Given the vulnerability of nitrate films, it should not be surprising that individuals like Cemil Filmer burned or destroyed their material. However, the Army or the Ministry of Culture with a stock preserved by the Mimar Sinan University's Centre of Cinema and TV would be expected to be more efficient in such an archival project. As a matter of fact, it was only in 2011 that the first steps for the restoration and digitalization of 600,000 metres of nitrate films as a joint project of Mimar Sinan University and the Ministry of Culture were taken. The sword-girding ceremony of Sultan Vahdettin from 1918 is a news film with Ottoman Turkish subtitles recently discovered in this archival project. It is not clear who the producer of the film is, yet there are traces of evidence to suggest that the producer is pro-state. The Funeral of Sultan Abdul Hamid, another film re-discovered, given the exact matches of frames, should be considered misidentified and a part of the Sword-girding Ceremony.

In fact, Ottoman sultans had been acquainted with the camera long before 1918. In 1905, the Friday following an assassination attempt that targeted him, a cameraman was allowed to film Sultan Abdul Hamid as reported by his daughter, Şadiye Sultan.[1] Three years later, the first Friday after the Young Turk Revolution, he was filmed again. His successor, Sultan Mehmed V Reşad has been filmed both by local (the Manaki Brothers in 1911, in Bitola and Thessaloniki), and foreign cameramen (Pathé, Eclipse-Klein). The first film, from 1905, is still considered lost (if it ever existed), but all those moving images mentioned above are now available in various archives in Macedonia, France and Russia, which allows a comparison with the rediscovered record of Vahdettin.

Given that the Manakis' films of Sultan Reşad have remained unedited until 1996, none of those films have intertitles in Ottoman Turkish, except the record of Vahdettin's sword-girding ceremony, due to their target public. The florid language of the inscriptions hints at the representational strategies in this local production – 'The fabulous and embellished arch of triumph erected in the name of the city'; 'The special committee addresses congratulation on behalf of the people of Istanbul and the delivery of oration': potential Ottoman viewers were supposed to join their fellow countrymen in the recognition of the new ruler's legitimacy. However, the inscriptions are not the only distinguishing feature; apparently the focus of interest was not the same for a foreign and a local camera, as Paul Desdemaines Hugon instructed in 1915, in his Hints to Newsfilm Cameramen: '… if you were taking the visit of the King of England to Berlin, for Berlin, you would take close-ups of the King … But if you were taking the same subject for London … the close-ups of the King would be almost superfluous.' In the recording of *Vahdettin*, multiple local cameramen – soldiers randomly captured throughout the footage – were in charge in following the high-lights of the ceremony: the sultan's arrival at Eyüp; his visit to the ancestral tombs; his recognition by the townsmen are all filmed. Their intention was not to stress ethnographic exotica, unlike the cameramen of Pathé, who in 1908 shot scenes of the carriages of the harem women of almost equal length as those of Sultan Abdul Hamid's carriage. On the other hand, in the immediate physical surroundings of the Sultan, the eminent figures of the Committee of Union and Progress, Enver Paşa, Talat Paşa and Cemal Paşa were shown in close-ups suggestive of the power they shared with the Sultan. Conversely, Abdul Hamid has been filmed with no identifi-able figures around his carriage. Actually, Sultan Vahdettin would probably never have realized that the cameras were recording the last imperial consecration ceremony in Ottoman history. These recordings let us see this historic moment, but also promise new debates and operative paradigms of the history of cinema during the transition period from the Empire to the Republic, with conti-nuities and discontinuities between them, and a sprouting visual language to be discussed.

Saadet Özen

Notes

[1] Cited in İbrahim Yıldıran, 'Selim Sırrı Tarcan ve Türk Sinemasının Erken Dönem Tartışmalarına Katkı', *Kebikeç* No..27, (2009), pp. 221-230. Original resource: Hanzade Sultanefendi, *Osmanlı Hanedanı Saray Notları 1*, Tekin Yayınevi, 2002.

SCI-FI & FANTASY

Discussions of Turkish national cinema have traditionally focused on the complex relationship between film and national identity, with a particular emphasis on films which are seen to represent Turkish culture and society. Yet, what of those cinematic cycles which clearly engage with imported forms? In recent years, a number of scholars and fans have attempted to raise awareness of the rich tradition of 'Turkish Fantastic Cinema' – a Yeşilçam genre which had previously been omitted from histories of Turkish cinema due to its dependence on borrowed characters and stories.

The beginnings of the genre are usually dated to the 1950s with the appearance of a number of films which transplanted imported characters onto Turkish soil, including *Tarzan İstanbul'da/Tarzan in Istanbul* (1952), *Drakula İstanbul'da/Dracula in Istanbul* (1953), and *Görünmeyen Adam İstanbul'da/The Invisible Man in Istanbul* (1955). Meanwhile, fantastical elements also appeared in local adventure films such as the giant spider in *Balıkçı Güzeli* (*Handsome Fisherman*, 1953) and the flying carpet in *Üç Baba Torik/ Three Fat Fish* (1953). Nevertheless, it was not until the golden age of Turkish popular cinema, between the early 1960s and the late 1970s, that the genre really started to take off. During this period, annual film production rose to a peak of 301 films and a number of different cycles appeared including local variations of science fiction, horror, and superhero films.

Many of these titles were produced to capitalize on interest surrounding the release of Hollywood films such as when director Kunt Tulgar directed *Süpermen Dönüyor/The return of Superman* (1979) a year after the global success of Richard Donner's *Superman* (1978). While partly inspired by such blockbuster successes, the direct antecedents to the aesthetic style of Turkish fantastic cinema were actually the American movie serials of the 1940s and 1950s. Indeed, many of these low budget quickies borrowed heroes directly from the serials in films such as *Baytekin Fezada Çarpışanlar/Flash Gordon: Battle in Space* (1967), *Zorro Kamçılı Süvari /Zorro: The Rider with the Whip* (1969), and *Casus Kiran/Spy Smasher* (1968) while some were even loose remakes such as *Yılmayan Şeytan* (The Deathless Devil, 1972) which reworked the 1940 Republic serial *Mysterious Doctor Satan*. Furthermore, Turkish film-makers were not only borrowing from American popular culture, but also produced films featuring European characters such as the French

Left image: *Three Mighty Men*, 1973, Tevfik Fikret Uçak © Tual Film.

criminal *Fantômas in Fantoma Istanbul'da Buluşalım/Fantômas: Appointment in Istanbul* (1967) and the Italian criminal Killing in *Kilink Istanbul'da* (*Killing in Istanbul*, 1967). It was in 1973 that this trend towards imitation reached its peak with *3 Dev Adam/3 Giant Men* which brought together Captain America, Spiderman and the Mexican 'luchador' Santo in a single film.

It is important to note, however, that while these films generally borrowed iconography, they rarely attempted to recreate the plotline or setting from their sources. With a few notable exceptions such as *Şeytan* (*Satan*, 1974), which did closely recreate the plotline of *The Exorcist* (1973), albeit with the Catholicism replaced with Islam, the majority of these hybrid texts would use recognizable character designs and costumes but would place these characters into situations far removed from their source material. *3 Dev Adam*, for example, opens with a scene in which the criminal mastermind Spiderman tortures a young women who is buried up to her neck in sand, a depiction of the character which is very different from Stan Lee and Steve Ditko's comic books. Moreover, the masked hero films often contain sequences of sadistic violence coupled with sleaze which meant that even straight-laced comic book characters such as Superman use their powers to ogle scantily clad women.

Produced on a very low budget and with a quick turnaround, these Yeşilçam titles were often rushed into production to capitalize on the latest trend and relied on an industrial mode of film-making that meant that leading stars would often work on several productions at the same time. These quickie production methods meant that Turkish fantastic films tended to be structured around a series of set pieces with little attempt to integrate them into a coherent narrative. Furthermore, the borrowings were not solely restricted to iconography since a number of films actually used borrowed music, such as with the unlicensed use of the James Bond theme in *Yılmayan Şeytan* and the music from *Enter the Dragon* (1973) in *Kılıç Aslan/Lion Man* (1975).

Today, audiences within Turkey and around the world often treat these films as a form of naïve camp which is to be simultaneously celebrated and ridiculed. The combination of poor costumes, cheap special effects and broad, melodramatic performances mean that the films are marked by a distinct lack of realism and this has meant that many titles such as *Dünyayı Kurtaran Adam* (*The Man Who Saves the World*) (1982) have come to be celebrated as classics of trash cinema. What this particular reading protocol can sometimes neglect, however, is that Yeşilçam was also drawing on narrative traditions that date back to the Turkish shadow plays of the Ottoman period – utilizing various recognizable character archetypes and paying little regard to verisimilitude or Western notions of 'realism'. Furthermore, while the films have often been dismissed as purely imitative, closer examination reveals that films such as *Turist Ömer Uzay Yolunda* (*Ömer the Tourist in Star Trek*, 1973) and *Ayşecik ve Sihirli Cüceler Rüyalar Ülkesinde* (*Aysecik in the Magical Land of the Dwarves*, 1971) exhibit a more complex relationship with their source texts than the fan appellations 'Turkish Star Trek' and 'Turkish Wizard of Oz' would suggest.

Turkish Fantastic Cinema almost died out in the 1980s and 1990s as the industry went into decline. A combination of the shift towards pornography and increasing competition from television meant that a number of studios went out of business in this period. More recently, however, the genre has undergone a revival with a number of success stories including the science fiction blockbuster *G.O.R.A.* (2004) and the horror titles *Araf/The Abortion* (2006) and *Semum* (2008). There have even been attempts to cater to the burgeoning fandom surrounding golden-age Yeşilçam with the production of belated sequels such as *Dünyayı Kurtaran Adam'ın oglu/Turks in Space* (2006). With this rise in interest in science fiction and fantasy, it is worth considering what this genre can tell us about Turkish national cinema. While it would certainly be possible to pick out traits to suggest that these films exemplify a specifically Turkish take on international genres, I contend that this would not be the most productive approach. Instead, these films point to the fluid, transnational nature of cinema. While it may be difficult to pinpoint the 'Turkishness' of films which are so heavily invested in intertextual reworkings of global cinema, it is for this same reason that the films are so rich for investigating the ever-more globalized flows of media and culture. In other words, while it would be possible to use a national paradigm to make claims for a film like *3 Dev Adam* as a quintessentially 'Turkish' text, it would ultimately be more productive for us to consider how this reworking of Captain America, Santo and Spiderman may actually destabilize notions of a discrete national cinema.

Iain Robert Smith

Dracula in Istanbul

Drakula İstanbul'da

Studio:
And Film

Director:
Mehmet Muhtar

Producer:
Turgut Demirağ

Screenwriters:
Ümit Deniz
Ali Rıza Seyfi (novel 'The Impaling Voivode')

Cinematographer:
Özen Sermet

Duration:
112 Minutes

Cast:
Arif Kaptan
Annie Ball
Bülent Oran
Ayfer Feray

Year:
1953

Synopsis

In contemporary Transylvania, Azmi visits the ancient and sinister Bisthiç Hotel, where he learns that he has been invited to Count Dracula's castle. He takes a car for half of the journey; then a coach. The longer he stays at the castle, more Azmi realizes that there is something very sinister about the Count; eventually he discovers that the Count is a vampire, fond of feeding babies to his female vampire companions. Dracula thinks that Azmi knows too much and attacks him, but the young man escapes in the nick of time.

The action switches to İstanbul, where Azmi recovers in bed from his ordeal. His girlfriend Güzin, a night-club singer and dancer, spends most of her leisure time in the company of her inseparable female companion Şadan. The two women's lives seem happy and contented – until Şadan encounters Count Dracula. No one knows what is wrong with her, until her doctor discovers that she has become one of the undead. Nothing can be done to save Şadan, but the doctor, Azmi, and Şadan's boyfriend Turan resolve to destroy the vampire once and for all – even if it means putting Güzin's life in danger.

Critique

The screenplay for the novel was based on a 1928 novel *Kazıklı Voyvoda* (*Vlad the Impaler*) by pulp writer Ali Rıza Seyfi. The plot more or less follows the Bram Stoker text, but there is no Renfield character, while Güzin (the 'Mina Seward' character), played by Annie Ball, is transformed into an exotic dancer who regularly strips in front of the camera. Dracula/Drakula is played by Atıf Kaplan as a middle-aged, balding figure impeccably dressed in top hat and tails. The film makes an explicit connection between Dracula and the historical character Vlad the Impaler (1431-1476), who resisted the Ottoman forces, while imposing cruel punishments on his enemies.

To non-Turkish viewers, *Drakula İstanbul'da* might seem almost laughably bad, with its cheap, tatty sets and over-the-top per-formances. Such assumptions overlook the film's significance in Turkish film history. The early 1950s were a time of prosperity; the number of films produced each year increased rapidly, which led to the emergence of new stars such as Ayhan Işık. In this kind of environment, directors such as Mehmet Muhtar wanted to prove to local audiences that Turkish film-makers could emulate any-thing that their Hollywood counterparts had done. Hence *Drakula İstanbul'da* remains largely faithful to Stoker's book – save for one significant alteration. In an Islamic context – even in the Turk-ish Republic, which adopted largely secular values – the use of a crucifix to repel Count Dracula might have seemed unnecessarily provocative. Hence Azmi (Bülent Oran) and Turan (Cahit Irgat) have to make do with cloves of garlic.

The film's nationalist message is reinforced by associating Drakula with Vlad the Impaler, enemy of the Ottomans. On this view he represents a potential threat to the social *status quo*. It is the duty of all good men – Azmi and Turan in particular – to fulfil their duties as Turkish citizens and remove the threat by driving a stake through his heart. Director Muhtar is obviously aware that most of his audiences would have been unfamiliar with the Dracula story (even though it had been available in translation ever since 1925, as well as in Seyfi's adaptation). Hence he includes long expository sequences designed to summarize the story – in one sequence Azmi sits in Count Dracula's study reading the book, while his voice can be heard on the soundtrack. In another sequence, Nazmi, Turan and the doctor discuss at length the best means to resist Dracula; and eventually decide to pick garlic cloves. Both scenes impede the plot development, but they fulfilled an important function for filmgoers at the time of the film's original release.

While based on Hollywood models, *Drakula İstanbul'da* is squarely aimed at local audiences, incorporating several conventions characteristic of Yeşilçam cinema. The acting-style is broad, not to say melodramatic: Count Dracula is particularly fond of speaking his lines in an elevated tone reminiscent of the old British melodrama expert Tod Slaughter. However, Kaplan's interpretation would have been instantly recognizable to anyone familiar with *Karagöz*, or Turkish shadow theatre, in which all characterizations were necessarily two-dimensional in stories invariably pitting heroes against villains. Yeşilçam inherited this tradition and popularized it once more for audiences who were just beginning to enjoy film-going as a mass leisure pursuit.

Yeşilçam also perpetuated the *Karagöz* tradition of repetition, a strategy designed to render stories accessible to all types of audience, irrespective of whether they could read or write. *Drakula Istanbul'da* includes several close-ups of Count Dracula's eyes glittering in close-up as he stares into the camera lens. The camera tracks backwards to reveal him walking slowly yet ominously towards his victims, his face fixed in a wolfish grin. On other occasions we see Azmi endlessly walking up and down corridors in Count Dracula's lair; this shot is repeated later on, as Güzin treads nervously around her house in search of the Count. Yeşilçam adopted a relaxed approach towards genre classification. Films were not conceived as comedies, or tragedies per se but, rather, included elements designed to appeal to everyone. Hence tragic stories were likely to incorporate scenes of comic relief or musical interludes which had little or nothing to do with the plot, but could be enjoyed in themselves. *Drakula İstanbul'da* includes at least three scenes where Güzin performs exotic dances at the Minerva Club in varying stages of *déshabillé*. While these moments might seem incongruous in terms of the story (Güzin is certainly not the naive virgin of Stoker's tale), I suggest that this is not Muhtar's principal concern. Rather, he conceives Annie Ball as a sex symbol reminiscent of Marilyn Monroe, designed to appeal to young male film-goers. By today's standards, *Drakula İstanbul'da* has dated badly. Nonetheless it is an important text, evoking a time when

Turkish cinema was in the process of establishing itself as a viable alternative to Hollywood.

Laurence Raw

GORA: A Space Story
GORA

Studios:
BKM
Böcek Yapım

Director:
Ömer Faruk Sorak

Producers:
Necati Akpınar
Nuri Sevin
Gökhan Tuncel

Screenwriter:
Cem Yılmaz

Cinematographer:
Veli Kuzlu

Art Director:
Bahattin Demirkol

Composers:
Rahman Altın
Ozan Çolakoğlu

Editor:
Mustafa Preseva

Duration:
127 Minutes

Cast:
Cem Yılmaz
Özge Özberk
Özkan Uğur
Şafak Sezer

Year:
2004

Synopsis

Arif is a local tourist guide and carpet salesman, who, in his free time, likes to fake UFO photos to make a living from the pulp magazines. One day, two aliens who pretend to be customers abduct him. The mastermind behind the abductions is commander Logar, whose grandfather was traumatized by humans centuries ago. Logan carries a grudge and enslaves the humans. Arif arrives at the home planet of GORA as a prisoner and he meets another fellow Turk, Bob Marley Faruk. Later, he also befriends an android called 216, who is also the maid and best friend of the planet's princess Ceku. Meanwhile the palace politics starts influencing the GORA administration. The King has only one daughter and commander Logar wants to rule the land by marrying this daughter Ceku. Ceku, who is romantic, like humans are, cannot tolerate Logar. Just as GORA is about to be destroyed by a giant ball of fire, and all else has failed, Arif steps in and applies methods he learned from watching the film *The Fifth Element*. Arif steps in with the princess between the holy stones, kisses the princess, and saves the planet. Logar breaks his promise to release Arif and his friends and they decide to escape from prison. Ceku helps Arif, Faruk and 216 to escape. At the end of the film, Arif beats Logar and marries Ceku. They decide to settle on earth and live happily ever after.

Critique

GORA is a product of the *new televisual production regime* in Turkey. GORA represents the coming together of two products of television in Turkey: the technical excellence of the television infrastructure and the new, popular television talent. The year 1999 was a turning point for cinema in Turkey as digital post-production facilities came in line with their American counterparts in terms of quality. These facilities were used mostly for commercial productions. The investment made in the 1990s to produce quality domestic commercials also worked well for film-makers. GORA is the brainchild of two men who came to fame on television: Cem Yılmaz, a young stand-up comedian who had also appeared in commercials, and Ömer Faruk Sorak, a TRT-trained (public television) steadicam operator turned commercial cinematographer. In 2002, Sorak and Yılmaz embarked on a project the scale of which was unheard of before in Turkey. As a sci-fi parody film, GORA has a dual ambivalent edge. In terms of form, it tries to prove its worth formally by borrowing from, referring to, and imitating some of the visual elements in American science fiction films. In terms of content and theme, GORA renders such borrowing secondary, as it wants to present its own pride in Turkish culture. An example of this ambiva-

GORA: A Space Story, 2004, Ömer Faruk Sorak.

lence is the long shot of the space ship in *GORA*, a direct reference to all *Star Wars* movies that open with a long shot of a spaceship. This iconic image is imitated and domesticated, and its visual influence is reinforced by our knowledge of American sci-fi films. The shot is significant in two ways: It fits our expectations of a sci-fi film with spectacular visual effects. In addition, it serves the ideological function of boasting, and showing off that Turkish film-makers can create this special-effects shot. The references in *GORA* to previous Turkish science fiction films and characters represent a process I call *repatriation*. Repatriation is the recycling of intertextual references to the genre films of the 1960s and 1970s by the new televisual production regime of the 2000s. In *GORA*, Arif's look is iconic: that of a Turkish man of Anatolian origin. His manners and moustache especially reflect the look of Sadri Alışık, who was one of the stars of Turkish cinema between the 1950s and 1980s. In Arif's last shot, after he lands back on earth, he is dressed in the costume from Sadri Alışık's *Ömer the Tourist* movies. This positions the viewer to recall these films and the character to fully appreciate Cem Yilmaz as he recreates the look of Ömer of the 1970s.

GORA redefines the way in which the classical debates of the sci-fi genre employ the dichotomy of East-West, low-high in favour of the spiritual, the human, and the emotional. *GORA* displays concerns regarding the mechanization of humanity – what technology would do to humans – and is proud to present human qualities like emotions as superior to mechanical, technological and rational qualities. Arif and Faruk, the two Turks on planet GORA, remain the most innovative, active, and powerful figures among the thousands of people who have been kidnapped by Gorans.

Murat Akser

Iron Claw the Pirate

Demir Pençe: Korsan Adam

Studio:
Metin Film

Director:
Çetin İnanç

Producer:
Işık Toraman

Screenwriters:
Kamil Erşahin
Erdoğan Şahin

Cinematographer:
Rafet Şiriner

Duration:
85 Minutes

Cast:
Demir Karahan
Feri Cansel
Nebahat Çehre
Yıldırım Gencer
Behçet Nacar

Year:
1969

Synopsis

Demir Pençe, his sidekick Mine and partner Yıldırım, take on the criminal organization run by the infamous Fantomas. When Demir Pençe proves to be too much of a disruption, Fantomas decides to move to İstanbul and work with the Turkish mafia to eliminate Demir Pençe. In a gunfight with Fantomas' men, Yılmaz is murdered. Demir Pençe decides to avenge his death by going after Fantomas directly. Meanwhile, Yılmaz's brother Yıldırım also begins to plot his revenge. Eventually, the two join forces to track down Fantomas, in the process having to confront the seductive female assassin Cansel as well as the man with the steel arm, Behçet!

Critique

Demir Pençe Korsan Adam/Iron Claw: The Pirate is an incredibly entertaining film as long as the viewer can set aside his selfish need for narrative coherence. Director Çetin İnanç is best known for his ridiculous *Dünyayı Kurtaran Adam*, which has gained a cult following around the world as the 'Turkish Star Wars'. İnanç learned the craft of film-making from working with Yılmaz Atadeniz and soon became a director in his own right. İnanç is not half the storyteller that Atadeniz is. Indeed, he often seems to actively encourage narrative confusion, but his films have a chaotic feel to them that – whether intentional or not – often make them worth viewing. He is also more bloodthirsty than Atadeniz. Whereas Atadeniz might tear his heroine's blouse and smack her around a bit, İnanç is more likely to strip her naked and stab her in the heart.

Unlike Atadeniz, İnanç did not have quite the same passion for the masked hero films and made only a handful of contributions to the genre. His first was his very own Kilink film entitled *Killing Caniler Kralı*. That was followed by *Kızılmaske* – an adaptation of Lee Falk's comic strip *The Phantom* that was released the same year as another film with the same title directed by Tolgay Ziyal. Two of his masked hero films featured an original character called Demir Pençe or 'The Iron Claw.' In truth, there is very little to distinguish him from *Casus Kiran, Uçan Adam or Maskeli Şeytan*, other than the fact that he has played by Demir Karahan rather than masked hero mainstay İrfan Atasoy.

The plot is virtually identical to *Kilink İstanbul'da* – there is a scientist, microfilm, a master criminal and a hero bent on avenging someone's death. Perhaps because the material is so familiar, İnanç does his damnedest to keep the audience as confused as possible. The first twenty minutes are nearly impossible to follow. After multiple viewings, it becomes clear that İnanç has either edited scenes in the wrong order or shot the film so improvisationally that he unwittingly wrote himself into a corner from which he had no way of extricating himself. Clocking in at 85 minutes, *Demir Pençe* is practically an epic for the masked hero genre. While the viewer's patience may be tried during the incoherent opening scenes, the plot starts to settle down about twenty minutes in.

What makes *Demir Pençe* unique and worth viewing is İnanç's use of the popular character Fantomas. Created in France in 1911 by Marcel Allain and Pierre Souvestre, Fantomas quickly became one of the most popular fictional characters in European history as well as an inspiration to the burgeoning surrealist movement. Film director Louis Feuillade gave birth to the movie serial by adapting five of the Fantomas books for his film company, Gaumont. The character had remarkable staying power. Films featuring the character were being produced until the late 1940s. After the French occupation, however, interest in Fantomas began to wane and the character vanished from movie screens for almost two decades. When he finally reappeared in Andre Hunabelle's big-budget, sci-fi, spy-fantasia trilogy from 1964-1967, the character once again became a worldwide sensation. Fantomas purists, however, were seriously irked. This new incarnation of Fantomas was too silly, too playful and too light-hearted for hardcore devotees of the original stories.

When Turkish film-makers began to pilfer heroes and villains to populate their work, Fantomas was toward the top of the list. The result was a trio of unauthorized films that featured Fantomas taking on various pop-culture icons – *Süpermen Fantoma'ya Karşı/ Fantomas vs. Superman, Fantoma İstanbul'da Buluşalım/Fantomas: Appointment İstanbul*, featuring Batman, and İnanç's *Demir Pençe: Korsan Adam*.

Audiences outside Turkey were largely unaware of the cinematic delights taking place inside its borders, otherwise, Fantomas fans would have been pleased to know that, while their beloved character was taking a drubbing at the foolish hands of Andre Hunabelle, he was being celebrated in all his sadistic glory by Çetin İnanç. Fantomas allowed İnanç to give his violent imagination full rein. *Demir Pençe* has an air of sleaziness about it that Atadeniz's films do not. Feri Cansel – abandoning her normal role of the heroic sidekick – plays one of Fantomas' ill-fated accomplices who performs a nearly-nude dance that is surprisingly explicit for the genre. Toward the end of the film – in a burst of transgressive violence – Fantomas dispatches two of the major characters with such brutality that Allain and Souvestre would be proud. *Demir Pençe: Korsan Adam* is not a perfect film – Çetin İnanç's casual approach to narrative makes sure of that – but there are enough oddball elements to make it an enjoyable contribution to the masked hero genre.

David Lee White

Kilink in Istanbul

Kilink İstanbul'da

Synopsis

Master criminal Kilink has returned to Turkey, having been revived from a comatose state by his sidekick, Suzy. Kilink disguises himself as a manservant to a brilliant scientist that betrayed him in the past. Kilink kills the professor and makes off with a secret formula. The professor's son, Orhan, swears vengeance by his father's grave and

Studio:

Atadeniz Film

Director:

Yılmaz Atadeniz

Producer:

Yılmaz Atadeniz

Screenwriters:

Çetin İnanç
Yılmaz Atadeniz

Cinematographer:

Rafet Şiriner

Composer:

Necip Sarıcıoğlu

Editor:

Mustafa Kent

Duration:

70 Minutes

Cast:

İrfan Atasoy
Pervin Par
Suzan Avcı
Mine Soley
Muzaffer Tema

Year:

1967

is visited by a kindly old man that gives him the power to become a superhero called 'Flying Man' when he utters the magic word 'Shazam!' Flying Man and Kilink pursue one another through a series of encounters until Kilink imprisons Orhan and takes off with the professor's colleague and his daughter to his secret island. The film concludes with Kilink having the upper hand. Orhan finally comes to the rescue in the film's follow-up, *Kilink Ucan Adam*.

Critique

Director Yılmaz Atadeniz makes his mark on the burgeoning Turkish movie scene and creates one of the most memorable subgenres in exploitation cinema – the masked hero film. *Kilink Istanbul'da* was not the first film in the genre – that honour goes to *Örumcek Adam/Spider Man* in 1966. But Atadeniz's contribution caused a sensation. Kilink (or, rather 'Killing') is the sadistic master criminal that starred in a series of 'photo-romans' – adult-themed comic books that featured actors in staged photographs, rather than illustrations. Sex and violence were the photo-roman's chief allure. While the photos never veered into the realm of pornography, the *raison d'être* for these magazines was to depict leering master-criminals ogling bound women in torn blouses.

Adapting the adults-only photo-romans for the screen was a surefire recipe for success. However, while Atadeniz borrowed imagery from them, his main inspiration were American movie serials from the 1940s like *Captain Marvel*, *Flash Gordon* and *The Crimson Ghost*. *Kilink İstanbul'da* was to be Atadeniz's homage to the American serials from his childhood. To that end, he crafted a story filled with the tropes of a twelve-chapter serial play – secret weapons, brilliant scientists with beautiful daughters, long bouts of fisticuffs and masked heroes and villains with secret identities. These plot devices and character archetypes would go on to be staples of the masked hero genre, with plots and characters so interchangeable that local Turkish actors – many of whom would be become Atadeniz's defacto stock company – would special-ize in playing the same archetype over and over again. To make matters more confusing – or more fun – the actors often used their real names; as if fully-written characters did not tally with the production budget. Atadeniz's go-to guy for superheroics was İrfan Atasoy – a square-jawed he-man with sensitive eyes. He is terrific here, playing an inspired combination of Batman, Superman and Captain Marvel with the bizarre name Uçan Adam (the Flying Man). Atasoy would go on to make several masked hero films – perfectly embodying the tonal balance that Atadeniz was trying to achieve – a cheapjack blast of nostalgia with a dash of adult titillation.

The plot of *Kilink İstanbul'da* is nothing special. The last fifteen minutes start to drag and the lack of any kind of action scene at the film's conclusion is a disappointment. What keeps the film afloat is Atadeniz's affection for the genre. The fight scenes are right out of the Saturday Serial playbook, with lots of flailing fists, overturned furniture and gun-play. The torture scenes, while containing an undeniable strain of misogyny, are still relatively tame. Atadeniz was certainly capable of brutal film-making (*Four For All*, for instance) but in these films, the spirit of childhood takes over just as things are starting to get a little too 'adult.'

Uçan Adam is a neat creation – a masked crime-fighter avenging his father's death while sporting an 'S' on his chest and getting his powers by shouting 'Shazam!' He's like a one-man Justice League. The showstopper here, however, is Kilink himself. Clad in a skintight skeleton costume with a full facemask that stays on even when he is making out with women, Kilink is a delicious addition to the ranks of sinister cinema. The film was shot, edited and released in a matter of days, and it shows. You can almost hear the record player needle hitting the vinyl during music sequences. The post-dubbed voices sound like they were recorded in a tin can and the music seems to change abruptly with every edit. But it all adds to the film's charm. The viewer is advised to watch *Kilink İstanbul'da* with the same affection he would give to a mouldy comic-book discovered in a moth-eaten box in his grandfather's attic. While we are lucky that *Kilink İstanbul'da* has survived, it has not survived in very good shape. The only print comes from Atadeniz's personal collection. Every frame is scratched and some scenes are in tatters. The biggest drawback, however, is the film's lack of an ending. Thankfully, Onar films dug up an incomplete print of the film's direct sequel *Kilink Uçan Adam*. After an incoherent recap of the first film, *Kilink Uçan Adam* spends its second act wrapping up the storyline from *Kilink İstanbul'da*. The final section of the film, in which Kilink attempts to steal a princess's jewels, no longer exists. Atadeniz wrapped up his Kilink trilogy with one of his best films – *Kilink Soy ve Öldür*, which dispensed with the Flying Man completely in favour of a more traditional action/spy thriller in which Kilink served as both hero and villain at the same time. Further films by other directors pitted Kilink against Mandrake the Magician, Frankenstein, Django and other pulp archetypes. There were eleven films in all, although only four survive.

David White

Kılıç Aslan
Kılıç Aslan

Studio:
Uğur Film

Director:
Natuk Baytan

Producer:
Memduh Ün

Synopsis

Suleiman Shah, ruler of the Seljuk Empire, through trickery is assassinated by Antoine of the crusaders, who usurps his kingdom. The Shah's right-hand man escapes with the only heir, a babe-in-arms. Relentlessly pursued through the forests by the crusaders, he manages to lose the Shah's son – to a family of lions! Many years pass and rumours abound of a wild man living in the forest, raised on raw meat, roaring like a lion, swinging from vine to vine, fighting with tree trunks he has plucked out of the ground with the ease of a maiden plucking flowers, but on the whole seems a little shy and disappears without a trace.

Meanwhile, Antoine has become the very symbol of hatred throughout the region and a band of rebels, longing for the glori-

Screenwriter:

Duygu Sağıroğlu

Cinematographer:

Mustafa Yılmaz

Duration:

90 Minutes

Cast:

Cüneyt Arkın
Bahar Erdeniz
Yıldırım Gencer

Year:

1975

ous days of their beloved Shah, begin to investigate the origins of this mysterious lion man. For the bloodline of Suleiman Shah carries a unique trait – the mark of the lion – a mark that has been finally identified. Captured by the rebels, educated in heritage, speech and arms, the lion man sets out to claim the kingdom that is his birthright, aided with steel claws.

Critique

Natuk Baytan was one of the most prolific directors in the Yeşilçam system who mainly excelled in delivering fast-paced action, adventure films throughout the 1960s and 1970s. Baytan established himself as a film-maker who had not relied on the constant zoom lens, as had others, but fashioned his action scenes with the use of tracking sequences and a variety of medium- to long shots. His style reached its peak with an early 1980s' box-office hit titled *Topragin Teri*, where his camerawork demonstrated some startling spaghetti western influences which he had honed over the years, in particular those of Sergio Leone and Enzo G Castellari.

Kılıç Aslan, like many Turkish adventure films from this era, has no original soundtrack. In fact, one can immediately identify Lalo Schifrin's groovy *Enter the Dragon* score, as well as tunes from *Planet of the Apes* and other *foreign* films. Used unsparingly, of course. However, given Natuk Baytan's energetic style, where the camera's hyperactivity matches its athletic star Cüneyt Arkın's, the 'borrowed' soundtracks accommodate the scenes tolerably and should not prove bothersome, unless you work in copyright law. At first, the influence is plain enough: a redressing of Edgar Rice Burroughs' most appreciated pulp creation, Tarzan, to suit a medieval setting. Apes are replaced with lions and Kılıç Aslan's wardrobe is enough to rattle Johnny Weismuller's bones. We have a beautiful brunette Jane-alike too, who teaches our hero to say important things such as water and bread. Our protagonist is a fast learner for he soon romances her with the finesse of Don Juan. Interestingly, the film is based on a real warrior king, Kılıç Aslan II, the son of Suleiman, who fought wave after wave of crusaders. Of course, Turkish film-makers have put much 'no man's land' between fact and fiction. In short, Kılıç Aslan II was not reared by lions nor was he known to fight with claws.

Equally important, *Kılıç Aslan* was dubbed in English and French and was distributed under the title *Lion Man* during the 1980s' VHS era. These particular versions had dull public-domain orchestral scores that ultimately failed in accommodating the fast pace onscreen. Later, an unofficial sequel by the name of *Lion Man and the Witch-Queen* was released. The film starred an American actor Frank Morgan in the title role. Even though a second sequel was promised at its closure, no further adventures were forthcoming. This review would be incomplete without mentioning that the plot of *Kilic Aslan* was recycled for the film *Aybice Kurt Kizi*. This version starred Canan Perver as a warrior-girl reared by wolves in the forest. Perver was previously Turkey's answer to Linda Blair in Metin Erksan's Islamic rendering of *Şeytan*.

Ayman Kole

Ömer the Tourist in Star Trek

Turist Ömer Uzay Yolunda

Studio:
Saner Film

Director:
Hulki Saner

Producer:
Hulki Saner

Screenwriter:
Ferdi Merter

Cinematographer:
Çetin Gürtop

Composer:
Rauf Tözüm

Editors:
İsmail Kalkan
Mevlüt Koçak

Duration:
80 Minutes

Cast:
Sadri Alışık
Erol Amaç
Cemil Sahbaz
Ferdi Merter
Kayhan Yıldızoğlu

Year:
1973

Synopsis

In *Turist Ömer Uzay Yolunda* (*Ömer the Tourist in Star Trek*), the starship Enterprise crew visits a planet to bring supplies to a colony. The colony is under the supervision of Doktor Krater, who protects his wife Nancy, a salt-draining monster who kills Enterprise crew members. As a means to protect his wife, Dr Krater uses a time travel/teleporter machine and kidnaps Ömer the Tourist from earth in order to frame him for the deaths. Captain Kirk invites Ömer to the Enterprise under the supervision of Dr McCoy and Mr Spock. Ömer, like a troublesome child, plays with the ship's controls, confuses its computer with strange questions, and drives Spock mad with his illogical conclusions about life and everything else. Eventually, the shape-shifting, alien monster gets on to the Enterprise where it is spotted by Ömer, who, with Spock's help, beats the monster. Ömer is sent back to earth with a present, Spock's long Vulcan ears, and an ability to use the Vulcan neck grasp.

Critique

The plot of the film reflects the expectations of the sci-fi film audiences of the era: low production values and imitation-quotation of American films in stylistic qualities (special effects as both form and icon), and narrative qualities (plot, character, pseudo-scientific dialogue) as well as discursively (materialism vs. spiritualism). *Ömer the Tourist in Star Trek* debuted even before the official Hollywood film adaptation of the *Star Trek* TV series in 1979. The film is a fusion in terms of creating viewer expectations in that its core material is both cinematic and televisual. The film is one of many in a series of Ömer the Tourist films: a comedy series in the travelogue tradition of the *Road To* series with Bob Hope and Bing Crosby. It is the story of an encounter between technology/West and emotion/East in which a typical Turkish man – undereducated, working class – travels abroad and sees all the different cultures and people in foreign lands. His interactions with these people and their customs create the comedy. *Ömer the Tourist*, in that sense, refers to the Turkish people's prejudices towards other countries. In *Ömer the Tourist in Star Trek*, Ömer encounters cultures that are alien in many senses of the word – the American technological culture of the future and the alien culture of a foreign planet. Ömer stands out as the odd man in the film.

In Turkey circa 1973, Ömer represented Turkish people who could only watch the wonders of technology as Americans and Soviets flew their astronauts to the moon and brought them back. This was during the height of the cold war when both the United States and the Soviet Union commanded nuclear weapons that could destroy an entire country without losing any of their own soldiers. During the period, Turkey was a country that had also adapted to technology as an industrializing country, though the kind of technology described in American sci-fi films could not be achieved by Turks in the near future. Even though it was only at the level of film fantasy, Ömer travelled to those distant places representing Turkish practical wisdom and solving problems that even the coldly-rational Vulcan's super intellect could not. In terms of imitation, the plot of the film is borrowed directly from the very first episode of *Star Trek* entitled 'The Man Trap,' which aired in the United States on 8 September 1966. While the plot of Ömer the Tourist is similar to the original episode, the names of the characters were *domesticated* – so Mr. Spock and Captain Kirk become Mister Spak and Kaptan Körk. The extent to which the plotline, characters, and costumes are duplicated, positions the viewer to see a genuine sci-fi story; however, the desire to tell a story that is an exact duplicate also points to an inferiority complex in the face of the technologically-superior, *other* cinema. Ömer's presence as a typical, low-tech, emotional easterner signifies an attempt to mock reason but, at the same time, he is presented as a stand-in for an audience that is imagined to be in awe of the technology on screen.

Murat Akser

Spy Smasher

Casus Kıran

Studio:
Atadeniz Film

Director:
Yılmaz Atadeniz

Producer:
Yılmaz Atadeniz

Screenwriter:
Yılmaz Atadeniz

Cinematographer:
Rafet Şiriner

Duration:
67 Minutes

Cast:
İrfan Atasoy
Sevda Ferdağ
Suzan Avcı
Yıldırım Gencer
Erol Gunaydın

Year:
1968

Synopsis

The villainous Mask takes control of the Black Glove gang and infests Turkey with its network of spies. The patriotic Spy Smasher and his partner Sevda – the daughter of the local police detective – don masks and motorcycles to break up the spy ring. After Sevda is kidnapped by the Black Glove, Spy Smasher rescues her and liberates a secret tape with vital security information on it. The Black Glove attempts to recover the information by kidnapping a scientist, leading to a conflict between the Black Glove, the Mask and the Spy Smasher.

Critique

By the time he made *Casus Kıran*, Atadeniz had the masked-hero formula off pat. Hire actors you know, write a screenplay that includes a hero, a villain, a female sidekick, a scientist and a secret formula, weapon or microfilm, mix thoroughly with the same half-dozen music cues and figure out which scenes to shoot at the water tower, the living room, the nightclub and the torture dungeon. *Casus Kıran* is so much fun that it is tempting to call it Atadeniz's best film in the genre. In truth, however, ranking them really depends on the personal preferences of the viewer. For instance, is Feri Cansel your favourite heroic sidekick or are you more of Sevda Ferdağ kind of guy? If it is the former, check out *Maskeli Şeytan*. If it is the latter, *Casus Kıran* is where you want to be. The devil is in the details.

Atadeniz's first little detail was coming up with a new hero. He had already used Kilink, Zorro and the Flying Man, so he turned his attention back to his beloved American serials. Spy Smasher was introduced as a comic-book character in the second issue of Fawcett Publication's *Whiz* Comics in 1940. In 1942, he became the second comic book hero (after Captain Marvel) to earn his own Saturday serial, directed by William Witney. It remains one of the most entertaining of all the American chapter plays and it is easy to see why Atadeniz pilfered it for inspiration. Atadeniz did not adapt the serial directly (as he would later when he remakes *The Mysterious Dr. Satan as Yılmayan Seytan*), but came up with his own storyline that was basically a rehash of the plot of *Kilink İstanbul'da*. The film is wall-to-wall full of all sorts of cinematic mayhem – car chases, gunfights, you name it. The antagonist of *Casus Kıran* is The Mask – a neat, pulpy creation right out of an early issue of Detective Comics. Clad in a suit and fedora with a full, white face mask, the character looks like a pulp illustration come to life. He is no Kilink, to be sure, but when combined with Spy Smasher's black cape and Sevda's short-shorts, Atadeniz films virtually every frame with comic-book style. Whereas other Turkish film-makers had abandoned the nostalgia factor completely, choosing instead to make their masked hero films exercises in swinging sixties sadism, Atadeniz took Casus Kıran in the other direction. While there are still whiffs of adult-themed play (you cannot make a masked hero film without the occasional nude whipping scene after all) Casus Kıran remains light-hearted. Atadeniz was also a better storyteller than many of his peers. While it may seem an odd compliment to give, at least his films have all their scenes in the correct order.

İrfan Atasoy is on hand, once again, as the hero. He looks a little tired, this time around, but once he pops that mask on his face and hops on his motorcycle to the scratchy sounds of surf-guitar, you will be in pulp heaven. One of the character archetypes that did not appear in Kilink İstanbul'da is the bumbling, goofy, idiot that tries desperately to help our hero and almost always screws up. Usually, these characters – and the actors playing them – test the viewer's patience. But Erol Gunaydın is a genuinely funny actor who manages to maintain an acting career in Turkey to this day. For an even better example of his work in the genre, see Atadeniz's later film *Yılmayan Şeytan*. Probably because it was easier for Atadeniz to film outside of the city, Casus Kıran has a very remote feel – almost as if Turkey had been mysteriously depopulated for some reason. In addition, when you watch enough of these films in quick succession, it becomes a thrill to see the same locations over and over again. In this case, the water tower from *Maskeli Şeytan* makes an appearance. It is like spotting Hitchcock in one of his famous cameos.

Surprisingly, the film ends with a whiff of tragedy as a major character – one in need of saving throughout the film – is shot and killed in the final moments. Atadeniz does not dwell on the heartbreak, however. Spy Smasher and Sevda jump on his motorcycle and drive off, quickly followed by the familiar 'Son'. Spy Smasher was enough of a success that Atadeniz followed it with a sequel in 1970 entitled *Casus Kıran Yedi Canli Adam*. It is more of the same – fast-paced, frenetic and fun. After all, it is a Yılmaz Atadeniz film.

David Lee White

Superman Returns

Süpermen Dönüyor

Studio:

Kunt Film

Director:

Kunt Tulgar

Producer:

Kunt Tulgar

Screenwriter:

Necdet Tok

Cinematographer:

Abdullah Gürek

Duration:

80 Minutes

Cast:

Tayfun Demir
Güngör Bayrak
Yıldırım Gencer
Eşref Kolçak
Nejat Özbek

Year:

1979

Synopsis

Tayfun, a fresh university graduate, learns from his parents, when at his family's farm house, that he is adopted. After learning of his unearthly past, Tayfun goes to a cave where his father's ghost explains to him that he is indeed Superman, the last survivor of the planet Krypton. After learning that he is Superman, Tayfun starts exploring his powers by flying above Turkey. In the meantime, a Turkish professor, who studies a strange meteoroid from the planet Krypton, claims to make the most important discovery, while some others plan to get a hold of the meteoroid to use it to transform metals into gold. Tayfun starts working at the newspaper *Dünya* (World) where a co-worker, Alev, is the professor's daughter. After the kidnapping of her father by the gold-hunting evil guys, Alev also finds herself under threat but Superman rescues her. Falling in love with Superman, Alev refuses Tayfun. However, later, unable to contact Superman, Alev finds herself asking Tayfun for help to hand the Kryptonite to the evil guys in return for her father. Once again Superman shows up: he rescues the professor and Alev, after she is kidnapped once more. Despite Alev's insistence, at the end, Superman flies into space to find Krypton.

Critique

Süpermen Dönüyor (Superman Returns) opens with several shiny plastic Christmas tree ornaments which are hung from the ceiling and framed against a black curtain. As the handheld camera moves through them with shaky movements, a narrator introduces Krypton before the opening credits. *Süpermen Dönüyor* is a low-budget, trashy, simplistic, and imitative costumed-hero film adaptation, just one among many Turkish adaptations of fantastic heroes borrowed from the West, including remakes of Tarzan, Dracula, Zorro, and Batman. As such, it is a laughing stock for many – excerpts from this film have been seen by over two million people on YouTube. Once a trash film is isolated from its particular production, distribution, and exhibition hub, its reception also changes. Instead of reading this film through an ironic distance and pointing out its mistakes, *Süpermen Dönüyor* presents a specific way of responding to the Western popular cinemas by both remaking or adapting and redoing those cinemas.

Süpermen Dönüyor unites elements from Yeşilçam's mode of film production, culture-specific tropes from Turkey, and a pretentious Hollywood-style film language. More than being a failed imitation, the film reproduces the domestic storytelling conventions and their filmic instances in the opening scene. By setting the expectations of the spectators low through a voice-over narration coupled with simple visuals, Süpermen Dönüyor's naive film language is not its weakness but, instead, its strength because, here, the visual aids the narrative. This was also coupled with the Turkification of Superman, which renders him Turkish through various visual and narrative tropes. Much like Yeşilçam melodramas, Tayfun is introduced at the beginning of the film as the son of a low-class peasant family who later falls in love with the daughter of a professor at the newspaper. In line with his rural characteristics, before he leaves the family house, the Kryptonite is taken out of a wooden cast wrapped in lace and his family prepares some food for him before he embarks upon his long journey. Such elements place Tayfun within a rural Turkish setting, part of a folk tradition with a good upbringing, and, most importantly, allow us to identify with him as a Turk. The director of the film, Kunt Tulgar, in a personal interview in 2002, accepted that both the Kryptonite in lace (signifying the dowry) and the food in a sack represent Turkish customs.

In the film, the scenes showing the flight of Superman are handled by the shots of a Superman-costumed Ken-doll which are alternated with the horizontal upper body shots of the actor who plays Superman, while both are placed in front of a back-projected screen showing various aerial touristic images of Turkey taken from a plane and mostly borrowed from a promotional film of Turkey directed by Claude Lelouch. The coming together of these back-projected images from a French director's film with a homemade Turkish Superman doll is indeed symptomatic of the popular cinema of Turkey, of Yeşilçam in the years between 1950s and 1980s (See Arslan 2011). This practice is at the core of cinema in Turkey, which brought together traditional performances including two-dimensional shadow plays and storytelling conventions with the Western, realistic vocabulary of film-making.

As such, *Süpermen Dönüyor* is a typical Yeşilçam product, an instance of a culmination of different styles of film-making which presents us with a new vocabulary. It is this play between two cultural traditions, this in-between situation where such trash films are located. In this respect, the films are also very often playful. Tayfun, in exploring his Superman powers, notices that he can see people naked. But the girls he sees naked are, indeed, wearing bikinis. However, Tayfun's friend Naci, unaware of Tayfun's newfound abilities as Superman, thinks that he cannot see the girls naked. Thus he says, 'What's up? Do you wish you were Superman?' Indeed, Naci is right next to Superman. It is this play of identities which is at stake in Yeşilçam's costumed-hero films – a Turkish superhero that is not convincing enough, even to his/her friends, yet, in fact, *is* the superhero. This is what is at stake in the interplay of a Ken-doll in an American superhero costume sewn by a Turkish woman, the director's wife, and acted by a Turkish actor, with the back-projected images of Turkey's touristy sites. If this is to be found trashy, excessive, and transgressive, then this claim is extendable to almost all of Yeşilçam as a popular cinema laced with simultaneous illusionism and anti-illusionism, realism and non-realism.

Savaş Arslan

Tarkan: The Viking Blood

Tarkan Viking Kanı

Studio:
Arzu Film

Director:
Mehmet Aslan

Producer:
Nahit Ataman

Screenwriters:
Sezgin Burak
Sadık Şendil

Cinematographer:
Cahit Engin

Duration:
88 Minutes

Cast:
Kartal Tibet
Seher Şeniz
Bilal İnci

Year:
1971

Synopsis

Tarkan, gallant warrior of the Huns, finds himself in the middle of yet another hair-raising adventure. Renegade Viking Toro falls under the employ of a mysterious Chinese princess named Lotus, who plots to kidnap Yonja – the daughter of Attila the Hun. Tarkan, beaten during an unsuspected attack on a Hunnish fortress, recuperates and sails to the land of Vikings to rescue Yonja and settle the score. Vengeance is two-fold this time, as Tarkan's loyal companion, Kurt, a wild wolf from the steppes of Asia, is slain. Swashbuckling from one death trap to the next, Tarkan meets Ursula, a leader of a band of warrior women who has her own personal vendetta against Toro.

Critique

Based on the popular comic strip, Tarkan made his film debut in 1969 starring Kartal Tibet, and directed by Tunç Başaran. For the sequels, Başaran was replaced with Mehmet Aslan – a director known for many quickie B-grade action films throughout the 1960s. As a result, the sequels could not match the superiority of the original as Aslan's direction fell short in capturing the much-needed flair. More likely, the producers intended to cash in on the popularity generated by their successful first outing, as the budget seems smaller in comparison. This sequel also appears rushed and handled with less care. At first glance, the budget constraints do hurt the film. For instance, the costumes worn by the actors, be it Vikings or Huns, resemble cut-to-size bathroom mats (they probably were) or rugs, the many colours do not blend and this makes for some visual awkwardness, especially for viewers familiar with Hollywood spectacles. The overdone wigs scream *look at me*, and the actors give it all they have as if contending for lavish exaggeration trophies.

In retrospect, this was a common problem, since most of the directors, including Aslan, worked in black and white films in the 1950s and 1960s. When an abrupt jump was made to colour films in the 1970s, many film-makers had not adapted well and, therefore, were unable to use colour in a sophisticated manner. Thus, the cheap sets were more noticeable – something they could get away with in beautiful black and white. Naturally, costumes showed their obvious limitations whilst little thought was given to using shades and shadows to create atmosphere and deliver a stylish product. Further, a rather primitive understanding of lighting was also evident in these low-budget Yeşilçam adventures. Although some directors were able to adapt and renew themselves efficiently, Aslan was a plodder. Yet, taking all of the above into consideration, perhaps this is as close a production can get to a real-life comic strip (whether by intention or chance)! Once these grounds are accepted, it is easy to overlook the many imbalances and enjoy it for what it really is: a moving storyboard. So, wigs off!

It is important to note that its star Kartal Tibet was Cüneyt Arkın's cinematic rival. In 1965, when Tibet starred as *Karaoğlan*, another swashbuckling comic-strip hero by Suat Yalaz's pen, the scene was set for comic-book inspired feature film competition. Hence, Arkın made *Malkoçoğlu*, and both pulp characters became successful box-office franchises. The 1970s saw stars Tibet and Arkın once again matching muscle for muscle, with Tibet's *Tarkan* series against Arkın's *Kara Murat* films. With his slightly slanted eyes and Tartaric features, Kartal Tibet was an ideal choice for Central Asian heroes such as *Tarkan* and *Karaoğlan*, whereas Arkın, with his European looks, became a box-office drawer in Ottoman-era adventures like *Malkoçoğlu* and *Kara Murat*.

Ayman Kole

Tarkan: The Viking Blood, 1971, Mehmet Aslan.

The Deathless Devil

Yılmayan Şeytan

Studio:
Atadeniz Film

Director:
Yılmaz Atadeniz

Producer:
Yılmaz Atadeniz

Screenwriter:
Seçil Erok

Cinematographer:
Sertaç Karan

Composer:
John Barry & various
(unauthorized)

Duration:
84 Minutes

Cast:
Kunt Tulgar
Mine Mutlu
Erol Taş
Muzaffer Tema

Year:
1972

Synopsis

No sooner has the adoptive father of young Tekin revealed to him his true parentage – telling him that he is actually the son of a masked crime fighter by the name of The Copperhead – he falls victim to an assassin's blade. Said assassin turns out to have been an emissary of the mysterious criminal mastermind Doctor Satan, the very man responsible for the death of Tekin's real father. With The Copperhead's chainmail mask in hand, Tekin determines to adopt the crime fighter's identity in order to track Satan down and bring him to justice. Meanwhile, Doctor Satan is bent on obtaining the remote control device created by Professor Doğan by any means necessary. The madman has already built one killer robot and, by means of Dogan's device, hopes to command an army of similarly diabolical machines for the purpose of ruling the world. Until The Copperhead can succeed in uncovering his hidden lair and putting a stop to his treacherous plan, no one, especially not Dogan and his beautiful young daughter Sevgi, is safe.

Critique

It is almost impossible to overstate the influence of the classic American movie serials upon Turkish pulp cinema of the 1960s and 1970s, and especially upon the career of director Yılmaz Atadeniz. Atadeniz not only drew heavily upon such serials for inspiration but also, on at least two occasions, helmed direct remakes of them, proving in the process that he was a true connoisseur of the form. Both the 1942 *Spy Smasher*, which served as the basis for Atadeniz's 1967 *Casus Kıran*, and 1940s' *The Mysterious Doctor Satan*, which provided the model for Yılmayan Şeytan, are widely considered to be among the best American serials made. Both were directed by one of the acknowledged masters of the form, William Witney (in the case of *Doctor Satan*, in collaboration with frequent co-director John English) and produced under the auspices of Republic Pictures, the studio that refined the process of making serials into a finely-tuned art form during the 1930s and 1940s.

   With *Yılmayan Şeytan*, Atadeniz pays affectionate homage to his source material while at the same time making liberal use of those few advantages he had over the makers of the original. The first is his use of colour, which allows the director to take the action of the 1940 chapter play out of its monochrome original context and place it within a comic book world exploding with bright primary hues. The second is Atadeniz's reliance on Turkey's relaxed censorship standards at the time to update what was originally intended as a Saturday afternoon diversion for children with a somewhat sleazy grindhouse sensibility. Atadeniz's otherwise faithful treatment of the text notwithstanding, you can rest assured that the square-jawed hero of the 1940 Doctor Satan was never seen openly ogling a mini-skirted female's rear end, or describing himself to a lingerie-clad potential bedmate as 'hot and horny'. In the best Turkish pulp cinema tradition, *Yılmayan Şeytan* glides over its considerable narrative and technical hiccups by virtue of sheer velocity. While having to compensate for the usual threadbare production values, Atadeniz's direction is sure-handed throughout and, with the exception of some particularly unwelcome narrative ballast from Erol Günaydın in an execrable comic relief role, admirably maintains a consistent, breakneck pace. Nonetheless, the film's story, when held up to close inspection, reveals itself to be one held together more by holes than by such niceties as the relationship between cause and effect. Action is its own justification here, and, once one surrenders oneself to that logic, it is possible to forgive – or perhaps overlook altogether – even such visual non-sequiturs as a fistfight whose location switches rapidly back and forth between interiors and exteriors without rhyme or reason.

Perhaps the affinity that Turkish film-makers like Atadeniz felt for the Republic serial mill can be explained in part by the latter's lean economy and shrewd instinct for recycling; a model which Atadeniz and his peers followed admirably. However, while Republic's craftspeople tended to cannibalize their own work, reusing props, costumes, and footage from their previous productions whenever possible, Turkish pulp film-makers took advantage of both their own under-the-radar status and the vagaries of international copyright law to cast a much wider net. *Yılmayan Şeytan* provides an excellent example of this, not least by its choice of musical score. As was typical of the soundtracks to Turkish action films of its day, selections from John Barry's original scores to the James Bond films are pilfered, along with a wide selection of borrowed themes from other sources. On the visual front, Atadeniz proves that the greater cinematic world is also ripe for the plucking, simply and audaciously inserting scenes from the original 1940 *Doctor Satan* into a sequence in which his characters are watching part of the action play out on a black-and-white monitor.

In the end, *Yılmayan Şeytan* is interesting not just for how it so successfully creates an enclosed comic book world within its very limited means but also for those moments in which the boundaries between that world and the real world beyond it break down. Such is the case in those location shot sequences in which we see The Copperhead and Dr. Satan – each a larger-than-life, colourfully garbed character firmly rooted in the realm of juvenile fantasy – walking the gritty Istanbul streets against a backdrop of bleak high-rise apartment blocks. In these moments, the film bears more than a passing resemblance to Vaclav Vorlicek's *Who Wants to Kill Jessie?*, in which figures from the protagonist's comic-fuelled dreams break free to run rampant on the streets of Prague. Like that film, *Yılmayan Şeytan* presents us with a kind of layered fantasy, showing us both an idealized pulp fiction universe and a version of our own world in which the fanciful products of that universe walk among us.

Todd Stadtman

The Exorcist

Şeytan

Studio:
Saner Film

Director:
Metin Erksan

Producer:
Hulki Saner

Screenwriter:
Yılmaz Tümtürk

Cinematographer:
Nihat Çifteoğlu

Duration:
105 Minutes

Cast:
Canan Perver
Cihan Ünal
Meral Taygun
Agah Hün

Year:
1974

Synopsis

In a suburb of İstanbul, 12-year-old Gül lives with her mother Ayten. Now separated from her husband – who does not want to speak to her – Ayten is being courted by rich playboy Ekrem, much to Gül's chagrin. Gül finds solace in mysterious objects from the occult, including an ouija board. The little girl starts to behave strangely; her condition worsens, despite all attempts to cure it. Eventually it turns out that she has been possessed by the devil. Anyone foolish enough to stand in her way is ruthlessly mutilated. The only person able to cure her is Tuğrul, a trained psychologist who has published a book on exorcism. Like Gül, however, Tuğrul experiences family problems, as he feels guilty for having committed his mother Fatma to a lunatic asylum. Nonetheless he resolves to try and cure Gül, enlisting the help of an exorcist who doubles up as an imam. Together they embark on a series of treatments, both violent and non-violent. However Tuğrul ends up paying the ultimate sacrifice for his actions, both past and present.

Critique

Erksan's film lifts most of its plot, characters and situations from William Friedkin's *The Exorcist* (1973). It is now regarded – especially by western critics and/or viewers – as a hilarious piece of trash with rudimentary special effects and over-the-top performances. A different picture emerges, however, if the film is looked at in its context of production. From its earliest days Yeşilçam cinema had a history of remaking Hollywood films of all genres: one of the most successful examples being Capra's *Pocketful of Miracles* (1961), released as *Elmacı Kadın* (1971). By the late 1970s, *Star Trek*, *Star Wars* and *The Exorcist* had all been remade. However Yeşilçam directors did not simply imitate Hollywood, rather, they appropriated the films to their local contexts, both thematically and stylistically. This is evident in *Şeytan*, where director Erksan reconceives the story as a family melodrama (a staple component of Yeşilçam cinema). While Ayten (Meral Taygun) makes every effort to care for her daughter Gül (Canan Perver), the child has no proper father to look up to. Ayten's husband has absconded, while boyfriend Ekrem (Ekrem Gökkaya) treats Gül as a plaything to be teased rather than loved. Consequently Gül becomes vulnerable to corruption by a perverted father-figure – i.e. the Devil. The child is transformed from a happy-go-lucky schoolgirl into a monster, cursing and swearing at every opportunity and taking revenge on Ekrem by breaking his neck. Gül's condition is an extreme representation of what happens when parents break up, leaving their children uncared for.

Şeytan explores the same theme through Tuğrul (Cihan Ünal), a trained psychologist who allows his mother Fatma (Sabahat Işık) to be consigned to a lunatic asylum. Fatma dies there, leaving Tuğrul to rue his decision. Just like Gül's father, he has willfully neglected one of his own family members. The only way Tuğrul can redeem himself is to exorcize the devil out of Gül – even if it costs him his life. In stylistic terms, *Şeytan* is replete with techniques characteristic of Yeşilçam – repeat shot/reverse shot sequences, zooms in and out from the characters' faces, and abrupt transitions between individual scenes. Such devices may look amateurish, but they provided a kind of visual shorthand for hard-pressed Yeşilçam directors, working on tight budgets with only two or three weeks in which to shoot their films. More importantly, such devices show how Yeşilçam cinema consistently challenges western-formulated conventions of narrative and/or sonic coherence. In place of logic, with plot and characterization based on a relationship of cause and effect, *Şeytan* foregrounds the notions of repetition and dissonance, punctuated throughout with repeated snatches of the opening bars of Mike Oldfield's 'Tubular Bells' (originally commissioned for the Hollywood *Exorcist*). What we see bears little relationship to what we hear: once possessed by the Devil, Gül's lip-synching looks positively amateurish as she mimes the lines delivered on the soundtrack by a middle-aged man. This type of structure has some fascinating consequences. On the current (2008) American DVD release, the English subtitles continually make jokes at the film's expense. Gül speaks various languages, including Latin and French, but it is clear that the translator cannot understand what she is saying. On one occasion the subtitles ask 'La Plume de ma Tante, maybe?' and later on they make a derisive comment about Gül's presumed lack of linguistic competence ('what a linguist!'). On another occasion the subtitles abandon the task of trying to translate the Turkish, inviting English-language viewers to 'search Google' instead. Such jokes reveal how little the translator understands about the ways in which Yeşilçam cinema challenges the prevailing cinematic hegemony. Films like *Şeytan* do not set out to be 'comprehensible' – as western viewers might understand the term – but unfold according to their own logic.

More significantly, *Şeytan* tries to educate as well as entertain its viewers. In this version, the exorcist (Agah Hün) recites lines from the Koran rather than the Bible, reminding us that God's grace will be bestowed on those who subject themselves to His authority. By such means individuals can protect themselves from diabolic penetration. Both Gül and Ayten understand the significance of this lesson – at the end of the film they are shown entering a mosque, their heads covered with scarves. Gül sees the imam in the corner and runs towards him; to her surprise, she discovers that it is the exorcist. This comes as a surprise both for her and for viewers: in an earlier sequence he had apparently died of a heart attack in a valiant if doomed attempt to purge the devil out of the little girl. Yet perhaps the exorcist's reappearance proves just how benevolent God can be. If people respect his status as the father of everyone (the family theme recurs yet again), then they too might have the chance of resurrection.

Laurence Raw

The Man who Saved the World

Dünyayı Kurtaran Adam

Studio:
Anıt Film

Director:
Çetin İnanç

Producer:
Mehmet Karahafiz

Screenwriter:
Cüneyt Arkın

Cinematographer:
Çetin Gürtop

Art Director:
Nuri Kırgeç

Composer:
Kunt Tulgar

Editor:
Necdet Tok

Duration:
102 Minutes

Cast:
Cüneyt Arkın
Aytekin Akkaya
Füsun Uçar
Hüseyin Peyda

Year:
1982

Synopsis

The film begins with a story of how the earth was destroyed by a nuclear holocaust. Some men who survived this disaster have brought pieces of the earth together and reconstituted it by using their brainpower. However, humankind has a very powerful and destructive enemy in an alien wizard who lacks one essential thing, an ability humans have: the collective wisdom, compassion, and knowledge of humankind. Repeatedly, the wizard attacks the earth and destroys it. Repeatedly, the world is reconstituted by mankind. Finally, the elders of the earth decide to send a team of star fighters to attack and destroy the wizard. The team of two men Murat and Ali represent a united earth (and are both Turkish). Murat and Ali first encounter some savage people, and then are ambushed by the wizard. They fight their way out, aided by a wise man and his daughter. The wise man takes them to important religious sites and shows them meteor craters coming from earth. He then explains the wizard's story and tells them what the wizard is looking for. It is a golden sword where all of mankind's power is stored and a brain where mankind's wisdom, passion, and love reside. The shape-shifting wizard steals the brain and the sword and kills Ali. Murat then melts the sword and brain given by the wise man into a hot golden fluid, puts both his arms into it, and takes them out as golden gloves. Now in possession of the wisdom and strength of the world, Murat faces the wizard in a final confrontation. He beats the wizard, saves the earth, and avenges the death of his best friend.

Critique

The Man Who Saved the World is reportedly the worst film ever made, according to a poll of movie buffs. The judges of the poll suggest that, by comparison, Ed Wood's *Plan 9 From Outer Space* (1959) is tame in its illogical narrative progression and narrative absurdity, but *The Man Who Saved the World's* reputation is undeserved. It is a coherent narrative with a three-act structure, executed with professionalism and sincerity. In an interview, Cuneyt Arkin, the star and co-writer of the film, indicated that his intent was to parody sci-fi films and television series that took place beyond the stars, such as *Star Wars* and *Battlestar Galactica*. The film gained a cult audience, travelling university campuses and reducing students to tears of laughter. What made the film so notorious was its attempt to tell a classic sci-fi story but its inability to do so for lack of proper sets and costumes, in addition to the actors' extremely idiosyncratic, even comedic, tongue-in-cheek performances. The storyline is very fragmented and often jumps from one scene to the next. Just as *Omer the Tourist* stole clips from the original *Star Trek* series, *The Man who Saved the World* borrowed footage from *Star Wars* and the music from *Raiders of the Lost Ark*. *The Man Who Saved the World* again aims to imitate and borrow from American sci-fi films. There are spaceships, laser weapons, exploding planes, and scrolling titles reminiscent of Star Wars. There is extensive use of borrowed footage from American sci-fi films such as Star Wars. American sci-fi also used recycled footage to a limited degree in the 1950s. However, Turkish use of borrowed footage is excessive, as though compensating for its lack of advanced technology not only in the film industry but also in the country itself, and once again displaying an inferiority complex in terms of the superior other in cinema. Overall, *The Man who Saved the World* is a bold and daring science fiction film that was an inspiration for the new Turkish cinema's sci-fi films since the 1990s. *The Man who saved the World's* serious tone created a comedy effect on a first viewing. Yet, different viewings of the film would offer depth into the psyche of Turkish film-makers of the 1970s and how Yeşilçam cinema dared to rival Hollywood.

Murat Akser

The Nameless Knight

Adsız Cengaver

Studio:
Erman Film

Director:
Halit Refiğ

Producer:
Hürrem Erman

Screenwriter:
Halit Refiğ

Cinematographer:
İlhan Arakon

Art Director:
Annie G Pertan

Editor:
Hilmi Güver

Duration:
83 Minutes

Cast:
Cüneyt Arkın
Nebahat Cehre
Altan Günbay

Year:
1970

Synopsis

Set in ancient Samarkand, the scheming Vizier Jabbar usurps the throne and has the former ruler publicly executed by beheading. In the following moments, the severed head utters a prophecy that, in light of his treachery, Jabbar in turn will be vanquished by one of his heirs. To render the prophecy useless, Jabbar rids himself of concubines in a series of paranoid murders to avoid any chance of offspring. Yet, a boy of mysterious origin survives and is nurtured by a peaceful fisherman's family who call him Adsız, meaning *nameless*. Many years later, armed with a genie's magic sword, Adsız is committed to put an end to Jabbar's injustices once and for all. Unaware of his true heritage, Adsız, aided by a female warrior companion, embarks on a journey full of black magic, peril, romance and swordplay. However, his invincibility is linked to the magic sword that cannot be used against someone of his own blood. As stories of a *hero with no name* spread like wildfire through the countryside, the power-crazy Jabbar, with the assistance of witchcraft, seeks to destroy his dedicated nemesis before a full-scale rebellion is ignited against his kingdom.

Critique

Halit Refiğ is an important director for his film *Gurbet Kuşları* (1964), a drama focused on the problems of internal migration of peasants to big cities. Another controversial production is his 1966 film *Harem'de Dört Kadin* (1966), with the sub-plot of the Young Turk movement inside Palace walls. Incidentally, Cuneyt Arkin starred in both films, although in lesser roles. In fact, Refiğ is credited with discovering Arkin, a star who became one of the most popular action icons in Turkish cinema. Naturally, by 1970, Arkin was a household name and his popularity had spread to Iran, too, where he was known as Fahreddin. Therefore, it should come as no surprise that producer Hürrem Erman decided to make the film far more marketable in the Middle East by involving Iranian talent and partially shooting the film in that country. Technically, the film is armed with a bigger budget, and the special effects were done at Rank Studios, London. Refiğ proves to be very competent, employing a lot of long- and wide shots, taking full advantage of the Cinemascope format. It is hard to believe that this is Refiğ's first Cinemascope production, as he is quite comfortable and gives one of his strongest directorial efforts. As for his screenplay, Refiğ has dreamed up a fantasy world where East/West fables and mythologies blend brilliantly. Therefore, Adsız Cengaver can owe to *Aladdin's Lamp* as much as it does to *King Arthur*. For instance, he gives the viewer a genie released from a bottle who, in turn, rewards the young Adsız with a magic sword. However, the sword is then thrust into a stone from which the boy must withdraw it when his time has come to rule. The introduction of Adsız's aide-de-camp Altınay, the female warrior, is reminiscent of Lancelot. Adsız meets a Knight upon a bridge, they joust with lances. As can be understood, this is borrowed and then filtered delicately to suit the eastern setting. Refiğ also mixes in ancient Turkic folklore represented by the hero's 'name'. According to Central Asiatic tradition, boys remained nameless until they earned themselves one by performing heroic deeds. The hero in Adsız Cengaver remains *Adsız* that is, nameless, until he overthrows the villain and earns the title Adil Han. Moreover, there are essences of the story of Moses. In order to escape murder, the baby Adsız is placed in a basket by his mother and left to drift down a river, where he is eventually safely found by a family who raise him as their own. It must be noted that this idea was recycled again in another Cuneyt Arkin costumed adventure titled *Battal Gazi'nin Oğlu* (1974).

Another departure is the main conflict itself. In most costumed adventure films made in Turkey during the 1960s and 1970s, such as *Karaoğlan* (1965), *Kılıç Aslan* (1975), *Battal Gazi Destanı* (1971) and *Köroğlu* (1968), the hero is motivated by revenge for the harm done to his father, which can be either torture, inflicted disability, but more often death at the hands of the villain. However, in *Adsız Cengaver* the conflict is about fulfilling a prophecy and, therefore, the fight to the death is between son (hero) and father (villain). Given that Turkish cultural values emphasize the importance placed on the paternal figure as *backbone of the house* and *bread-winner*, the storyline is indeed unique in its departure from countless Turkish adventure films.

Ayman Kole

The Serpent's Tale

Karanlık Sular

Synopsis

Karanlık Sular opens with a prologue explaining that the film is based on fragments of a lost manuscript by a nineteenth-century Islamic calligrapher named Mehves. Although fictional, this framing device helps set up the looping, elliptical narrative structure of the

Studio:

Temasa

Director:

Kutluğ Ataman

Producer:

Kutluğ Ataman

Screenwriter:

Kutluğ Ataman

Cinematographer:

Chris Squires

Art Director:

Sita Sayin

Composer:

Blake Leyh

Editor:

Annabel Ware

Duration:

82 Minutes

Cast:

Gönen Bozbey-
Daniel Chace
Metin Uygun
Eric Pio

Year:

1995

film which is set in contemporary Istanbul but is very much haunted by the past. Containing a series of interweaving and overlapping stories, *Karanlık Sular* follows Richie Hunter as he meets a mysterious young man named Haldun who gives him an ancient compass to take to his mother Lamia's mansion -- only to find out from Lamia that her son Haldun has actually been dead for years. We then follow Lamia as she attempts to track down this man claiming to be Haldun, convinced that the compass is linked to two untranslatable manuscript fragments that he had left her. Complicating this attempt is the involvement of a vampire known as 'Theodora the Byzantium Queen', and an older man named Hasmet, who proposes that Lamia marry him and dispose of her mansion for insurance money. As the film loops around these narrative strands, it soon becomes clear that everything is not as it first seems, and that Lamia is far from being the only person interested in deciphering these manuscript fragments.

Critique

While much of the output of Turkish Fantastic Cinema is often dismissed as being ridiculous or laughable, *Karanlık Sular* stands out for its serious tone and its genuine artistic flair. Directed by Kutluğ Ataman straight out of film school, the film clearly demonstrates his ambition to be seen alongside the greats of European Art Cinema. Bearing comparison with the work of film-makers like Michelangelo Antonioni and Alain Robbe-Grillet whom Ataman cites as inspirations, *Karanlık Sular* exhibits a mastery of the form which is all too rare in the few horror films produced in Turkey. Indeed, Ataman has since had a varied and successful career, with his follow-up film *Lola+Bilidikid* (1998) being selected to open the Panorama section of the 49th International Berlin Film Festival and his work in contemporary art being nominated for the Turner Prize in 2004.

An arthouse vampire story, the film follows a circular form of dream logic and functions more on the level of symbolism than storytelling – therefore lending itself well to an analysis of implicit levels of meaning. Given the theme of culture clash set in the decaying world of Istanbul, the more convincing interpretations focus on the symbolic value of the various cultural representatives. From such a perspective, Lamia (played brilliantly by Gönen Bozbey) can be seen to represent the haunting presence of the Ottoman empire in Istanbul, while Hasmet, on the other hand, represents the new Turkish republic with its pragmatic rejection of this Ottoman past. Similarly, the 'Byzantium Queen' Theodora symbolizes the Byzantian heritage still present in present day Turkey, while Richie Hunter (Daniel Chace) can easily be seen to represent the presence of American imperialism. On this level, the film is very much embedded in the particular cultural context of 1990s' Istanbul with the resultant clashes between forces of tradition and modernity.

In many ways, the closest comparison would be with the work of directors like David Lynch and Alejandro Jodorowsky, where imagery and symbolism override a sense of coherent narrative development. This emphasis on imagery is helped by the beautiful cinematography from Chris Squires, who has since worked as a steadycam/camera operator in Hollywood on such titles as *The Usual Suspects* (1995) and *I Heart Huckabees* (2004). There is an artistry to the compositions which really captures the sense of hidden depths behind the façade of modern-day Istanbul – tensions which are referred to in the film's Turkish language title literally as 'Dark Waters.' Cinephiles should also look out for a cameo from Giovanni Scognamillo, perhaps the most important film historian in Turkey and author of the book *Fantastik Türk Sineması*.

Admittedly, however, some aspects of the film are less successful. In particular, the decision to shift between English and Turkish as the primary language may function well on a conceptual level – capturing that theme of overlapping cultures which runs throughout the film – but the execution is poor and only serves to heighten the stitlted nature of some of the performances. Furthermore, the elliptical nature of the narrative curves back on itself like an Ouroboros (a mystical symbol depicting a serpent eating its own tail) which helps explain the international title of *The Serpent's Tale* but does little to bring the narrative strands to a satisfying conclusion. Nevertheless, these perceived failings are actually the result of the admirable conceptual ambition of the film; an ambition which certainly results in a film that rewards further viewings.

To date, the film has struggled to find an audience with that level of engagement. On release in Turkey, the film was a notorious box office flop, selling only 1,738 tickets on its release despite almost universal critical acclaim. There are a variety of reasons for this – not least the general slump in Turkish cinema viewing in the mid-1990s – but primarily the issue seems to be that the subject matter was too lowbrow for the arthouse crowd while the treatment was too highbrow for the genre crowd. Indeed, at the time, this was one of only a handful of Turkish horror films ever produced in the country. More recently, the genre has come into fashion with titles like *Araf* (2006) and *Dabbe* (2006) having great success at the box office. Given this shift in tastes, it can only be hoped that the recent limited edition DVD release from the Greek distributor Onar Films helps bring this lost classic to a wider audience.

Iain Robert Smith

Three Mighty Men

Üç Dev Adam

Studio:
Tual Film

Synopsis

Turkey has become the latest base of international operations for the criminal syndicate run by the evil mastermind Spiderman (who would look just like the well-known American comic book hero of the same name but for the imposing, caterpillar-like brows poking out of the eye holes in his mask). Fortunately, help is on the way in the form of masked Mexican wrestler Santo, Captain America, and Captain America's sexy female associate Julia. It seems that the gang has been doing a handy business trafficking in stolen

Director:

Tevfik Fikret Uçak

Producer:

Ridvan Tual

Screenwriter:

Doğan Tamer

Cinematographer:

Orhan Kapkı

Composers:

John Barry & various (unauthorized)

Editor:

Hüsamettin Üren

Duration:

81 Minutes

Cast:

Aytekin Akkaya
Yavez Selekman
Doğan Tamer
Deniz Erkanat
Teyfik Sen
Mine Sun
Altan Günbay

Year:

1973

Turkish artefacts and distributing counterfeit currency, and that both Mexico and the US have become caught up in their web. Once in Istanbul, Captain America teams up with local lawman Orhan to investigate a mysterious yacht anchored offshore, while Santo follows the money. Meanwhile, Juliet goes undercover in the glamorous world of Turkish high fashion.

Spider-man is soon feeling the heat, and rushes to wrap up his operations before fleeing the country, but first he is determined to get payback against the meddling superheroes. At first it seems that the heroes are gaining the upper hand, until they discover that they may be dealing with more than one Spiderman.

Critique

3 Dev Adam was among the first examples of Turkish pulp cinema to gain the attention of Western cult cinema enthusiasts, and, in the years prior to its official release on DVD, was enthusiastically traded on homemade VHS tapes and DVD-Rs on the so-called 'grey market'. The film exhibits the same lax attitude toward international copyrights seen in other Turkish cult favourites, but its appeal goes somewhat beyond that of entries like *Seytan* (popularly known as 'The Turkish Exorcist') and *Badi* (popularly known as 'The Turkish ET'). While those last-mentioned films generated a sort of 'so bad its good' fascination on the part of fans via their attempts to duplicate specific Hollywood properties with only a minuscule fraction of those films' budgets and technical means, *3 Dev Adam* takes more of what would now be called a 'mash up' approach, seemingly seeing the entirety of pop culture's more disreputable regions – comic books, Mexican *lucha* films, movie serials – as a field from which to freely pick and choose its elements.

In keeping with this mash-up aesthetic, *3 Dev Adam*, once having pilfered its iconic characters, takes the further liberty of altering them to whatever degree suits its needs, much as a mash-up artist in the world of music would alter the pitch or tempo of a sample. Thus, the teenage American superhero Spiderman is transformed into a cackling villain from the 'far east' who rapes, murders and steals, and Captain America's blonde, stereotypically 'all American' alter ego becomes something altogether more swarthy, definitely the product of a more cosmopolitan part of the US than the mythical Midwest. Perhaps most radically, the film takes Santo, the ring persona of the wrestler Rodolfo Guzmán Huerta, and completes his migration into the world of fiction, divorcing him from his real-world roots and giving him a handsome young alter ego who conducts many of his heroic duties *sans* mask (something the real Guzman never did, either on screen, in the ring, or in public appearances). Also interesting is how the film drags these somewhat corny characters into a world that is so markedly dark and adult, dotted as it is with strip clubs and sleazy bars, and infused with the threat of sexual violence. Even Captain America, with his taste for highballs and openly beyond-professional relationship with his sexy sidekick, seems like more of a product of this world than he does the realm of juvenile fantasy. And keep in mind that

Three Mighty Men, 1973, Tevfik Fikret Uçak © Tual Film.

this was years before figures like Frank Miller would introduce such noirish, adult elements into the world of comics proper.

On the technical side, *3 Dev Adam* is crude, but far from artless, and even displays the occasional stylistic flourish. One instance of this is a fight that takes place in a mannequin warehouse, which calls to mind both Kubrick's *Killer's Kiss* and Seijun Suzuki's *Underworld Beauty*. The action owes the typical debt to the old Republic serials but, in its recklessness and enthusiasm, still has that certain 'back yard' quality that will undoubtedly be familiar to anyone with childhood memories of tying a blanket around their necks and emulating the exploits of their favourite comic book hero. In this childish context, the film's often quite bloody violence is somewhat shocking in conception, but also leavened by the ludicrousness of its execution. At one point, a nod is made toward Orwell's *1984* by having a cage containing a hungry rat strapped to the face of one of Spiderman's under-performing minions. However, the 'rat' in this case is actually a fairly sated looking guinea pig, and the 'cage' is actually a long clear plastic tube through which the animal ambles listlessly toward the face of its screaming victim, giving this scene the distinction of being the first cinematic instance of death by Habitrail.

One final point that sticks out about *3 Dev Adam* is the oddly rationalist approach it takes to its superheroes. At one point, Captain America – who, like Santo, spends a great deal of the film in his civilian guise, making no attempt to conceal his identity – is asked to explain why he wears a costume. He responds that it is part of his strategy to draw out Spiderman, whom he describes as 'a child-minded lunatic' who 'wears a costume all the time'. Later, we get that familiar piece of shtick in which a drunken derelict, in this case upon seeing Captain America and Spider-man run by, takes a disbelieving look at his bottle and then tosses it aside. Clearly, *3 Dev Adam* takes place in a world where such figures are not supposed to exist. Despite their scepticism, however, its makers were too generous to deny such fanciful tropes to an audience that had apparently by this time developed quite an appetite for them.

Todd Stadtman

WOMEN'S FILMS

The concept of *Women's films* is difficult to define. It suggests films made by, addressed to, or concerned with women, or all three. The term is a complex critical, theoretical and institutional construction. It can be employed to suggest a kind of uniformity while used in relation to the body of work produced by women film-makers. There is, however, another element in play here, and that is the female spectator. For instance, melodramas (at times referred to as women's weepies) are associated with a feminine spectator, as they are perceived to belong to a genre that speaks to a female audience. Therefore, they inscribe femininity in their address, thereby constructing a female point of view, which motivates and dominates the narrative. The term, then, may carry the implication that women's issues are of major significance; and that there is a woman at the centre of the film. Taking into account all the interpretations of the concept of women's films, we focus here on films about, made by, and for women. A change in the gender of the film-maker may or may not make a difference in representing women; however, the presence and visibility of women film-makers in the cinema of Turkey is worth celebrating.

Some of the films here may be characterized as women's films, but also they may well fit into different genres and styles. For instance, the discussion on Eylem Kaftan's *Vendetta Song* could well have been moved to the section on transnational cinema. Tomris Giritlioğlu's *Güz Sancısı* could have been examined under the category of (historical) drama. As suggested by the term to describe Atıf Yılmaz, 'director of women's films', it is not always women behind the camera. Yet, at the same time, not all films directed by women deal with women's issues, or target the female audience. Contemporary women film-makers tend to focus on a range of issues around political, cultural and ethnic identity and memory. Yeşim Ustaoğlu's films, for instance, tend to focus on the concepts around identity, memory, the past and, at times, trauma. One other concept, 'honour', is a recurring motif in Turkish films: there are countless narratives which treat the concept as an integral part of representing womanhood or relationships between men and women. Since the 1990s there has been an increase in the number of films which attempt to critique the concept as well as the practice of so-called honour-based violence. Handan İpekçi's *Saklı Yüzler* (*Hidden Faces*) (2007) focuses on honour crimes in the South East of Turkey and Aydın Sayman's *Janjan* (2007) and Oğuz's *Mutluluk*, which

Left image: *Pandora'nın Kutusu*, 2008, Yeşim Ustaoğlu © Film Yapim.

is discussed in this section, are recent films that directly focus on honour-based violence. Eylem Kaftan's 2005 bio-documentary *Vendetta Song* is also a case in point, as it explores practices of honour killings, arranged marriages as well as gender inequalities.

As evidenced by the current academic writings on the topic, in recent years there is an increase in the number of silent women characters.[1] What underlie this silence are different levels and types of violence – verbal, physical, emotional. Yet, silence may signify a choice, a resistance, even a type of rejection of speaking the language of the male. We also include films from the 1980s, as this decade was crucial in establishing links between the feminist movement and cinema. It is in this period that an increased tendency to focus on women's lives and issues is evident.[2]

Eylem Atakav

Notes

[1] For a detailed discussion on the relationship between silence and the representation of women in Turkish cinema, please see Güçlü, Ö., 'Silent Representations of Women in the New Cinema of Turkey', *Sine/Cine: Journal of Film Studies*, vol. 1, No. 2, Autumn, (2010), pp. 71-85 and Suner, A., *New Turkish Cinema: Belonging, Identity and Memory*. London: I. B. Tauris, 2010.

[2] For a detailed discussion of the 1980s feminist movement and cinema in Turkey, and for a detailed discussion of many of the films in this category, please see Atakav, E., *Women and Turkish Cinema: Gender Politics, Cultural Identity and Representation* (Routledge, 2012).

After Yesterday Before Tomorrow

Dünden Sonra Yarından Önce

Studio:
Eks Film

Director:
Nisan Akman

Producers:
Eriş Akman
Nisan Akman

Screenwriter:
Eriş Akman

Cinematographer:
Erol Sayıbaşı

Art Director:
Erol Sayıbaşı

Composer:
Onno Tunç

Editor:
Tamer Eşkazan

Duration:
84 Minutes

Cast:
Zuhal Olcay
Eriş Akman
Sedef Ecer

Year:
1987

Synopsis

Gül is a successful film director. Her marriage to Bülent, who is also a director, looks ideal from outside until Pelin, Bülent's assistant, decides to pursue him. After a long conversation with Bülent, about their marriage, Gül consents to giving up her job and becoming a housewife, at the same time as starting to think about having a baby. However, this becomes a challenge when she realizes that she is not happy. One day she sees bruises on the face her of her cleaner, Mübeccel. When she finds out that Müubeccel was a victim of domestic violence, Gül decides to go back to work and direct a documentary film about domestic violence. In the meantime, Bülent and Pelin get even closer, as Gül does not spend much time with Bülent. At the end of the film, we see Gül walking alone in an empty street at night, having left Bülent's possessions with Pelin, suggesting that she has given up on her marriage.

Critique

One of the most remarkable films in representing working women in Turkey is *Dünden Sonra Yarından Önce*, which mainly deals with the lack of communication between a married couple. What makes this film unconventional in terms of its representation of women is that the film does not endorse for women the solution of leaving their jobs (and becoming good housewives) for the sake of keeping a happy marriage. On the contrary, it proposes an alternative with a protagonist, Gül (Zuhal Olcay), who claims that she needs to work in order to be independent. The film engages with issues that arise from the feminist movement of the period. It explores the para-doxes inherent in simultaneously being a career woman and wife through the story of Gül, a successful film director at the peak of her career. Moreover, the film proves important with its overt refer-ence to the feminist movement of the 1980s in Turkey as well as its exploration of women's rights. In exploring a conflict experienced by urban women – that is, career versus family – the film represents the professional woman and wife as two distinct and disconnected options, presented as an either/or dichotomy. The focus here is on the patterns of marital negotiation in an urban, high-class marriage in which the wife has a demanding job and, hence, does not seem to devote herself to her home and husband, even though she is in love with him. In addition there is an exploration of how the power dynamics of an urban marriage are constructed and negotiated, and through which mechanism these dynamics are maintained, reinforced and challenged. Furthermore, women's chances of suc-cessfully combining career and family are scrutinized in the film. Through a focus on sexual politics, *Dünden Sonra Yarından Önce* looks at how female identity is constructed; it represents the elite, urban career woman as someone who cannot distance herself from independence and who cannot be convinced that her life should be focused around marriage and the family. Moreover, the film provides a critique of the class differences of women as well as looking at the urban woman versus rural woman. Yet, it still fails to give voice to the women in the documentary film that its main character directs. Overall it tells a story about the resurgence of the need for a woman to make a choice. It proves to be subversive, with its at times feminist discourse, because it assigns subjectivity to the female by letting her question the validity of her choice, not just of a man, but of a direction in her life.

Eylem Atakav

Bliss

Mutluluk

Studio:
Ans Production

Director:
Abdullah Oğuz

Producer:
Abdullah Oğuz

Screenwriters:
Kubilay Tuncer
Elif Ayan
Abdullah Oğuz

Cinematographer:
Mirsad Herovic

Art Director:
Tolunay Türköz

Composer:
Zülfü Livaneli

Editors:
Levent Çelebi
Abdullah Oğuz

Duration:
105 Minutes

Cast:
Talat Bulut
Özgü Namal
Murat Han

Year:
2007

Synopsis

Mutluluk tells the story of Meryem, a 17-year-old woman from a small village in Eastern Turkey. Meryem is found unconscious by the side of a lake. Because of shock and because of the identity of the rapist (her dad's cousin) she cannot talk about it. Thinking that she has given up her virginity before getting married and brought shame to the family, they decide to condemn Meryem to death. Initially, she is put in a barn and left in the dark for days and is given a rope to hang herself so that the family does not have to deal with it. She does not hang herself. Because her name is not registered in the citizen's directory, it becomes even easier to kill her. The duty of 'cleansing' the family 'honour' falls upon her rapist's son Cemal, who has just returned from his obligatory army duty. His job is to take Meryem away from the village to İstanbul and kill her there. Once they reach the city, in a traumatic and disturbing scene, he forces her to jump off a tall building. As she is about to fall down Cemal decides to save her. Unable to return to the village they run away. Eventually, they meet İlhan, a retired professor, who lives on the boat he owns. Meryem and Cemal start living on the boat with İlhan. With the help of İlhan, Cemal realizes his love for Meryem. At the end of the film, when he finds out that Meryem's rapist was his own father, he goes back to the village to kill him.

Critique

Mutluluk focuses on the concept of 'honour' through the story of Meryem (Özgü Namal). In the opening sequence of the film we see her body in the distance; she does not move. We are led to believe that she is dead until she is picked up by a local shepherd and until we see her looking scared and bruised in a barn. As the shepherd walks through the village, people start gossiping about what might have happened to her. Her family, influenced by her dad's cousin (who is actually the rapist), and the villagers think that she brought it upon herself, thereby bringing shame to the family and the village. Women's chastity and its relation to so-called family honour are recurring themes in films in Turkey. In fact, religious values are significant determinants in cultural practices and customs and these do tend to get represented in films and other media. As experienced in many patriarchal regimes, honour

is typically perceived to be residing in the body and sexuality of women; protecting this honour and policing female activities relating to marriage, sexuality or love are perceived to be the primary roles of the male or the male members of a family or a community. The film, in this sense, can be regarded as one of the current and most revealing films on the topic. The brutality of rape is captured in the film even though it is not overtly shown to us – it is implied but not necessarily displayed. When Cemal (Murat Han) decides to save Meryem rather than killing her, he does not know exactly what happened to her. Meryem does not talk much throughout the film. Silence is commonly associated with the representation of women in the cinema of Turkey, and Meryem remains silent about what happened to her, until the end of the film when she is kidnapped by Cemal's father; she re-lives and reveals through her screams the traumatic and violent experience she had. She is asked several times throughout the film who did what to her, but she remains silence – a silence that requires maturity for a young woman who is only seventeen. Meryem and Cemal's journey is about subverting customs and tradition. This journey is also accompanied by an intellectual, middle-class man, İlhan (Talat Bulut), who offers them a different experience from their own. An experience that is westernized both ideologically and materially. The film brings together three characters that would otherwise not even know about each other, and exhibits the diversity of cultural traits within one country. The film overall is significant as a text that sheds light on the issues of 'honour' killings and violence against women. Through the journey of Meryem and Cemal the film tells us that change in practices and customs is possible.

Eylem Atakav

How can Asiye Survive?

Asiye Nasıl Kurtulur?

Studio:
Odak Film

Director:
Atıf Yılmaz

Producers:
Atıf Yılmaz

Screenwriters:
Nuran Oktar
Barış Pirhasan
Atıf Yılmaz

Cinematographer:
Kenan Davutoğlu

Art Director:
Metin Deniz

Composer:
Saper Özsan

Editor:
Mevlüt Koçak

Duration:
105 Minutes

Cast:
Müjde Ar
Ali Poyrazoğlu
Hümeyra Akbay

Year:
1986

Synopsis

Asiye is a musical. The main characters (mainly people who work in the brothel or in the shops around it) put together a play throughout the plot for one of the other characters: the president of the *Struggle against Prostitution Association*, Seniye Gümüşçü, a rich, middle-aged and snobbish woman, decides to pay a visit to this brothel, in response to a letter she receives from one of the prostitutes called Asiye. However, there is no one in the brothel with that name. The 'actors' of this play choose the name Asiye in their attempt to tell the life story of a woman who falls into prostitution. The narrator is Selahattin, who works in the brothel and directs the play within the film. The film on the whole tells the story of Asiye and her fall into prostitution.

Critique

Asiye is different from those of classical Yeşilçam films since it questions the moral values of middle-class individuals who regard prostitution negatively. The film is successful in representing prostitutes as individuals who do this job in order to earn their living. It focuses more on the question of why and how women fall into prostitution in Turkey. While focusing on Asiye's (Müjde Ar) story and her descent into prostitution, the film not only exposes the oppression and exploitation of women in a sexist and male-dominated society but also questions how women survive from the sexual codification of patriarchy. The film can be defined as a 'fallen woman film', which seeks ways to subvert patriarchal ideology. Moreover, it can be seen as responding and contributing to the concerns of the women's movement of 1980s' Turkey. Indeed, in the 1980s, 'fallen woman' narratives are frequent in Turkish cinema, in accordance with the trend of focusing on individual women's lives who face difficult conditions because of rape, social pressures, running away from arranged marriages and strict traditions. *Asiye* is a significant film in its representation of a woman who falls into prostitution, particularly because it draws attention to (and at the same time attempts to question) the reasons that lead women to prostitution. It is illustrative of the ways in which patriarchal relations operate in society for women who do not have any financial, educational or social support. Asiye fights back against the condition of her oppression or, to put it broadly, the oppression suffered by women in a sexist society through gender inequity. Overall, the film not only deals with the issue of women's oppressed condition but also looks at capitalist relations in a patriarchal society. The patriarchal paradigm finds itself under attack throughout the narrative and the demands of patriarchal ideology and culture are represented in the film through the story of an individual.

Eylem Atakav

How can Asiye Survive?, 1986, Atıf Yılmaz © Odak Film.

Journey to the Sun

Güneşe Yolculuk

Studios:
IFR
Celluloid Dreams

Director:
Yeşim Ustaoğlu

Producer:
Behrooz Hashemian

Synopsis

Journey to the Sun tells the story of two lower-class youngsters, Mehmet from Western Turkey and Berzan from the Southeast, whose lives intersect in İstanbul. Mehmet is naive and apolitical. Berzan is actively involved in the Kurdish political movement. They come together after a football match when they are assaulted and chased by a group of nationalists: they become firm friends. Subsequently, Berzan loses his life during a raid on a Kurdish enclave. Because of his dark skin, the police misidentify Mehmet as a Kurd, and his mistaken identity causes him continued hardship. He and his girlfriend, Arzu, rescue Berzan's body from the mortuary, and Mehmet decides to take the body in its plain coffin to Berzan's eastern homeland. The film records his struggles throughout the long journey and, in conclusion, Mehmet seems to accept his imposed Kurdish identity.

Screenwriter:
Yeşim Ustaoğlu

Cinematographer:
Jacek Petrycki

Art Director:
Natali Yeres

Composer:
Vlatko Stefanovski

Editor:
Nicolas Gaster

Duration:
104 Minutes

Cast:
Nazmi Kırık
Nevruz Baz
Mizgin Kapazan
Ara Güler

Year:
1999

Critique

Journey to the Sun was the first of Yeşim Ustaoğlu's films to receive international acclaim. She wrote the script herself and found her cast among amateur actors at the Mesopotamia Kültür Merkezi (Mesopotamia Cultural Centre). The story was inspired by a news item in which she learned that the houses of Kurds living in Eastern Turkey were marked with a cross, thus identifying them for harassment and assault. As its name suggests, the film is a road movie, filmed almost twenty years after Şerif Gören and Yılmaz Güney's film Yol (1981). Ustaoğlu's characters embark on a journey during which she depicts the country in sharp relief. The film takes place when the Kurdish uprising had reached a peak of intense conflict. Mehmet (Newroz Baz), who represents an apolitical segment of the population, has no idea why Kurds are engaged in political activity, what they hope to accomplish, or what kind of troubles they are forced to endure. To enlighten him, a dramatic encounter is necessary. *Journey to the Sun* records that dramatic encounter. Mehmet's surname, significantly, is Black: significant because it is commonly assumed that Kurds in Eastern and Southeastern Turkey are dark skinned. Mehmet, in fact, is not Kurdish, but because of his dark skin he is taken into custody and tortured. When he is released, still suspected and labelled, his life has to change. He loses his job and cannot find another. Despite all this, he does not lose hope. He has a girlfriend, Arzu (Mizgin Kapazan), and he is befriended by a young Kurdish activist, Berzan (Nazmi Kırık). When Berzan is shot and killed, Mehmet and Arzu rescue his body from the mortuary and Mehmet, feeling threatened himself, decides to take the body to Berzan's distant Kurdish village. On the way, Mehmet finds himself in the same railway carriage as a young man on his way to do military service in the East. This fellow traveller asks Mehmet where he is going. Mehmet tells him, 'Zorduç,' the name of Berzan's village. When the young soldier asks, 'Are you from Zorduç?' Mehmet nods to signify 'Yes' and asks the soldier the same question. That the young man is from Tire is a revealing coincidence, because Mehmet is also from Tire. Mehmet says that he knows someone from Tire, a friend called Mehmet Kara. In this way, he fuses his own identity with Berzan's. At this point, having dramatized a Turk's empathy for a Kurd, Ustaoğlu takes the scene to another level. A gendarme comes to the carriage to conduct an identity check. He looks at their identity cards and sees that they are both from Tire. So he asks if they are travelling together. Yes, they say, they are together, even though the young soldier does not know that Mehmet is from Tire. This is the most important line in the film, symbolizing the desire of two peoples to live together in peace. Yeşim Ustaoğlu returned to the theme of the Other in later films, but *Journey to the Sun* was her pioneering landmark. For the first time, a Turkish director in a Turkish film discovered Kurds and portrayed them sympathetically.

S Ruken Öztürk

Journey to the Sun, 1999, Yeşim Ustaoğlu.

Kurtuluş Last Stop

Kurtuluş Son Durak

Studio:
Biber Yapım

Director:
Yusuf Pirhasan

Producer:
Ayşen Sever

Screenwriter:
Barış Pirhasan

Art Director:
Carlos Ritter

Composer:
Fırat Yükselir

Synopsis

The film tells the story of Eylem, a psychologist, who is dumped by her fiancé a couple of weeks before their wedding. She moves into a building with friendly neighbours, to whom she does not warm in the beginning. Throughout her depression and after a failed suicide attempt, the neighbours in the building look after her. The better she feels, the warmer she becomes towards the neighbours. Soon enough they start having regular meetings to talk about relationships and men and, more importantly, violence against women. They then decide to take revenge and stand up against violence of all kinds. Yet, things do not go quite right because they accidentally kill some of the men they deal with. Soon, the police and then the media get involved in their fight against all forms of violence against women.

Critique

Kurtuluş Son Durak challenges the idea of women as silent images and absent characters without agency. It is a dark comedy that focuses on the issue of violence against women. It tells the stories of six women living in different flats in an apartment block and how they use their solidarity to fight against violence. The protagonists of the film come from different ethnic, religious, cultural and economic backgrounds. This is suggestive of the fact that

Editor:

Aylin Zoi Tinel

Duration:

106 Minutes

Cast:

Belçim Bilgin
Demet Akbağ
Nihal Yalçın
Ayten Soykök
Damla Sönmez
Asuman Dabak

Year:

2012

the concept of Turkish woman is not and should not be considered as a single entity. Yet, what bring these different women together are the different forms of violence they face from men; and violence resonates at different levels – verbal, physical, and psychological – throughout the narrative. What is also thought-provoking is that none of these characters are seen outside the private domain. Eylem (Belçim Bilgin) attempts to commit suicide after being dumped and betrayed by her fiancé; Vartanuş (Demet Akbağ) is devoted to looking after her ill father and does not have a life of her own; Goncagül (Nihal Yalçın) is depressed about having an affair with a married, macho man; Gülnur (Ayten Soykök) gets beaten by her husband every night; Tülay (Damla Sönmez) is depressed after seeing her mother being beaten; and, finally, Füsun (Asuman Dabak) is an optimistic character married to a man who is stereotypically represented as weak. What is visible throughout the film is an effort to engage in self-expression in a radical and communal manner. The film challenges discourses around womanhood and violence against women through the use of comedy. The narrative presents a positive transgression of gender norms and enables the characters to articulate personal issues around violence in the public sphere, particularly towards the end of the film when the media suddenly becomes interested in this group of women's activities within the apartment block. The female transgression and solidarity between women in the film allows them to take the subject position as they critique patriarchal values and political and institutional structures that oppress them. The generic choice here is of crucial importance, as the film uses comedy as a strategy. Using comedy makes its main message more accessible to the mass audience. The film is a promising step in new Turkish cinema's representation of women, as it presents a shift from patriarchal, constraining and violent spaces to a shared space of female collectivity and solidarity. It is also a positive step because a change at the level of representation of women is essential in making a corresponding change in reality.

Eylem Atakav

Kurtuluş Last Stop, 2012, Yusuf Pirhasan.

Life on their Shoulders

Sırtlarındaki Hayat

Studios:
Ustaoğlu Film Production
Silkroad Production

Director:
Yeşim Ustaoğlu

Producer:
Yeşim Ustaoğlu

Cinematographers:
Ali Rıza Movahed
Yeşim Ustaoğlu
Özcan Alper

Composers:
Ozan Aksoy
Grup Helesa

Editors:
Thomas Balkenhol
Yeşim Ustaoğlu
Emmanuelle Mimran

Duration:
39 Minutes

Year:
2004

Synopsis

This is the story of people who live in the wild mountains of Black Sea region of Turkey. It records their annual journey up misty mountains to feed their cattle in the summer months, a journey they have been making for centuries. This seasonal migration requires climbing almost around five kilometers up the mountain. The film tells the story of women who work very hard in this journey – hence carrying 'life on their shoulders'.

Critique

The film is Yeşim Ustaoğlu's only documentary. Although it was filmed in 2002, prior to *Bulutları Beklerken/Waiting for the Clouds*, a feature film shot in the same location, the post-production procedures were not completed until 2004, when the feature film was also released. The location is the Black Sea region of Northern Turkey, which is famous for its wild nature and natural beauty. Ustaoğlu spent her childhood and went to university there, so she was already familiar the Laz people who inhabit the mountain valleys. Her camera dwells mostly on the women, who typically work harder than the men. In the summer, whole families take their animals to the high plateaus and live there among the clouds until Autumn. The documentary is about their climb up the mountain. The journey is one of Ustaoğlu's main themes. The journey in *The Life on Their Shoulders* is steep and the load is heavy. In the first scene, families close their homes and prepare for the journey. Women in traditional clothes, along with their menfolk and their animals, labour upwards, leaning on their staves as they plough through mud at the very edge of cliffs. Their destination is like heaven, a wild and green wetland. The last scenes show preparations for their return. This journey continues like a loop in their lives. Through amazing camera work we watch men singing, drinking tea, and smoking, but the women do not have a moment of rest. It is they who load up the animals and carry similar loads on their own shoulders. Ustaoğlu portrays the women through revealing details: zooming to the wrinkled hand of a woman as she talks, or framing the face of a woman who looks old while still quite young. Her selective close-ups make us feel close to the women. *Life on Their Shoulders* not only documents how hard the women in the Black Sea region work, but also confronts various other problems they experience, such as early marriage, illiteracy, many children, and diverse health problems. These women are worn out early, and become old quickly. In contrast to the hardships of the women, the director shows us the beauty of the Black Sea region; its green and misty nature plays a major role in the documentary, which speaks to us in a poetic and lyrical language.

S Ruken Öztürk

Mine

Mine

Studio:
Delta Film

Director:
Atıf Yılmaz

Producers:
Atıf Yılmaz
Sadık Deveci
Ömer Kavur

Screenwriters:
Atıf Yılmaz
Deniz Türkali
Necati Cumalı

Cinematographer:
Salih Dikişçi

Art Directors:
Atıf Yılmaz
Salih Dikişçi

Composer:
Cahit Berkay

Duration:
84 Minutes

Cast:
Türkan Şoray
Cihan Ünal
Hümeyra Akbay

Year:
1982

Synopsis

The film tells a story of one woman (Mine) and two men: the husband Cemil, who does not love or listen to or talk in the way she wants and/or needs; and the other man, the lover İlhan, who can do all those things. Mine was forced into an arranged marriage with Cemil, who is much older than her. She is not loved by her husband, and she does not love him; yet she performs her 'duties' as a housewife including housework, serving visitors and cooking meals. They live in a small village with a tiny population, where the husband works as the manager of the train station. The villagers tend to gossip a lot, and the men in the village, young and old, including the mayor, the engineer, and the builder, have a crush on the beautiful Mine. Mine, on the other hand, is highly uncomfortable and self conscious about their admiration. Things begin to change in the village with the arrival of İlhan, a novelist and intellectual who comes to the village to visit his sister, Perihan, an independent-minded single woman who is the village teacher and who happens to be Mine's only friend.

Critique

Mine is one of the pioneer films dealing with women's search for independence. It looks at the relationship between women and society and their search for freedom from the oppressive conditions imposed by strict patriarchal traditions. The film was highly significant in making a link between the 1980s' women's movement and the cinema in Turkey since it sought to represent the particular experience of a woman caught in gendered power relations in a sexist environment. Mine contributes to a new understanding of women's sexuality with its focus on the notion of female identity. Türkan Şoray, who until then has been performing 'virtuous' woman characters, is shown naked for the first time in this film while taking a significant part in the creation of a new understanding of female sexuality and identity. *Mine* is a woman who, although inherently passionate, is not understood by those around her; neither by her husband nor the neighbourhood. This, however, changes with the arrival of İlhan on the scene. Although she spends her life with the wrong man in an unhappy marriage, at the end of the film, she comes to be understood and appreciated by a masculine yet sensitive male. Although the film is about a woman who gains new forms of self-expression by taking control of her sexuality, one might read the film as a narrative about a threatened woman saved by the love of a man. *Mine* examines an individual's attempt to live out her desires either within these rules or despite them. In this context, the effect of representing the female experience in a patriarchal society becomes the main concern of the film. It focuses on the mental and physical suffering of a woman in her relationship with both her husband and the neighbourhood. In this way, the film points to a tension between female desire and a society that grants no agency to the female subject. It can be argued that the consistent focus on Mine helps to construct her as a subject who has desires and who tries to act on them. Yet, at the same time, throughout the film she is constantly 'looked at', and in order to avoid these looks and harassment she tends to stay at home rather than going out, and she almost always seems self-conscious of her every single move, particularly if she is in the public sphere. The film knowingly exaggerates this theme of being looked at to make a critique of the idea of objectification of female bodies.

Eylem Atakav

Oooh! Belinda

Aaahh! Belinda

Studio:
Odak Film

Director:
Atıf Yılmaz

Producer:
Cengiz Ergun

Screenwriter:
Barış Pirhasan

Cinematographer:
Orhan Oğuz

Art Director:
Şahin Kaygun

Duration:
100 Minutes

Cast:
Müjde Ar
Yılmaz Zafer
Macit Koper
Füsun Demirel
Mehmet Akan

Year:
1986

Synopsis

Serap, a theatre actress, takes a part in a TV commercial for a shampoo called 'Belinda' where she plays a typical middle-class woman, Naciye, with whom she has nothing in common, and in fact dislikes. On the day of the shoot, as the shower scene is being filmed, Serap finds that the crew has disappeared all of a sudden, and the set and everything in the scenario has turned into real life, including herself in the place of Naciye, mother and wife of the Gülveren family. At first, Serap thinks that it is a kind of dirty joke, but when she sees that her friends and boyfriend do not recognize her as Serap and there are other people living in her house, she understands that there is more than a joke: until this 'confusion' or 'nightmare' is over, she has to survive with a husband and two kids in a typical middle-class lifestyle. 'Mrs. Naciye is now in her warm hearth!'

Critique

What happens when all of a sudden you find yourself in the place of someone else, whose life is completely different from yours? The answer might be a nightmare or a farce. Director Atıf Yılmaz stunningly manages to pair up these two possibilities in a comedy. Renowned as a director of the women's films, Atıf Yılmaz once more tells a story of a woman in search of an identity with a class perspective but, of course, in his own way: with humour, irony and playfulness. The comedy of the film mainly arises from the big contrast between the lives of Serap and Naciye that is depicted so successfully in well-observed detail throughout the film: from the use of the jargon to food habits, from dress sense to choice of leisure activities. The strong dissociation of the inner and outer realities of Serap – being Serap, but being recognized as Naciye – is portrayed with humorous irony that is most apparent in the scenes where Serap faces (gendered) class-based differences for the first time, followed by her need to adapt to them in order to survive in her role as Naciye. It is crucial to mention that the successful, humorous depiction of the lifestyle differences between the two characters also has a lot to do with the well-written dialogues, which illustrate sharp observations of middle-class lifestyles in 1980s' Turkey. Müjde Ar gives an impressive performance as Serap, a challenging multifaceted character with many nuances. Also, Macit Koper's brilliant performance as Naciye's typical middle-class husband Hulusi is worth mentioning, as his character makes the audience understand Seap's – and thereby Naciye's – suffocation. One of the modernist elements of the film, and something rarely used in Turkish cinema of this era, is the interplay of the real and the fantasy/dream/performance boundaries by the characters who are in very 'unlikely' or 'unrealistic' situations. This technique was used in different ways in Yılmaz's other women's films such as *Adı Vasfiye* (*Vasfiye is Her Name*) (1985), *Hayallerim Aşkım ve Sen* (*My Dreams, My Love and You*) (1987) and *Asiye Nasıl Kurtulur?* (*How can Asiye be saved?*) (1986). In *Aaahh! Belinda*, what the 'real' story is or what 'really' happened to her is left obscure. Moreover, this playfulness is supported by the scenes where Serap seems to adopt Naciye's role. Each of these scenes is followed by a line or a tone, gesture or gaze that reveals that she was performing in order to survive in this 'wild middle-class jungle' until she finds a way out. These elements maintain the tension throughout the film, as well as portray Serap's in-between situation. Moreover, the meta-fictional references in the film, such as the TV commercials we see or hear in the background in most of the scenes, not only constantly remind us of the scenario that Serap is trapped in but they also blur the boundary between the real and the fiction, as if the director wants the audience to see that he is playing with the idea of reality.

Both Serap's and Naciye's entrapment in the scenario of middle-class gender roles is once more emphasized in the film through a reference to the play 'Asiye Nasıl Kurtulur?', which tells the story of a prostitute who cannot be 'saved' no matter what she does in such a gender order. How can Serap and Naciye be saved? The answer is revealed near the end of the film. Though the women are very different, Serap learns to be Naciye through time and practice. In the wonderful scene where Serap gives the recipe of Imam Bayıldı (a traditional Turkish dish) to her dinner guests, it is revealed that she 'becomes' (accepts) the woman in the scenario at the end. The nightmare scenario becomes her 'reality' as she 'is' Naciye from that moment on. Accordingly, one of the other important features of this film is the humorous ironic style, which enables not only a scenario in which (some) women are trapped in Turkish society but also lets its absurdity become visible. Furthermore, it illustrates a new perspective that points out not only the different gender roles and positions that emerge from the class intersections but also the performative feature of gender, which is learned through time, practice and imitation, just like a role. Finally, whilst the films of the decade are generally considered as proof the Turkish cinema's decadence, due to their lack of aesthetic thematic or cultural originality, *Aaahh! Belinda* comes very close to becoming one of the cult classics through its unique and avant-garde style and approach. If it fails in one aspect, however, it is that its closed cathartic ending contradicts the narrative style throughout the film.

Özlem Güçlü

Pains of Autumn

Güz Sancısı

Studio:
ÖzenFilm

Director:
Tomris Giritlioğlu

Producers:
Bahadır Atay
Fatih Enes Ömeroğlu

Screenwriters:
Nilgün Öneş
Etyen Mahçupyan
Ali Ülvi Hünkar
Tayfun Pirselimoğlu

Cinematographer:
Ercan Yılmaz

Art Directors:
Nilüfer Çamur
Naz Erayda
Erol Taştan

Composer:
Tamer Çıray

Editors:
Ulaş Cihan Şimşek
Mark Marnikovic

Duration:
112 Minutes

Cast:
Murat Yıldırım
Okan Yalabık
Beren Saat
Belçim Bilgin

Year:
2009

Synopsis

Tomris Giritlioğlu's film, *Pains of Autumn*, is a historical drama based on Yilmaz Karakoyunlu's book of the same name. The film takes place in Beyoğlu district of İstanbul and represents the İstanbul of 1955. The Greek neighbourhood within Beyoğlu is portrayed through daily events, shops, characters, their costumes, dialogues, and neighbour-relations. The film depicts the relations in between Turks and Greeks while carrying out the depicted story of a Turkish man, Behçet, who falls in love with his Greek neighbour, Elena, within the context of the turmoil of political events of those times. Family relatives of both Behçet and Elena represent certain political and socio-economic figures of society. Behçet's father, Kamil Efendi, is a rich landowner with strong ties to the government while some other relatives are involved with pro-nationalist groups. One of the main characters, Behçet is portrayed as a conservative man who is also sensitive to the political developments and potential threats in Turkey. In parallel to the events of the time, Cyprus is one of the discussion issues. Some of their family friends are members of the Cypriot Turkish Association. Elena, as a Greek prostitute, is under the control of her grandmother and is her grandmother's tool in maintaining strong ties with important members of society. In spite of this, Elena and Behçet, as neighbours, get closer to each other and it turns into a love affair. This is a clear threat for his father and his political party. In the political turmoil of 1955 in Cyprus and with news reports of the bombing of Atatürk's house in Thessaloniki, tension turns into violence on the sixth and seventh of September. All these developments carry this love affair to a horrible end.

Critique

Historical dramas reveal realities about the forgotten corners of histories, and the histories of forgotten ones. Those films embody almost first person, eyewitness accounts of people. They carry personal knowledge and experiences of people of those times. Through psychological analysis of periods and history, they construct the time- and space dimensions of knowing. Viewers experience and explore characters, locations, and events of those times. During the process of this experience of a psychological analysis of history, viewers in movie theatres are like captives of those histories and become part of the film-maker's ideological point of view. In this historical drama, the director Tomris Giritlioğlu embraces historical topics of 1955 in İstanbul. Giritlioğlu builds her historical drama through individual lives, community conflicts, social movements, power issues, and politics. While structuring the period's story into film, human conflicts and Behçet and Elena's love affair exist within each other.

Through the constructed images of those times and events, Giritlioğlu does not only tell a story but reveals, and at the same time accentuates, a political argument about those events. *Pains of Autumn* makes use of historical drama as a genre that allows the audience to experience history rather than limiting them to written official histories. The film can be regarded as her self-reflexive inquiry about the historical and dramatic aspects of the events, in mixed form of drama and analysis. Giritlioğlu stresses that there may be more than one sort of historical truth and the historical films like *Pains of Autumn* can be a useful tool to represent those realities.

E Nezih Orhon

Pains of Autumn, 2009, Tomris Giritlioğlu @ Özen Film

Pandora's Box

Pandora'nın Kutusu

Synopsis

Upon learning that their mother, Nusret, who lives in the Black Sea region of Turkey, needs help, three siblings, two sisters and a brother, who live in İstanbul, set out on a journey together. During this journey their opinions and their feelings about one another are

Studios:
Ustaoğlu Film Production
The Match Factory

Director:
Yeşim Ustaoğlu

Producers:
Yeşim Ustaoğlu
Muhammet Çakıral
Serkan Çakarer
Behrooz Hashemian

Screenwriters:
Yeşim Ustaoğlu
Sema Kaygusuz

Cinematographer:
Jacques Besse

Art Directors:
Elif Taşçıoğlu
Serdar Yılmaz

Composer:
Jean Pierre Mas

Editor:
Franck Nakache

Duration:
112 Minutes

Cast:
Tsilla Chelton
Derya Alabora
Onur Ünsal
Övül Avkıran
Osman Sonant

Year:
2008

revealed. Thus Pandora's box is opened. The three, with their different personalities, take their mother, an Alzheimer's sufferer, back to İstanbul. She stays with her elder daughter, who is married and has a decent family life in a decent home. Caring for the mother is not easy, however, and problems arise among the siblings. The younger sister is having a difficult affair with a married man. The brother is an unemployed misfit who shuns an orderly lifestyle. The elder sister's son feels empty and yearns for a meaningful life. Events, as they unfold in Istanbul, hinge on a clash of personalities embedded in a clash of generations, producing severe and traumatic conflict.

Critique

Yeşim Ustaoğlu's latest and internationally-acclaimed film, *Pandora'nın Kutusu/Pandora's Box*, depicts a personal quest for one's own identity and a desire to embrace the other. She also explores themes of alienation and lack of communication in this realistic, intensely urban narrative. Among its several characters is an old and sickly mother, Nusret, who, in need of care, goes to live with her three children and one grandson. The elder daughter, cold and strict, tries to take responsibility for the others, but in fact she interferes in their lives, especially in her son's. Her brother lives an errant life, and her younger sister is struggling to maintain a relationship with a man who is having an extramarital affair. The grandson, like his unruly uncle, is searching for freedom. What makes the film interesting is that it makes the viewer anticipate what will happen when the peasant mother joins her urban family. Contrasts and conflicts are inevitable when the director transports the urban family to the countryside and then brings the peasant mother to the city. There, the actress Tsilla Chelton performs wonderfully, like a fish out of water, even though her dialogue is sometimes hard to understand. Perhaps it would have been better if she had fewer lines. Anyone able to disregard the fact that she is foreign will agree that Chelton's performance is as real and believable as can be. Contrasts and conflicts multiply throughout the film: it brings the oldest and youngest together; demonstrates that getting married does not change anything in an impossible relationship; and pits characters who adapt to the norm against those who oppose the norm. What I like most in this film is the relationship between the mother and the camera, which seems to share her every mood. The camera, like the old mother, looks for green among the towering blocks of buildings; it zooms over the bends of mountain roads and highways, hoping to catch a glimpse of green or the sea. No one in İstanbul understands the aging mother, who is stranded in the great city far from home. Only her grandson seems able to communicate with her. Finally he hears her longing for a peaceful death in her village, and so they take her there. In the end, on a high plateau near the Black Sea, she is happy and ready to die.

S Ruken Öztürk

Pandora'nın Kutusu, 2008, Yeşim Ustaoğlu © Film Yapim.

The Frogs

Kurbağalar

Studio:
Gülşah Film

Director:
Şerif Gören

Producer:
Selim Soydan

Screenwriters:
Özden Çankaya
Osman Şahin
Erdoğan Engin

Synopsis

The story takes place in a small village in Western Turkey. The villagers are low-paid factory workers or local wage labourers. Men in the village collect frogs at nights around the nearby river to sell them to the local factory, which makes use of the skins of frogs in their production.

After her husband's death, Elmas has to work and do her husband's job at the same time as cultivating the land they own, to survive, to pay her husband's debt and to look after her son. The issue here is that both of these jobs are done by men, yet Elmas, representing a strong and independent-minded woman, is happy to take on the challenge. However, the locals are not happy with this. Elmas attracts sexual attention from the male villagers as a widowed woman. Ali, who returns to the village after serving a prison sentence, has had feelings for her since before her marriage. After a night together he leaves Elmas, as he decides he does not want to be with a widow.

Cinematographers:
Erdoğan Engin
Turgay Aksoy

Art Director:
Erdoğan Engin

Composer:
Atilla Özdemiroğlu

Editor:
Mevlüt Koçak

Duration:
82 Minutes

Cast:
Hülya Koçyiğit
Talat Bulut
Yaman Okay

Year:
1985

Critique

Şerif Gören's *Kurbağalar* deals with issues including widowhood and the concomitant absence of the male; the gendered division of labour in peasants' lives in rural Turkey; suppressed sexuality under religious rules; and the importance of the meaning of female chastity in a patriarchal society. It looks at how womanhood is structured in the absence of the male and the kind of pressures that shape women's identity as well as the means available to women to resist oppression. *Kurbağalar* is a film that focuses on the absence of the male through the story of Elmas, which is represented in the context of religion and tradition. The film is significant in the sense that it constitutes an attempt to deconstruct the idea of a woman's social identity being reduced to that of her husband and her family. Despite allowing her a degree of freedom (at work and at home) she is reduced to a piece of female flesh; an object of desire not only in the eyes of the males of the village, but also women, since women start seeing her as a threat to their marriages and relationships. Even though the film allows room for exploring the experiences and living strategies of women in widowhood, through Elmas's character it affirms that, as a distinct system of male dominance, village life determines women's survival strategies as well as influencing their forms of resistance and struggle. Among the structural features of this form of patriarchal relations are patterns of deference based on age, distinct male and female hierarchies and a separation of spheres of activity. The film explores the predicament of a widowed woman, who must break from tradition and act independently because she lacks the security the tradition is supposed to offer. *Kurbağalar's* representation of the village woman concurs with this dual identity.

Eylem Atakav

The Play

Oyun

Studios:
Sine Film
Umut Sanat

Director:
Pelin Esmer

Producer:
Pelin Esmer

Screenwriter:
Pelin Esmer

Synopsis

Ummuye, Behiye, Ummu, Fatma K., Cennet, Saniye, Fatma F., Zeynep and Nesime are nine peasant women living in Arslanköy, a mountain village in southern Turkey. They spend their days working hard in the fields, on the construction site and at home. To lighten the burden of life, these women come together for a wholly different reason. They intend to write and perform a play based on their own life stories. They gather at the local high school, though they were shy of even stepping into it until that day, and they work with the principal, Hüseyin. They reveal their life stories that they were even afraid to tell themselves and to confront. For days on end, under the curious gaze of the village men, they work tirelessly, discussing and creating, with much fun, a play: *The Outcry of Women*. *Oyun* is about the development process of this play and the changes the women experience during this period.

Cinematographers:

Pelin Esmer

Özlem Özbek

Mustafa Ünlü

Composer:

Mazlum Çimen

Editor:

Pelin Esmer

Duration:

70 Minutes

Cast:

Behiye Yanık

Cennet Güneş

Fatma Fatih

Fatma Kahraman

Hüseyin Arslanköylu

Year:

2005

Critique

Oyun consciously manipulates the distinctions between fiction and nonfiction. For the majority of men portrayed in the documentary, the act of rehearsing and performing a play might be nothing more than a distraction from the 'real business' of rural life in the farming village of Arslanköy near Mersin. However the women involved in acting and performing the play *Kadının Feryadı* (*The Outcries of Women*) understand that while reality is constructed through fictitious discourse, it is also lived in a way that needs to change for many of them. With the help of Esmer's camera, the nine women in *Oyun* recount their struggle for self-determination to viewers who will never experience them; and by doing so demonstrate just how complicated the notions of 'femaleness' and 'femininity' actually are.

The women have spent all their lives serving their husbands at home and on the land; and for the first time they are given the opportunity to tell their stories to a wider audience. We learn about Zeynep Fatih, who recalls the harrowing experience of taking her child to the hospital alone, while being heavily pregnant with another child. With no money to pay for any medical treatment, she eventually gives birth alone, her husband nowhere to be seen. Nesime Kahraman grew up in a village, but her father sent her to Ankara to acquire an education; although her ambition was to become a teacher, she was forced to return to her community and now works as a hairdresser, where she feels very much the outsider with her city mannerisms. In *Kadının Feryadı* Nesime achieves her ambition by playing a teacher who is so concerned for Aytül (one of her students) that she is prepared to risk a beating by confronting Aytül's brutal father Recep. Ümmü Kurt plays Recep by drawing on her own experiences of living with a partner who acts according to patriarchal logic.

As the play unfolds, so distinctions between past, present and future are collapsed into a continuous present, giving the women the chance – perhaps for the first time – to confront their pasts and forge new meanings out of them for their collective future. Esmer shows the women *constructing* alternative meanings for themselves through writing, rehearsing and performing the play. Playing Recep's abused wife Emine, Zeynep Fatih understands the power of silence; in a significant exchange with her real-life husband, she vows loyalty to him but refuses to admits whether she loves him or not. Unable to discern the meaning of her words, her husband emphasizes the fact that 'She [Zeynep] really loves me but she can't show it …] As much as she loves me, I love her that much too.' At the same time, Esmer makes no judgment on the two of them; it is clear from their body language that husband and wife are very much in love with one another. This is one of the film's paradoxes: just as we think we have made a judgment on the characters (in this case, the wife challenging her husband's authority), Esmer invites us to question that judgment.

This paradoxical strain – where the women fulfil their roles as wives and mothers, yet also progress towards self-discovery – runs throughout the film. Fatma Kahraman admits that she has limited opportunities to learn her lines, as she has to entertain guests at her family home. At the same time she relishes the experience of being involved in rehearsals and performance; this is emphasized through frequent close-ups of her face wreathed in smiles as she tries to create her character. Several of the women admit that their husbands oppress them: family secrets (for example, domestic abuse) are not to be disclosed in public. On the other hand, they are perfectly willing to tell their secrets to their director Hüseyin Arslanköylu (the high school principal) to be included in a performance in front of the entire village. More importantly, the women are perfectly willing to question Hüseyin's suggestions, and follow their own instincts instead.

Through the film Esmer challenges the dualistic, oppositional nature by which gender is traditionally framed – particularly in rural societies – showing, instead, that there are multiple and often paradoxical constructions of 'femininity'. At the end of *Kadının Feryadı*, another woman appears disguised as a police officer, pronouncing that theatre as an illegal activity. When no one listens, s/he suggests that theatre is not appropriate for women, emphasizing his point by beating one of the performers with his baton. By this time, however, we have learned so much about the women and their attitudes that such phrases seem irrelevant. Nesime (Zeynep Fatih) sums up the women's experiences by quoting a song by the Turkish folk-singer Mahsun Kırmızıgül (which describes life as a matter of dressing well) and demanding that they should be accepted as individuals on their own terms.

Laurence Raw

Vendetta Song

Adı Güzide

Studios:
DLI Productions
National Film Board of Canada

Director:
Eylem Kaftan

Producers:
Abbey Jack Neidik
Irene Angelico
Germaine Ying Gee Wong

Screenwriter:
Eylem Kaftan

Cinematographer:
Eylem Kaftan

Synopsis

Vendetta Song is a documentary about Eylem Kaftan's journey from Montreal to Istanbul and then to a remote Kurdish village in Eastern Turkey. The reason for this journey is to unravel the 30-year-old mystery behind the murder of her aunt, who was shot in the name of so-called honour. Her aunt Güzide is the central character of the film, yet we never see her image or hear her voice. As the director strives to understand the patriarchal relations and power struggles, the audience is presented with a variety of interviews and people. The film also points out the differences between Eastern and Western Turkey as well as providing diverse picture of women of Turkey.

Critique

Eylem Kaftan's bio-documentary *Vendetta Song* explores honour killings, gender inequalities, the traditional practice of arranged marriages and the semi-feudal social structure in Eastern Turkey within the context of Islamic tradition. The film critiques gender politics through its feminist discourse whilst at the same time

Art Director:

Eylem Kaftan

Composers:

Stéphane Allard

Jean-François Ouellet

Dave Gossage

Jason Lang

Editor:

Jeremiah Hayes

Duration:

52 Minutes

Year:

2005

attempting to deconstruct the at times misperceived connection between Islam and violence against women. Whilst doing so it also places emphasis on tradition rather than religion. *Vendetta Song* is a significant film that calls for an analysis of its exploration of honour killings, gender inequalities, the traditional practice of arranged marriages and the semi-feudal social structure in Eastern Turkey within the context of Islamic tradition. The film also problematizes the relations of the West to the East (both within and outside Turkey) as the narrative is structured as a travelogue of a woman travelling from Canada to Istanbul and then from Western to Eastern Turkey. *Vendetta Song* proves to be an interesting example which adopts quite complex and critical stance on the question of 'honour'. The film closely scrutinizes the past for clues about the present. The biographical structure, which is common to many feminist documentary films and documentary codes used throughout the film, permits identification on the part of the female spectators with the women in it. With an emphasis on the lasting effects of the past, the film critiques the present. The power of the film is in its success in documenting aspects of the reality of a collective and gendered oppression. Although the film is powerful in focusing on patriarchal structures, it at times gives the feeling of a tourist gazing at what happens in a world unknown to her. As she travels in Eastern Turkey, the director/narrator takes photos of people she sees. Her camera sometimes becomes her visa symbolizing her status as a tourist exempt from the normal rules and codes. The use of photographic images is significant in creating the idea of difference.

The film also focuses on the practice of bride price. The director is presented with a headscarf by the daughter of the family she stayed with during the filming of some of the scenes. Until this point we have not seen her in a photograph; as her frozen image appears on the screen she tells us that she 'felt at once degraded, yet strangely flattered' when she was seen with her headscarf by some men in the village, who thought her bride price would be equivalent to 'one thousand sheep, one hundred Kalashnikovs, fifty camels and ten horses'. In her own photo, then, she becomes static, hypostatized, reified, frozen: she becomes an object of the camera as soon as she is confirmed as a 'member of the family'. This scene is crucial in the construction of a feminist critique of this patriarchal customary practice which commodifies women. What is most interesting is the fact that the main character of the film, Güzide, the reasons for whose murder the director is seeking, is an absent and invisible character, as no picture of her exists. *Vendetta Song* plays a significant role in revealing what is happening in the East in women's lives with strict customary practices.

Eylem Atakav

Vendetta Song, 2005, Eylem Kaftan © DLI Productions.

Waiting for the Clouds

Bulutları Beklerken

Studios:
Ustaoğlu Film Production
Silkroad Production
Flying Moon Film Production

Director:
Yeşim Ustaoğlu

Producers:
Setareh Farsi,
Behrooz Hashemian

Synopsis

Ayşe feels lost and alone, and becomes distanced from everyone in the village after the death of her elder sister Selma. She only continues to speak with Mehmet, an 8-year-old boy, who likes listening to her stories. After days of silence and isolation, Ayşe starts speaking in Greek and telling the story that she had suppressed for 50 years: that her real name is Eleni and she had been adopted and protected by a Turkish family during the First World War when her family, Pontus Greeks, were deported by force. She had 'forgotten' her real name, language, identity and past for 50 years. Furthermore, she had been living with the guilt of abandoning her brother in the deportation. Set in Tirebolu, a small port-town in the Black Sea Region, in 1975, *Bulutları Beklerken* tells the story of a woman's journey to find her silenced past and identity.

Screenwriters:

Yeşim Ustaoğlu

Petros Markaris

Cinematographer:

Jacek Petrycki, P.S.C

Art Director:

Selda Ülkenciler

Editors:

Timo Linnasalo

Nicolas Gaster

Duration:

92 Minutes

Cast:

Rüçhan Çalışkur

Rıdvan Yağcı

Ismail Baysan

Dimitris Kaberidis

Year:

2003

Critique

Inspired by the novel, *Tamama*, by Georgios Andreadis, which is based on a true story, director Yeşim Ustaoğlu once more draws attention to a suppressed point in the official history of Turkey through the story of an elderly woman. While Ustaoğlu makes the audience confront silence, loss and traumatic experience of the Other in the first half of the film, she calls the concepts of home and belonging into question in the second part where Ayşe (Rüçhan Çalışkur) goes on a journey to her homeland to find her long-lost brother and her roots. Furthermore, with the sub-stories of Mehmet's friend Cengiz's father and of Thanassis the Red, the director weaves a story portraying the hatred towards the ethnic minorities and communists deeply ingrained in everyday life and culture in the given time frame. However, Ustaoğlu still seems to entertain hopes of the possibility of establishing a new relation to the Other by displaying a close friendship between Ayşe and Mehmet, who is eager to listen to her-story. On the other hand, while *Bulutları Beklerken* tells Ayşe's (inner) journey to her traumatic past, language and identity, revealing bit by bit her 'silenced' story, it creates, and prioritizes, a counter-memory against the official discourse. Yet this counter-memory does not only emerge from the content. Indeed, the director's stance also has a lot to do with it: rather than speaking on behalf of the Other, Ustaoğlu lets her character speak of her story. At the beginning of the film, Ayşe tells Mehmet a fairy tale about a girl whose family is kidnapped on a snowy winter night by *Karakoncolos*, a dark creature from an ancient regional myth who kidnaps people from their houses while they are asleep. After the days of isolation and silence, when Ayse begins to talk in her mother tongue, Greek, she tells the traumatic experience of the forced deportation of her family to Mehmet, in a long monologue sequence that makes the audience understand that the girl of the fairy tale is her, and the tale is her narrative of a counter-memory. Furthermore, the use of archival footage at the beginning and end of the film serve to connect the narrative of the counter-memory, suggested by the film, with the real. In this it brings History into question. Likewise, the scene where Ayşe remembers and hears the voices of people walking in the forced deportation, illustrates the gap in History. By providing her point of view, the audience is made to connect with her counter-memory as well. Accordingly, the 'affect' of the film exactly emerges from the director's talent in 'silently' portraying Ayşe's story – a story composed of silence, loss and trauma – with the narrative threads that makes the audience face the gaps and silences in the History. Moreover, in contrast to the majority of its counterparts, this film tells its story through a female protagonist, which becomes an important detail as it reveals that the film not only provides a counter-memory, but also a *her-story*, against the official discourse of his-story. However, the most important feature of this film is not only the content and narrative tools that manage to perform as a kind of counter-memory, but also the way that director Ustaoğlu chooses to tell this painful silenced story. The film gains its power from its minimalistic cinematography and composition and from its humanistic style – this accords well with the choice of telling a minor story where silence is the main motive, thereby serving to 'humanize' the (her) story and allowing the audience connect with the experience, silence, fear, trauma and feeling of guilt of the protagonist throughout the film, which makes the film distinctive among its counterparts. For instance, in the end, as the open ending dissolves into the archival footage of the deportation, the film manages to connect the audience, but does not make them come to terms with the pain and burden of loss that Ayşe, like many others, suffers from. As such, the film does not fill the gap that it opened in the (his) story and leaves the audience with the burden of this confrontation with the so-far suppressed and forgotten traumas of the Other. *Bulutları Beklerken* is an important film in the contemporary cinema of Turkey, as it engages with one of the major silenced issues in the history of Turkey without necessarily being didactic. It is unique as it not only tells a story about/of the Other but does so in a successful humanistic style that makes the audience confront with, and moreover feel and relate to, the pain of the Other. Indeed, it is possible to suggest that this film paved the way for the others, such as *Bulutları Beklerken*'s assistant director Özcan Alper's first feature Sonbahar (2008).

Özlem Güçlü

BLOCKBUSTERS

The term blockbuster came to be used for Turkish cinema on three different occasions. The first was with high-grossing films that attracted crowds in the past glory of Yeşilçam cinema between 1950 and 1975. The blockbuster turn coincided with the end of the Yeşilçam mode of production. In 1988 veteran comedy director Ertem Eğilmez promised 'a film to end all films' and made a melodrama parody called *Arabesk*. It became the first ever film to cross the one-million-viewer barrier. Another veteran political film director Şerif Gören, the co-director of Palme D'or winner *Yol*, shunning the success of Hollywood's *Basic Instinct* from the previous year, made *Amerikalı* (The American). Paul Verhoeven's *Basic Instinct* eventually crossed the two-million-viewer barrier, an unprecedented feat in Turkish movie theatres. Goren made a comedy film, adding scenes parodying *Basic Instinct*, with the most popular actor of the period, Şener Şen. The film attracted around a million viewers itself which instantly qualified it as a blockbuster. It was no coincidence that both *Arabesk* and *Amerikalı* had Şen as their lead actor. Şen had seasoned himself as a versatile actor for the last two decades, appearing in supporting roles in 1970s' comedies and as the brooding character actor of arthouse films during the 1980s.

The star of the blockbusters was to make history with another director Yavuz Turgul. In 1997, the team made *Eşkıya* (The Bandit), which quickly became the highest grossing film of all time in Turkish cinema up to that date. The duo would go on to make more blockbusters like *Gönül Yarası* (2006) and *Av Mevsimi* (2010). With its 2.5 million viewers, *Eşkıya* attracted both audience and local producers' attention to local film-makers. The necessary support came from Özen film, the main distributor of Hollywood films in Turkey. Led by Mehmet Emin Soyarslan, who inherited the distribution company from his father, Özen film became the main distributor of blockbusters in Turkish cinema and co-produced record-breaking films like the *Recep İvedik* series.

The new wave of blockbusters was the product of a new production scene, which was shaped by the coming of television in Turkey. Television, like its counterparts in the US and Europe, had a traumatic effect on Turkish cinema. Audience size shrank from hundreds of millions to hundreds of thousands within a decade. Since 1974, TRT, Turkish Broadcasting Corporation, had dominated entertainment and television. The economic liberalization of the 1980s, under the Turgut Özal government, saw the development of

Left image: *Vizontele*, 2001, Yılmaz Erdoğan/Omer Faruk Sorak © Besiktas Kultur Merkezi (BKM).

another industry that profited from the coming of television: the advertising industry. The young film-makers who had witnessed a declining film industry instead directed their creative energies to making television commercials. Among them, the blockbuster directors of the future, Yavuz Turgul, Sinan Çetin and Mustafa Altıoklar, created some of the finest examples of TV commercials: small 'capsules of perfection', as Ridley Scott would call them. These new directors were also among the first to be university educated, and had attended state-run film institutes during the 1970s. Their style did not follow those who made films before them; instead they aspired to big-budget American films. These directors worked with advertising agencies and created a visually impressive style of vibrant colours and funny characters, which they would later carry on to their film-making practices. They also did what no director had done before: they actually owned film and lighting equipment, created their own casting agencies and operated their own studios. Commercial director Sinan Çetin's 'all-or-nothing' approach proved to be successful. After making unsuccessful arthouse films, he made the choice to direct a car commercial and invested his earnings in building a production empire. The accumulation of this production infrastructure would allow the new directors to invest in their own films with little or no capital. Çetin, in almost every interview, gives Ridley Scott as an inspiration as the British director also owns Pinewood studios and produces more films than he directs.

As film-school-trained commercial film-makers made their way, another type of actor-producer emerged in the persons of Cem Yılmaz and Yılmaz Erdoğan. Erdoğan had a successful theatre group and made sketches for television. He invested his earnings in the creation of BKM (Beşiktaş Kültür Merkezi), a total entertainment production company that produced theatre plays, films, concerts and even rock operas. Erdoğan accumulated a series of heartfelt characters and their stories that found life in the blockbuster of the new millennium: *Vizontele*. Yılmaz, on the other hand, was a stand-up comedian who had a successful show for nearly a decade. He was also a creative force in the weekly comic magazine *Leman*. Yılmaz and Erdoğan joined together in Vizontele. This was set in a remote Anatolian town and told the story of the coming of television in 1974. The film became a huge success and spawned a sequel *Vizontele Tubaa* in 2004. The nostalgic and naive look in a small-town setting, where the past two decades of decadence were forgotten, hit a chord with audiences. Erdoğan co-directed the film with Ömer Faruk Sorak and later began directing films on his own. In his recent directorial effort, *Neşeli Hayat*, he began to look into urban life of the rural immigrants in İstanbul. Yılmaz moved on to acting and directing both prestigious projects like Hokkabaz and occasional hit films, where he teamed with Sorak, like *GORA*, *A.R.O.G.* and *Yahşi Batı*.

Comedy film series of the past also found new life in the 2000s. Ferdi Eğilmez, son of the late director of *Arabesk*, was now in charge of the Arzu film school of comedy. He rebooted the series of *Hababam Sınıfı* in 2003. All three films in this series became huge hits. Parody films were among the most popular of comedy films. *Kahpe Bizans* and *GORA* made fun of the Yeşilçam films and demonstrated that they could rival Hollywood cinema in technology and style. With these blockbusters, audience segmentation also diversified. The old Yeşilçam films were made for families. They were shot on a shoestring budget and the tickets were cheap. The new Turkish blockbusters were expensive to make and ticket prices were accordingly high. These films had to appeal to everyone: urban/rural, young/old, male/female. They also took into account the audiences (Turkish immigrants) in Europe and in nearby Arab and Balkan states. Television series also helped to create film audiences. The adaptation of *Asmalı Konak* as a film became a huge success and made Çağan Irmak a major blockbuster director with *Babam ve Oğlum*. In addition, *Kurtlar Vadisi-Irak* produced sequels and spin-offs that turned into blockbuster films.

Two more stand-up comedians defined blockbusters of the post-2005 revival. Indeed, 2005 became the first year in two decades when Turkish films would gross more than American films at the box office. Şahan Gökbakar and Ata Demirer both produced successful franchises: *Recep İvedik* and *Eyvah Eyvah*. A total of five films made in both series attracted around 20 million viewers. Both actors had dramatic-theatre training and had previously made television sketches.Şahan Gökbakar's adaptation of the persona of Recep İvedik into cinema was an event celebrated by millions. Surprised at the bold-ness and sincerity of the İvedik character, audiences from all segments enjoyed the three İvedik films. Demirer, on the other hand, was already a successful actor in Plato Film-produced television series called *Avrupa Yakası*. Erdoğan's BKM supported Demirer's film project. *Eyvah Eyvah* appealed to the sensibilities of the people of the North-West. The vibrant funny musician character that Demirer created captured the imagination of mil-lions, and its sequel (*Eyvah Eyvah 2*) became the top-grossing film of 2011.

The daring attempt of a singer-turned-actor also re-defined the limits of daring in Turkish cinema. Mahsun Kırmızıgül, who followed the steps of his long-time friend and competitor Ibrahim Tatlıses, had been a very successful folk singer since the mid-1990s. In 2007 he gathered all his investments together and made *Beyaz Melek*. The film had a dozen veteran actors gathered from theatre and Yeşilçam. The film was a commercial success, attracting more than a million viewers. Film critics doubted Kırmızıgül's talent but he was unrelenting. After the success of *Beyaz Melek* he produced yet another blockbuster *Güneşi Gördüm* in 2009 – interestingly based on social issues of rural immi-grants in İstanbul. In 2011, Kırmızıgül employed veteran Hollywood actors and shot his next film, *New Yorkta Beş Minare*, partially in New York City. Kırmızıgül proved to be an able storyteller who bore comparison with Yılmaz Güney. His success opened way for other singer-directors like Özcan Deniz, who recently made a very successful directorial debut with *Ya Sonra*.

The future is ripe for Turkish blockbuster films. A series of historical adventure films with big budgets like Faruk Aksoy's *Fetih 1453*, *Kara Murat*, *Tarkan*, *Malkoçoğlu* and *Battal Gazi* franchises may redefine blockbusters in the next decade. The televisual pro-duction regime, with its film school trained commercial directors, stand-up comedians, and musician-actor directors, will thrive as more and more film theatres are opened in the heart of Anatolia within newly-erected shopping malls.

Murat Akser

Eyvah Eyvah

Eyvah Eyvah

Studio:
BKM

Director:
Hakan Algül

Producer:
Necati Akpınar

Screenwriter:
Ata Demirer

Cinematographer:
Gökhan Atılmış

Composer:
Fahir Atakoğlu

Editor:
Mustafa Gökçen

Duration:
100 Minutes

Cast:
Ata Demirer
Demet Akbağ
Özge Borak
Salih Kalyon
Bican Günalan

Year:
2010

Synopsis

Hüseyin is an amateur clarinet player living in Çanakkale with his grandparents. He plays at local weddings with his band. During a wedding, a girl gets choked and, trying to save her, Hüseyin is attacked by the father. He is taken to the infirmary and falls in love with the nurse Müjgan. One day his grandfather asks for money and he gets some from his grandmother's money box. There he finds the photo of his father and letters to his mother. He learns that his father is unaware of his existence. The grandparents hid the fact that he was born out of wedlock. He decides to go to İstanbul to find his father. He settles in with his family friend, tailor Ramiz. While waiting in his shop, a blond woman enters to pick up her stage clothes. It is Firuzan, a singer at a local club. She has a drunkard former lover, who harasses her all the time. Ramiz and Hüseyin decide to find his father. While waiting at Ramiz's shop Hüseyin is sent to deliver Firuzan's clothes. She asks for his help in a photo shoot, during which she hears him play the clarinet impressively and invites him to play for her; they become good friends. Firuzan joins in his search to find his father. During their search they witness a murder. They pretend to be blind to fool the criminals, who spot these witnesses. They escape but the mafia finds Firuzan through the posters on the street. Whilst running away from the mafia they have a car crash and both end up in the hospital, where, by a twist of fate, they find Hüseyin's father. At the end of the film they all manage to escape and hit the road (for potentially another journey) to Çanakkale together as, this time, Hüseyin plans to propose to Müjgan.

Critique

Eyvah Eyvah is a musical blockbuster using local town folklore in a colourful manner. Just like the other hit films by BKM, such as *Vizontele*, the festivity of the small town, the nostalgia and childlike innocence of the townsfolk are ever-present. It is the clash of town ideals in the city that makes the film so interesting and successful. The city is presented as a maze, a hell for a rural person like Hüseyin. Hüseyin feels uncomfortable in the crowds. The anonymity of the city overwhelms him and its cosmopolitan structure is alien to him. In a funny scene Hüseyin cannot order at a luxurious restaurant where all the food has European names and he keeps giving the food its authentic Turkish name. The town also has its bad memories. It is a place of shattered lives where Hüseyin had to grow up as an orphan, a representative of the generation after the 1980 military coup. Yet, he is also a Turkish Harry Potter, a grown-up child finding peace and happiness in small things in the midst of utmost harshness of the everyday reality of poverty. Ata Demirer as the feel-good easygoing musician is at the height of his acting and writing talent. He had previously shown his musical talents in another BKM film by Ezel Akay, *Neredesin Firuze?* Interestingly Demet Akbağ of the BKM tradition has carried the persona of

Firuzan from this film to new depth. The urban scenes in the film resemble some of the features of another Yılmaz Erdoğan film, *Organize İşler,* which dealt with rural immigrants in the city who had to deal with poverty and crime. Finally the diversity of the unique Çanakkale accent makes the dialogues funny. Fahir Atakoğlu's rendition of local gypsy music turned the film's soundtrack into another successful musical phenomenon. *Eyvah Eyvah* became one of the most commercially-successful films in Turkish cinema, with a sequel that matched its predecessor's success. With this film Ata Demirer established himself as a multi-talented star and his most recent work *Berlin Kaplanı* seems to cement his strong presence in Turkish film comedy.

Murat Akser

Eyvah Eyvah, 2010, Hakan Algül.

Eyvah Eyvah 2

Eyvah Eyvah 2

Studios:
BKM
UIP

Director:
Hakan Algül

Synopsis

Firuzan, a city club singer, who met the peasant Hüseyin in İstanbul, travels to his home town in Çanakkale with his new-found father. Upon arrival, Hüseyin wants to confess his crush on the local nurse Müjgan, but suspects that she is in a relationship already with the newly-appointed doctor at the town clinic. He decides to take the doctor out to find out about his feelings about Müjgan. However, the doctor is already engaged to someone else. We soon see Müjgan and Hüseyin meeting up and becoming lovers. They are happy; however, Müjgan's parents are not. Her father decides to

Producer:
Necati Akpınar

Screenwriter:
Ata Demirer

Cinematographer:
Gökhan Atılmış

Composers:
Fahir Atakoğlu
Serkan Çağrı

Editor:
Mustafa Gökçen

Duration:
107 Minutes

Cast:
Ata Demirer
Demet Akbağ
Özge Borak
Salih Kalyon
Bican Günalan

Year:
2011

take her to İzmir, where she can be away from Hüseyin. On the way, Müjgan opens Hüseyin's gift, which turns out to be a wedding ring. At the end of the film they manage to convince her father and Müjgan returns to the village for a big wedding. The film ends with a shot of the pregnant Müjgan sitting next to Hüseyin watching Füruzan thanking the couple for the adventure on a popular talk show.

Critique

Eyvah Eyvah 2 begins right where the first film ends. The first film centres around the adventures of the naive peasant Hüseyin in the big city. In the sequel, Füruzan finds herself at the heart of the countryside in a remote village. The nostalgia theme of the first film continues in the second. The small Çanakkale town is idyllic, representing a naive dreamlike place where a rural boy is in love with a city girl. The beautiful vista, sea and the old coastal town are used as landscape in the background of many shots. The remnants of the generation X's distaste of the post-1980 military coup is reflected in the military father blocking Hüseyin's love. Ata Demirer had long established himself as a television star with his recurring role in the Gülse Birsel-penned *Avrupa Yakası* as the spoiled son of a rich city couple. He also showed his ability to perform and create interesting characters in *Osmanlı Cumhuriyeti* (Gani Müjde, 2008), where he had played the fictional twenty-first-century Ottoman sultan. His interpretation of Hüseyin as a naive man finds new depth in *Eyvah Eyvah 2*. Hüseyin is more able and quick to find solutions to problems in his village than outside of it. In fact, to reinforce this idea, he is constantly referred to as the 'Thracian Shrek' throughout the film. The film plays on changing genres to avoid boredom and repetition. There is situation comedy, crime thriller and musical. The film also exposes human trafficking between Turkey and Europe. Smart, heartfelt, rhythmic and ecstatic, *Eyvah Eyvah 2* is a delightful film to see.

Murat Akser

Magic Carpet Ride

Organize İşler

Studio:
BKM

Director/Scriptwriter
Yılmaz Erdoğan

Synopsis

Samet's life takes a new turn just as he is trying to kill himself. He finds himself joining in with a group of thieves who steal cars and sell them to rich people. As an innocent and naive man, his first sale is not going to be easy as it looks, as he meets a clever young woman, who will not stop investigating this crime. Yet, behind Samet there is a team and behind that team there is the mafia. This is a funny yet at times noir-like story of a comedian whose life changes on the day he was supposed to die.

Producer:
Birol Akbaba (post-production producer)
Necati Akpınar

Cinematographer:
Uğur Içbak

Art Director:
Yaşar Kartoğlu

Composers:
Ozan Çolakoğlu
Yıldıray Gürgen

Editor:
Mustafa Presheva

Duration:
106 Minutes

Cast:
Demet Akbağ
Ebru Akel
Erdem Bas
Cemile Çam
Tolga Çevik

Year:
2005

Critique

Organize İşler (Magic Carpet Ride) starts out with a scene in which the protagonist, 'Superman Samet', the comedian Tolga Çevik, tries to commit suicide because he thinks he is boring, unoriginal and unsuccessful. Asım (Yılmaz Erdoğan), the head of a gang of professional automobile thieves, coincidentally saves him before he dies. This encounter changes Samet's ordinary and decent life, as he decides to quit his profession in order to pursue another career in Asım's world. Asım's 'humble headquarters' is an abandoned place in Beşiktaş that is squatted in by the new residents: his gang. This is their root space that we may define as the originary world. The gang's business is to steal cars from upper-class people and sell them back to them. In a sense, the idea behind it is reminiscent of Robin Hood or Superman, who also serve poor people by stealing from the bad-rich.

The gang's victims are an upper-middle-class family of three: the intellectual parents, Yusuf (Altan Erkekli), a sociologist/writer, and Nuran (Demet Akbağ), a professor of quantum physics and their young daughter Umut (Özgü Namal), a university student. This represents a nuclear intellectual family of the 2000s with reversed gender roles. Nuran's job is stereotypically regarded as a male profession; Yusuf is modern, westernized and is supportive of women's emancipation. Umut is a clever and witty young woman. Yusuf's book, titled *Societies With a Weak Sense of Unity and The European Union*, does not sell much at his book launch, but it wins him 20,000 Euros in a competition sponsored by the European Union. He gains market value without losing his virtue and goes through a transformation process. Yusuf and Nuran decide to buy a jeep for their daughter with the money. Riding happily together in the car, they get stopped by the police, only to find out that the jeep was registered as a stolen vehicle. After this scene, the film turns into a Turkish version of David Mamet's 1987 film *House of Games* (1987), which also contains academics, young university students as well as petty thieves and the mafia. The young, pretty daughter of the elite couple transforms into a lovely femme fatale in the sheltered spaces of İstanbul while she traces the thieves herself, instead of leaving it to the police. Samet is affected by the intrigues of this decent, beautiful young woman who is named Umut after the revolutionary youth of the 1970s. She cunningly pursues her aim, acting above the law of both the legal/formal (police) and the illegal/informal (mafia and the thieves). She asks the mafia boss Müslüm (Cem Yılmaz), who was also a victim of Asım's gang, to make the gang pay for their crimes. The final scene in the film is the same as the opening one: Asım and his swindler gang are in Mafia Müslüm's stable, kneeling on the ground with their hands tied behind them. Müslüm is playing golf at them, targeting their mouths as the holes. This is shot in film-noir style, but contrary to most films noirs, thieves and swindlers are punished by their equivalents instead of the police, above ground, on a sunny day. The film ends with all the balance restored and morality reassured. The family gets their money back; Umut expresses her fondness for Samet by going to see his stand-up show.

Magic Carpet Ride markets İstanbul as a cinematic city that unveils itself in a spectacular way. The city is shown from a birds-eye view through helicopter-camera shots. We encounter the funny-yet-bitter story of the metropolis through the story of a group of gangsters, an innocent man and an intellectual family. What is interesting is that the film converts specific locations of İstanbul into images and further into conventions of images, so that the city becomes the main protagonist of the film. Places like the Maiden Tower, Bosphorus Bridge, the Golden Horn, Taksim Square, skyscrapers and nightclubs are all shown to the spectator from above. *Magic Carpet Ride* flies over the city merging different genres and old and new narratives about the city, accompanied by the song 'I'm neither Superman, nor Clark Kent...', referring both to the director and the spectator.[1]

Deniz Bayrakdar

[1] A longer version of this article was previously published in Turkish, in Bayrakdar, Deniz & Akçalı, Elif. (2007) in *Türk Film Araştırmalarında Yeni Yönelimler VII* (ed. Bayrakdar, D.), İstanbul: Bağlam Yayınları.

My Father and My Son

Babam ve Oğlum

Studio:
Avşar Film

Director:
Çağan Irmak

Producer:
Şükrü Avşar

Screenwriter:
Çağan Irmak

Cinematographer:
Rıdvan Ülgen

Art Director:
Murat Güney

Composer:
Evanthia Reboutsika

Editor:
Kıvanç İlgüner

Duration:
108 Minutes

Synopsis

My Father and My Son is a melodrama about a left-wing activist journalist. The film tells the story of Sadık, whose wife dies while giving birth to their son, on the night of military coup of 12 September 1980. He is imprisoned and tortured during the coup for his political writings. When he finds out that he has a terminal illness as a result of the torture, he decides to return to his hometown where his parents live and leave his son Deniz in the care of his grandparents. Issues about the past re-emerge in the present in a quarrel between Sadık and his father when he returns 'home'.

Critique

In focusing on the military coup of 12 September 1980, which applied a systematic depoliticization in society, *Babam ve Oğlum* provides a melodramatic representation on the consequences of the traumatic past of a left-wing activist. The film is an instance in the growing body of films which attempts to come to terms with this national and political trauma. What is interesting about the film is its use of the child. The link between the coup and the child (and hence the political and the personal) is thought-provoking. The film, on the one hand, uses the child and his vulnerability as central to the narrative, thereby relying on the image of an innocent child and evoking emotion more than political consciousness; on the other hand, through the juxtaposition of images of torture applied to the adult and the child's imaginary world, it turns the personal into political. Deniz's mother dies on the night of the coup and his father is dying after serious physical torture for his political ideas. Both of the deaths are related to the political situation. Here, the

Cast:

Çetin Tekindor
Fikret Kuşkan
Hümeyra

Year:

2005

boundaries between childhood and adulthood are reinforced with emotion-evoking images. Melodramatic codes of staging and lighting, deep focus, distorted close-ups and expressivity of sound all coordinate to evoke appropriate emotional orientation to the text. Unaware of what will happen to his dad, Deniz becomes the central character in the narrative. Not only is the father victim of the coup, indirectly is also the child. He deserves our sympathy for his vulnerability. Throughout the storyline, as his helplessness is revealed more and more, the audience longs to protect him. This strong sense of compassion and tenderness also invites the audience to think about the reasons that put the child in this condition – hence the audience is invited to think about the consequences of the coup not only on the child but also on the mother and the father.

Babam ve Oğlum is one of the highest-grossing films in the history of cinema in Turkey, with around four million viewers.[1] It is also a film nationally and internationally recognized in festival circles with many awards, including the 2006 International İstanbul Film Festival's prestigious 'Best Film' award.

Eylem Atakav

[1] This information is retrieved from http://boxofficeturkiye.com/film/2005197/Babam-ve-Oglum.htm (Last accessed in August 2012)

My Father and My Son, 2005, Çağan Irmak.

Recep İvedik

Recep İvedik

Studios:
Aksoy Film
Özen Film

Director:
Togan Gökbakar

Producers:
Faruk Aksoy
Mehmet E. Soyarslan
Ayşe Germen

Screenwriters:
Şahan Gökbakar
Serkan Altuniğne

Cinematographer:
Ertunç Şenkay

Editor:
Erkan Özekar

Duration:
110 Minutes

Cast:
Şahan Gökbakar
Fatma Toptaş
Tülüğ Çizgen

Year:
2008

Synopsis

The film starts at a police station in the suburbs of İstanbul. Recep, a thirty-something drifter, is released from prison after a fight with the police. On his way home he sees a man dropping his wallet and picks it up. He later sees the owner of the wallet on the television as a hotel manager in Antalya. He decides to go to Antalya to personally deliver the wallet. On his journey, he camps at night, hitchhikes during the day. When he arrives at Antalya and hands the wallet back, the owner of the hotel, impressed by his honesty, offers him a week-long vacation for free. During his stay, Recep is enchanted by Sibel, who has a rich fiancé – a relationship imposed upon her by her overprotective mother. Not knowing about her engagement, Recep tries all sorts of things and at the end manages to win her heart. They realize they used to know each other from their childhood years but, because Sibel promises her dying mother that she will marry her fiancé, she cannot follow Recep. As he leaves she realizes her strong feelings for him, but it is a little too late.

Critique

Recep İvedik has been more than a blockbuster; it has turned into a cultural phenomenon. The film was made for a small sum, less than a million dollars, but grossed to be the greatest box-office winner to date. After the success of the film, Şahan Gökbakar, playing the famous lead character, made two sequels. His famous lines created what we can call a subculture. Recep was loved by millions, his laughing voice became a ring tone in cell phones and he even had an iPhone application quoting his lines. Recep İvedik as a character embraces the cultural diversity and problems of dislocated immigrant rural youths living in the suburbs of big cities. He is uneducated, unemployed, vulgar yet honest, modest, friendly and with some common sense and the belief that he can win the day. In many ways, he could be called the Turkish Borat, but Recep is more than that. Although there is toilet humour in the film, the character is way more complex and three–dimensional, as it had been developed on television shows years before. In fact, the Recep İvedik character was already famous due to television quiz shows where he appeared as a cameo and made fun of *Who Wants to be a Millionaire*. That episode was put on YouTube and reached millions of potential film viewers. Recep can also be a childlike figure and his actions are based on instant gratification of an ego that defies all social mores. The film is a teen's dream come true: women on the road waiting to be rescued (though this image can be rather problematic), partying with rockers and clubbers, enjoying a vacation in a five-star hotel and meeting your childhood sweetheart once again. Recep is a version of the common man making it big time.

The film is directed by Şahan Gökbakar's brother, Togan, a university-trained director who is technically proficient and well aware of the film traditions before him (and sometimes alluding to them). Recep is also very inventive with language. He can speak, even sing, in different Anatolian dialects. He has folk-tale character attributes like Keloğlan. He also continually makes popular-culture references to Turkish pop music. *Recep İvedik* can appeal to rich and poor, old and young, uneducated and the elite at the same time. In fact, this quality – its ability to reach across all class, gender and cultural background – gave it the right to claim the title of 'the best film to cut across all audience segments at the box office' in Turkish cinema.

Murat Akser

Recep İvedik 2

Recep İvedik 2

Studios:
Aksoy Film
Özen Film

Director:
Togan Gökbakar

Producers:
Faruk Aksoy
Mehmet E. Soyarslan

Screenwriters:
Togan Gökbakar
Şahan Gökbakar
Serkan Altuniğne

Cinematographer:
Ertunç Şenkay

Composer:
Oğuz Kaplangı

Editor:
Erkan Özekan

Duration:
110 Minutes

Cast:
Şahan Gökbakar
Gülsen Özbakan
Efe Babacan
Çağrı Büyüksayar
Zeynep Çamcı
Asiye Dinçsoy

Year:
2009

Synopsis

Recep is in his home neighbourhood in Güngören, İstanbul, where he visits his grandmother. His grandmother is an energetic and lively woman. She complains about Recep's idle ways. Grandmother orders Recep to find a job, get married, get a good reputation and be a good man. Recep starts looking for a job. First he becomes a pizza delivery man but he gets fired for eating half of the orders. Then he becomes a cashier in a supermarket. He gets fired again for ordering the customers around. Next, he works in a pharmacy and then becomes an air steward. He is fired 17 times in 20 days. He discovers that his cousin Hakan runs an ad agency created by his grandfather. He goes to the ad agency to claim his senior-partner position. After he has made several embarrassing scenes at the office he gets acquainted with the employees. To achieve his second goal, he befriends an internet junkie and finds about dating sites. He creates a dating profile and has his first date at a Starbucks. He mistakes another girl for his date and gets pepper-sprayed. On the business front, he decides to represent the agency in a deal with a Japanese company. He comes to the meeting with a kimono that has a *yakuza* symbol on and manages to deal. Even though all goes well for him on the job front, he cannot find love. Yet, in order to fulfil the promise he gave to his grandmother on her death bed, he takes one of the interns who works for him and presents her as his girlfriend. At the end of the film we see Recep sitting alone crying next to his grandmother's coffin.

Critique

The sequel to the incredibly successful *Recep İvedik* comes with a bigger budget and a more developed story. We get to see Recep (Şahan Gökbakar) in his own neighbourhood, where he is everybody's best friend. In the film, Recep's characters and actions are criticized by his grandmother, who represents authority and provides social criticism. He faces the challenging task faced by young men in the big city: finding a job. As Recep puts it, 'this is the problem of 18 million unemployed youths'. In line with this, the film makes fun of business practices and capitalist ideology, particularly through Recep's jokes. Recep's success as a newcomer to an old

Recep İvedik 2, 2009, Togan Gökbakar.

urban company is a commentary on new Anatolian capital coming to old city businesses and reshaping it. This is highlighted with the way in which he thinks about coffee: to him drinking foreign coffee at the heart of a coffee-producing country is too alien. His ways of trying to deal with the most exotic and alien practices range from yoga, golf and costume parties to his inability to eat sushi and caviar. Overall, the film offers an interesting and thought-provoking representation of 'Turkish-ness' in the face of both capitalism and eastern technocracy. It critiques the dispassionate capitalist ideology through comedic ploys, and by presenting us with a character, who, with his warmth, captures the hearts of audiences.

Murat Akser

The Hunting Season

Av Mevsimi

Studios:
Fida Film
Warner Bros

Director:
Yavuz Turgul

Synopsis

A severed hand is found in a river. Forensics finds that it is that of a teenage girl and they identify a fingerprint. A homicide detective, Ferman, takes on his final case of a murdered girl with his assistant İdris and a new recruit fresh out of college, Hasan. During their investigation they identify the girl through her criminal record. They locate her drug-addict boyfriend, acid Ömer, who denies the crime, in a night club. The girl, Pamuk, was living with Battal Çolakzade, a wealthy industrialist, as a teen bride. During another interview, Ömer decides to confess that it was one of Pamuk's brothers who killed her. İdris decides to sneak into Battal's mansion to gather evidence, but is shot by a security guard. Before he dies, he points to a clue to be seen in the surveillance footage. At the end of the film Battal admits to the murder of Pamuk, who was sacrificed as an organ donor to save his sick daughter, and commits suicide.

Producers:

Murat Akdilerk

Jefi Medina

Screenwriter:

Yavuz Turgul

Cinematographer:

Uğur İçbak

Composer:

Tamer Çıray

Editor:

Niko İsmail Canlısoy

Duration:

145 Minutes

Cast:

Şener Şen

Cem Yılmaz

Çetin Tekindor

Melisa Sözen

Okan Yalabık

Year:

2010

Critique

Examples of the crime genre are rare in Turkish cinema. Previous attempts include Gecelerin Ötesi (1958) by Metin Erksan, *Pars: Kiraz Operasyonu* (2007) by Osman Sınav and Behzat Ç. by Serdar Akar (2011). Yavuz Turgul tackled this genre many times with Eşkıya (1997) as a writer-director and with Kabadayı (2007) as a screenwriter. The film was released within a year of former Turgul protégé Uğur Yücel's *Ejder Kapanı* (2010), a noirish crime thriller that freely used stylistics of David Fincher's *Seven*. Though *Av Mevsimi* also borrows from Seven in terms of characterization (wise investigator and the rookie cop), it is a masterpiece in its own right in terms of story, character development and visual style. The film is narrated through the voice of the dead girl, an innovation in Turkish cinema. There are long, smooth, never-ending shots of the burial ground around the river, suggesting the transcendental point of view of the murdered spirit. The characters are well thought out and represent qualities of a good cop. Ferman,the hunter (Şener Şen), represents wisdom; the mad İdris (Cem Yılmaz) represents passion; and the youth Hasan (Okan Yalabık]) represents common sense and fear. The male characters' stories are delicately interwoven with their female partners'. Ferman's wife (Nergis Çorakçı), a saintly figure, is sick with kidney failure and, as a gracious woman, she rejects a donor in favour of a young girl. İdris' wife Asiye (Melisa Sözen) is fiery and fights İdris with fervour. Hasan's fiancée (Şefika Ümit Tolun) is motherly and protective of her love. The interaction of male characters with these women also shapes the story towards its eventual outcome: death in all fronts.

Turgul used a real-life detective during the research for the film. The interviews and notes by real policemen helped Şener Şen to create and perform Ferman. Rarely appearing on the silver screen for more than a decade, Şen is effortlessly natural and masterfully in command of his craft. Cem Yılmaz, long known for his comedic roles, wanted the role of Hasan and lobbied hard for it. His rendition of the Black Sea song 'Hayde' in the ballroom scene became an instant hit in Turkey. Çetin Tekindor as the obsessed hunter is at the height of his acting talent. Hasan, played by Okan Yalabık, gives a sense of freshness in the arrival of new acting talent. His inability to get rid of the scent of death on his hand is well played throughout the film. Yavuz Turgul is indeed an actors' director. His players freely leave themselves to his carefully-constructed and controlled acting style and the result is a well-balanced, stylistic film with unforgettable performances.

Av Mevsimi is about the dirty nature of police work – an emphatic look at the profession. It certainly opened the way for new crime TV series like *Behzat Ç*. Its central metaphor is the hunter and the hunted; between a hunter who hunts for fun and a real life one who hunts out of necessity. The film is a contemplation on the nature of men and the beast, of men and women, of sex and death. It is a crime film to end them all; a magnum opus by a great director and his team of talented craftsmen.

Murat Akser

The Hunting Season, 2010, Yavuz Turgul.

The Inter-national

Beynelmilel

Studio:
Beşiktaş Kültür Merkezi

Directors:
Sırrı Süreyya Önder
Muharrem Gülmez

Producer:
Necati Akpınar

Screenwriter:
Sırrı Süreyya Önder

Cinematographer:
Gökhan Atılmış

Art Director:
Çağrı Aydın

Editor:
Engin Öztürk

Duration:
105 Minutes

Cast:
Cezmi Baskın

Synopsis

The story is set in Adıyaman in Eastern Turkey, in 1982, where a group of local musicians experience financial problems due to the constraints of the curfew (and how their attempt at solving the problem resulted in their arrest). When the head of the local military orders the musical troupe to become a 'modern orchestra' that plays at formal occasions, both funny and tragic events arise. The General wants them to play for the arrival of the members of the military council. In the meantime, Gülendam, the lead maestro's young daughter, and Haydar, the boy she is deeply in love with, are influenced by the communist movement. The university student Haydar plans to protest against the council's arrival and he gets help from Gülendam. Their plan is to play the *Internationale* when the council arrives, and the film details how these two groups clash. In this regard, the film is a comedy with a serious underlying subject.

Critique:

Although *Beynelmilel/The International* is the first film made by the director, it is an accomplished piece. The film seeks to encourage the audience to reflect on a dramatic and traumatic issue while also making them laugh, and it mainly uses humour to criticize the militarist oppression. The story is well developed, and contains details, which represents aspects of the period in a realistic manner: Haydar (Umut Kurt) carrying books about socialism under a different cover; the banners hung in the streets which feature pictures of the military leaders; and the checking of identification cards in public places by military officers. In line with this approach, the characters are also realistically portrayed. The leading charac-

Özgü Namal
Umut Kurt
Nazmi Kırık

Year:
2006

ter, Gülendam (Özgü Namal), is a naive girl who has grown up in a small town. She learns about socialism and other political subjects from the books that Haydar brings her. Haydar, on the other hand, is a university student who strongly objects to the coup. He is fervent about the political situation of the country and he calls himself a revolutionist. In this regard, he represents socialist youth at that period in Turkey. He supports the rights of the ordinary people like factory workers and farmers, although his knowledge about them is solely theoretical. When his brother Servet (Sırrı Süreyya Önder) catches him reading a socialist magazine, he objects to Haydar's sympathy towards the movement by saying: 'We are just ordinary musicians. What is our relation to communism? What do know about farmers, workers?' Servet's reaction is intended to sum up the perspective of many young socialists in those years. The other important character in the film is the leader of the orchestra, Abuzer (Cezmi Baskın). He continues the tradition of playing music within the family and struggles to earn money together with his brother Tekin (Nazmi Kirik). He works so hard that he has blisters on his fingertips. Gülendam, his daughter, puts ointment on them every night. He stands for the real labourer that Haydar talks of theoretically. When the military officers arrest him and his friends while they are playing music illegally inside a truck, he loses the opportunity of earning money. Although the musicians are made the official orchestra of the military, it is not certain that they will be paid. In short, Abuzer and his brother start to run a nightclub with the permission of the military in order to earn some money. This event also indicates that one cannot do anything without the permission of the military. It is also important to mention that the building which is turned into a nightclub was a community centre just before the coup. At this point in the film, the statement that the coup is for the good of all people is effectively questioned: a place that worked to raise the cultural and the educational levels of the general public was closed on the order of the military, who instructed that it be used as a nightclub for entertainment. Haydar objects to the opening of the nightclub, claiming that it invites the exploitation of women's bodies. Hearing these words, Gülendam also reacts to his father and uncle by saying: 'Aren't you afraid of being slapped by our revolutionist public?'. These words are followed by a real slap, as Gülendam's father strikes him across the face. This slap can be understood as the slap of reality. The reality here is that Abuzer and his brother have to earn money to support their families and playing music is the only thing they can do. Furthermore, the nightclub is the only place where they can work under these strict conditions.

One crucial theme in the film is to do with the degree of suppression exercised by the military that may not just curtail freedom but may also result in absurdities. One of these absurdities is well exemplified by the ban on certain folk songs. The local musicians are made to play only permitted songs by signing an official permission form. During a wedding, one person asks them to play one of the forbidden songs. They can only play it 'silently'. While

The International, 2006, Sırrı Süreyya Önder/Muharrem Gülmez.

they are playing, a group of officers visit the wedding and they have to change the song to one that almost became a national anthem during those years. This shows the heavy hand of military on the daily life of citizens in both humorous and effective ways. As Haydar says in one of the scenes, almost all places in town are turned into military posts. The effect of the coup on social life had been handled in many Turkish films before. *Beynelmilel* is one of the few films dealing with this topic in a dramatic yet humorous way. However, humour in this film is not used to mitigate the serious and tragic effects of the coup. On the contrary, having a clear anti-militarist tone, the film asks the audience to question the oppressive effects of militarist regimes through a well-developed script and successful acting.

Funda Can Çuvalcı

The Mild West

Yahşi Batı

Studios:
Fida Film
Böcek Yapım

Director:
Ömer Faruk Sorak

Producers:
Murat Akdilek
Cem Yılmaz
Oğuz Peri

Synopsis

It is January 2010. Zeki and his friends are together when he claims that the boots he is selling belong to Turks who visited America in the nineteenth century, and starts talking about two Ottoman Turks: his grandfather Aziz Vefa from the secret service and Lemi Galip from the treasury who were sent by the Ottoman sultan to deliver a gift of a diamond to US President Garfield in 1881. While travelling on a stagecoach, they are robbed by the Sioux tribe and the diamond goes missing. The film is about their journey to find the diamond and their attempt to survive in the meantime. On the way, they meet a cowgirl, Suzan van Dyke, who will help them find the bad guys who stole their goods. When finally they find the diamond, we see them in the White House presenting it to President Garfield, who in return gives them a pair of boots. After telling a convincing story, Zeki tries to sell the boots for 20,000 dollars.

Screenwriter:
Cem Yılmaz

Cinematographer:
Mirsat Herovic

Art Director:
Hakan Yarkın

Composers:
Ozan Çolakoğlu
Ozan Özgür

Editor:
Çağrı Türkkan

Duration:
116 Minutes

Cast:
Cem Yılmaz
Ozan Güven
Demet Evgar
Özkan Uğur
Zafer Algöz
Yılmaz Köksal
Süleyman Turan
Uğur Polat
Mazlum Çimen
Cansu Dere

Year:
2010

Critique

Yahşi Batı is a daring parody by Ömer Faruk Sorak and Cem Yılmaz, the team which previously made *GORA* the sci-fi parody in 2004. The film is a proud statement about the mastery of cinematic technology in Turkish cinema. During the 1970s, following the example of spaghetti westerns, Yeşilçam cinema had tried to shoot Anatolian westerns with sheriffs, native Indians and the Western towns constructed outside Istanbul. The result was positive, beginning with the famed film Çeko (Çetin İnanç), in 1970. Yılmaz Köksal, who played the title role in that film, and veteran actor Süleyman Turan have brief appearances in *Yahşi Batı* as a homage. Here, Yılmaz follows the footsteps of Mel Brooks in *Blazing Saddles*. *Yahşi Batı* is also inspired partly by Jackie Chan's *Shanghai Noon*, where a nineteenth-century Chinese fighter finds himself in the Wild West. Several of the stereotypical western heroes known in Turkish popular culture also parade through the film: Pecos Bill, Gus from the TV series *Bonanza*, Billy the Kid, and Lucky Luke. There are also references to western films like *The Good, the Bad and the Ugly* and *Brokeback Mountain*.

The film is a self-reflexive parody as the English-speaking cast at the beginning of the film freeze the frame and switch to Turkish, playing with the filmic 'reality'. There are many stereotypical jokes about both Turks and Americans in the film that are repeated time after time, such as the 'knock knock' jokes told by Lemi, and the comments by Americans about 'Turks riding on camels'. There are also numerous references to Turkish pride in the film. The names and places are Turkified. For example, the sheriff has a thick Anatolian town accent. There are also references to traditional Turkish dramatic arts. When confronted by Suzan, Aziz and Lemi start playing Karagöz (Turkish shadow play), Ortaoyunu (Turkish theatre) and sing classical music to prove they are *authentically* Turkish. Aziz and Lemi also confront the 'native Indians' with the claim that 'all native Americans are descendants of Turks'. They also seem to 'invent' some brands, which are now known as American: kinetoscope, an early form of cinema; the formula for coke and fried chicken. The film plays on its main sponsor *Cola Turka's* motto – that it is a national drink as opposed to American coke. Later proven to be using Coca Cola's original formula, the film appeared with promotions related to this local brand. Local kebab stores served *Cola Turka* with *Yahşi Batı* glasses, *Cola Turka* cans gave free cell-phone minutes to drinkers who attended *Yahşi Batı*. The film also had major sponsors like Avea (cellular services), Ttnet (internet services), Türk Telekom (telephone services) and Ülker (food and beverage). Overall, *Yahşi Batı* is a great combination of film technology, Turkish national pride and the talents of Yılmaz and Sorak. The team is expected to reunite for the possible sequel that would take place in China suitably called *Yahşi Doğu*.

Murat Akser

Vizontele

Vizontele

Studio:
BKM

Directors:
Yılmaz Erdoğan
Ömer Faruk Sorak

Producer:
Necati Akpınar

Screenwriter:
Yılmaz Erdoğan

Cinematographer:
Ömer Faruk Sorak

Post-Production Supervisor:
Ali Taner Baltacı

Composer:
Kardeş Türküler

Editor:
Mustafa Preşeva

Duration:
106 Minutes

Cast:
Yılmaz Erdoğan
Demet Akbağ
Altan Erkekli
Cem Yılmaz
Cezmi Baskın
Bican Günalan
Erkan Can

Year:
2000

Synopsis

Vizontele is the story of the coming of television to a small village in Anatolia in 1974. The film revolves around the town fool, Emin, who is a self-professed mechanic. Emin lives on top of a hill alone and spends his time inventing eccentric devices on his own. The film narrates a broad cross section of life of the Eastern Kurdish town where we see the mayor and his wife, his sons, their wives and young lovers separated by necessities of state (military conscription). Life goes on idyllically with kids having fun, eating watermelons, falling from trees, and on rooftops trying to watch films for free in the local summer movie theatre. The government sends a television crew that delivers a television set to the town. The fear of losing his customers engulfs the local movie-theatre owner. The news of the 'the radio with pictures in every home' might have a devastating effect on his local cinema. The mayor, Nazmi, appoints Emin to take on the task of testing the new television set. After initial failures they climb on top of a mountain and get the first reception. Eagerly waiting for the first national signal, instead all they see is the neighbouring Iranian broadcast. After being exhausted, the group heads back to town where a local watchman accidentally changes channels and they suddenly see a proper image for the first time in their lives. The villagers gather in the mayor's house to watch television, and the very first news they receive is the invasion of Cyprus by the Turkish army, and the death of the mayor's son in combat. As the movie theatre gets emptier, the townsfolk now watch TV at home. Unable to claim her son's body back from the military, the mayor's wife, Sıti, buries the TV set to commemorate her fallen son.

Critique

Vizontele is both a commercial and subtly political film about today's Turkey. It also proudly shows off the capabilities of new Turkish cinema, as we see the images of the town and its people through hovering skycams. It is no coincidence that Yılmaz Erdoğan, the lead and creator of the film, chooses the coming of television to a small town in Van, in Eastern Turkey. Television is constantly referred in the film as a device that unites the people of the west to the people of the east, thereby creating a sense of uniformity and national identity. Yet, the inability to reach the TV signal points to the distance from the centre and alienation of the Kurdish citizens in the east. Ironically, the very same *technologically united nation* takes a victim with the death of the mayor's son. The film is also about lost values of the past. All this changes with the coming of television – a capitalist western invention that fuels consumption through commercials. The town changes to such an extent with the coming of TV that in the end the newlywed couples are given TV sets as wedding presents.

    Vizontele is also a film about the love of cinema where Yeşilçam audiences were lost immediately with the advent of television. The end of 'summer cinema' is deeply grieved over. There are detailed scenes from classic Turkish films throughout *Vizontele*. These films are about urban İstanbulites with pretty blonde girls, expensive cars and rich boys. It is ironic that Fikri (Cem Yılmaz) comments on the fake nature of kisses in these movies. Emin suffers from a neural condition that makes him involuntarily imitate people when they make repeated body movements in front of him. This is not coincidence and is symbolic of the protest against the imitation of western cinema (and a 'Western Turkish' lifestyle) instead of valuing the local (authentic) eastern lifestyle. There are constant references to Yılmaz Güney, the inventor of Kurdish cinema in Turkey, as we frequently see his image on the walls or in the posters of films around the local cinema. The film is also a product of the new tele-visual mode of production. The sketches Erdoğan nourished over a decade with his ensemble cast find new life on the big screen with *Vizontele*. The unrelenting persona of Erdoğan pops up in every scene. The prime cast of his television show *Bir Demet Tiyatro* shines with Demet Akbağ and others in the troupe. The existence of vulgar, everyday language and manners and the use of swear words derive from this previous television hit. So, the audiences are familiar with the actors. The stand-up comedian and block-buster writer-director Cem Yılmaz's presence in the film, as the local tailor and contractor Fikri, reinforces the comedy elements. In line with this new production regime, the cast is visually enriched by the inclusion of fashion models as actors with former *Miss Turkey* Zeynep Tokuş, and popular singer Yeşim Salkım. The film is episodic, very much in concert with Erdoğan's style of television sketches. He film uses digital visual effects expertise gained during ten years of commercial film-making. The film signs the birth of the directorial genius of both Erdoğan and Sorak, who would go on to make more blockbusters with *GORA*, *Yahşi Batı* and *Aşk Tesadüfleri Sever*. The colourful costumes and meticulous art direction are products of sponsorships and of the television-series expertise of the film crew. The additional success is generated from the strategy of opening the film during long holiday weekends – a distribution strategy that is antithetical to Hollywood. *Vizontele* can be seen as the musings of a childlike fool. It is Yılmaz Erdoğan's way of re-imagining childhood innocence. It is nostalgia that goes hand in hand in a pre-1980 military coup setting. *Vizontele* has made its mark in film history as a blockbuster, and is now referred to as a classic of new Turkish cinema.

Murat Akser

Vizontele Tuuba
Vizontele Tuuba

Synopsis

Vizontele Tuuba starts in October 1980, in a high school in Ankara. When the teacher asks the class to write a paragraph about their summer vacation, one kid starts narrating the events of June 1980. A family arrives on the bus to town. It is the leftist, exiled librar-

Studio:

BKM

Director:

Yılmaz Erdoğan

Assistant Directors:

Ali Taner Baltacı

Ozan Açıktan

Producer:

Necati Akpınar

Screenwriter:

Yılmaz Erdoğan

Cinematographer:

Uğur İçbak

Art Directors:

Yaşar Ziya Kartoğlu

Suzan Kardeş

Composer:

Kardeş Türküler

Editor:

Engin Öztürk

Duration:

107 Minutes

Cast:

Yılmaz Erdoğan

Demet Akbağ

Altan Erkekli

Tarık Akan

Tuba Ünsal

Tolga Çevik

Year:

2004

ian with his wife and disabled teen daughter Tuba. Not much has changed in the town since six years ago where we left off in Vizontele. This time, however, the youth is divided between socialists and Stalinists – representing the political tensions embedded in society at the time. In the meantime, when librarian Güner meets the mayor Nazmi, and finds out that there is no library in town, they decide to build one. In the meantime, Emin, still the town, meets Tuba, Güner's disabled daughter, who has a crush on him. The two quickly become friends. Nobody comes to the opening of the library, and knowing that people like the TV, Emin offers to install a television set at the library. They take the buried television set out of its grave. This solves the problem. However, on the night the television tube burns out, the September 12 coup takes place. Emin finds the library trashed and sees the military trucks nearby. The librarian's home is raided, and soldiers take him away. The movie theatre is closed. The kid goes back to school as the librarian's family leaves the town. Emin is sad that Tuba is leaving and gives his goggles to Tuba as a present. To show his affection for, her Emin writes Tuba's name on the hills and soldiers erase it thinking it represents the initials of another leftist organization.

Critique

Vizontele Tubaa takes the audience back to the same nostalgic town of the first film, Vizontele. This time the politics are more visible, as right-wing Adalet Partisi (Justice Party) and left-wing Cumhuriyet Halk Partisi (Republican Party) fight (physically and ideologically) over the nation's future. It is a time of turmoil, where political tensions are at a peak, as terror becomes everyday news. The iconic leftist actor Tarık Akan appears in the film as a leftist librarian. Another veteran actor, Nejat Uygur, also performs as the bigot Hacı Zubeyir. The film comments on the ever-growing grip of the state institutions in the form of military intervention. In a visit to his headquarters the commander remarks: 'If socialism is something good then we as the state will bring it, not the people.' The enlightenment project – that is the building of a new library – is destroyed by the military. The East and the West, once again, cannot come together as Tuba (who represents western values in her image) cannot stay with Emin, who represents masculinity and the East. Emin announces his feelings when he says: 'like all things that are good and beautiful, it leaves'. The film ends with the military vehicles leaving town. The divided left loses its battle. The only thing the two leftist groups in town could agree on is to raise their voice against the smoking ban imposed at the library. The goggles Emin gives to Tuba represent the new way of looking to the East from the West – a distorted view of the backward people the film aims to reverse. On another note, the film-maker is proud of his ethnic Kurdish origins – this is highlighted by the local ethnic Kurdish music that is present in the soundtrack.

The film continues the tendency to boast with technical mastery. The crane shots, the long take that lasts for a minute in the beginning are ways of showing off this mastery. Similarly, colourful cinematography exists with beautiful art direction. Ata Demirer appears as a stand-up comedian in a persona that will reappears years later in another blockbuster *Eyvah Eyvah*. Deniz Akkaya, Yasemin Ergene and Zeynep Tokuş are also present as TV celebrities. Former model and television commercial persona Tuba Ünsal uniquely leaves her mark by having her real name in the film's title.

Murat Akser

Drama is a broad category that covers a wide range of films. Drama in general and melodrama in particular are the prevailing genres in the history of cinema in Turkey. The films discussed in this category differ in their content and styles as well as their modes of production and release dates; yet there are certain elements or concepts that bring these films together. These films not only indicate the characteristics of the body of work by a variety of film-makers, but also represent aspects of different cultural, social and political realities in Turkey.

What is common to some of these films is the idea of coming to terms with the consequences of the 1980 coup. Indeed, the 1980s is a decade during which Turkish society and politics went through considerable transformation. The military intervention of 12 September 1980 repressed both the radical Left as well as the radical Right in Turkey, whilst aiming towards a period of systematic depoliticization in society. The significant work put forward by film-makers to confront this national trauma resulted in an outburst of films in Turkey, particularly since the late 1990s. The idea of collective childhood and the actual use of children in many of these films about the coup are worth developing. These films relentlessly try to come to terms with a traumatic past whilst at the same time interrogating questions of national belonging and identity. Through the use of children Turkish cinema presents a medium of memory. Throughout the narratives characters look for clues from the past to make sense of the present. An evident connection here is between public historical and political events and the personal. According to Asuman Suner, Turkish nostalgia films arrest the past in an image of frozen childhood as they reflect upon the ambivalences of longing and belonging (Suner 2010, 17). Suner also asks all the apposite questions about what she calls 'popular nostalgia films': 'How… can we characterise the peculiar act of memory that Turkish nostalgia films produce? … What does the peculiar representation of the past in these films tell us about the present condition of Turkish society? … What kind of cultural memory is performed in these films?' (ibid. 16). Some of the reviews in this section attempt to find answers to these questions through remarking upon the effects of the social, cultural and political changes on films.

İstanbul has always been a popular space and a recurring theme for drama in the cinema of Turkey. Stories around leaving or, predominantly, moving to the city are frequent in drama. The city, in these films, is a product of imagination and representation,

Left image: *Clouds of May/Mayis Sikintisi*, 1999, Emin Ceylan/Muzaffer Ozdemir, Nuri Bilge Ceylan © NBC Films.

which emerges as a cultural text or at times a character within narratives. As discussed by some of the reviews in this section, the city is rendered legible; it is constantly invented and reinvented. Its significance is related to what it represents for those who do and do not belong to it. The city, therefore, designates the space produced by imagination of the film-makers as well as the interaction of historically- and geographically-specific institutions and social relations.

The drama genre has most suffered from state censorship and local municipal storage laws. Governments, hesitant about communism and representations of social issues of all kinds, enforced a censorship law that established a board which gave a 'pass, reject or pass with revisions' status to films. Many dramatic scenes deemed too political were often cut from the films. As for the municipal services, the law required that they hold all film prints in warehouses, which eventually got burnt through neglect and all pre-1955 dramatic films were lost in successive fires. Throughout the 1960s, films by independent and political directors were banned. Notable examples, including *Karanlık Dünya* and *Yılanların Öcü* by Metin Erksan and later films by political director Yılmaz Güney, were banned. Even a state-sponsored historical prestige project by Halit Refiğ, *Yorgun Savaşçı*, was banned and all the negatives were burnt. Only after 1992 with the change of censorship law could Turkish cinema take off. The 1980s saw a series of personal films that critiqued the military coup. Films like *Uçurtmayı Vurmasınlar, Ses, Sen Türkülerini Söyle* and *Av Zamanı* told of the oppressive period through the eyes of its victims. The brooding, traumatized characters could never fit in the newly capitalizing society of the 1980s. The early 1990s saw the emergence of a new type of cinema, one that does not directly criticize the political conditions but turns inward. This new festival, arthouse, personal and inward-looking cinema owes its existence financially to support from a ministry of culture that was dominated by social democrats between 1991 and 2002 and by a Eurimages' agreement of the European Union. The next development was the rise of film schools that helped train a group of socially-engaged directors in the 1980s and the 1990s. Zeki Demirkubuz, Derviş Zaim, Yeşim Ustaoğlu and Nuri Bilge Ceylan are responsible for a dramatic and independent festival cinema that dominates the 2000s. Films like *Tabutta Rövaşata, Filler ve Çimen* by Derviş Zaim, *Masumiyet, 3. Sayfa* and *Kader* by Zeki Demirkubuz, *Güneşe Yolculuk* and *Araf* by Yeşim Ustaoğlu and *Distant, Three Monkeys* and *Once Upon a Time in Anatolia* by Nuri Bilge Ceylan created a new sense of cinema.

Thematically these films have a nostalgic look at the past; the narration is usually through the innocence of a child or a childlike figure. The small town and its desperate, depressive desolation (yet its bizarre innocence) is contrasted with the big city and its evils. Yet, there are new directors (from a variety of political and ethnic viewpoints) who open up new territories not tackled before. The Kurdish issue or the voicing of minorities, women, gays and underprivileged classes became the new dramatic frontier of Turkish cinema. Reis Çelik, Kazım Öz, Murat Saraçoğlu, Sırrı Süreyya Aydemir are among the directors who voice ethic concerns and issues around identity. For that very reason the term Turkish Cinema is often disputed, as it denotes an old cinema – one concerned with a nation-state united under one flag and language without ethnicities and classes. The recently-coined term 'Cinema of Turkey' came to be widely used by both film-makers and film critics, since film-makers united under the independent film movement started by films like Seyfi Teoman's *Tatil Kitabı* and Seren Yüce's *Çoğunluk*.

In the cinema of Turkey there are is also a wave of independent films which have become successful. These films are considered according to a variety of movements: the Social Realists (1961-1965); National Cinema Movement (1966-1979); Young Film-makers (1969-71); Festival Film-makers Era (1980s and 1990s); New Film-makers (1997 onwards) and the New Cinema Movement (2007 onwards). These movements have common elements: they are concerned with the alienated individual in the big city;

they have stylistic similarities with European art cinema; they reference literary master-pieces by Tolstoy and Dostoevsky every so often; and they are not widely distributed for commercial release but designed for festival audiences. The successive waves of independent film-makers show that Turkish dramatic cinema is looking for and trying out 'the new' in terms of themes, ideas and visual styles.

Murat Akser
Eylem Atakav

An Autumn Tale

Bir Sonbahar Hikayesi

Studio
Z Film

Director
Yavuz Özkan

Producer:
Aycan Çetin

Screenwriter:
Yavuz Özkan

Cinematographer:
Ertunç Şenkay

Art Director:
Figen Batur

Composer:
Cahit Berkay

Editor:
Sedat Karadeniz

Duration:
98 Minutes

Cast:
Zuhal Olcay
Can Togay
Sinem Üretmen

Year:
1994

Synopsis

Bir Sonbahar Hikayesi by Yavuz Özkan summarizes 'the 1980s autumn' as the whole country was awakened by the announcement of the military coup and its government. The film portrays the bleeding wound between one businessman and his wife, an academic, representing the division of labour between men and women of the upper-middle class.

Critique

The film begins with a car crash in the foreground and student uprisings and police intervention in the background. The young woman (Zuhal Olcay), who is trying to escape from the bullets, is hit by a red sports car. The driver, a handsome man, the embodiment of the yuppie generation, meets her by this coincidence. This beginning is meaningful, since the 1980s were the times when almost every relation was *par l'accident*. So, the young, pale, introvert beauty embodies the female academic and the handsome, extrovert man stands for the eager bank/stock market manager of the era. There is no escape from death except a love story. If they want to escape the bullets or the police pressure, they have to face the everyday life reality of the nuclear family. The story of the 'red car and love' saves them from the images and sounds of the ideologically-charged environment they lived in before they come under the protective shelter of romance. The woman is an academic at the Western Languages Literature Department. This information, given at the beginning, emphasizes her educational background, loyal attitude, her firm belief in the university and science, and her role in the society as an intellectual. Representative of a female intellectual of the 1980s, she wears greyish clothes, no make-up, carries an unhappy, melancholic air and drives a Volkswagen in contrast to her partner's expensive red car. She is an incurable romantic, and there lies her failure. She teaches like a poet, looking deep into a virtual sky while telling her stories from literature. After marrying the man, she finds out about his indifference towards political and social turbulence. Her inner struggle is intensified by her job at the university, where she speaks about Western Literature and the students, in turn, criticize her for being oblivious to the realities of the street. She lives with a dilemma: the harsh atmosphere of the university and the escapist passion/ love relationship with her husband. The husband offers to move to America, but the woman, as an existentialist and responsible academic, rejects the offer: 'If everything here, in this country would be OK, I would go to the US, but I'm an intellectual.' One night, she wakes up with the TV news announcing the military intervention. She gets very frustrated, as opposed to her husband, who perceives the *coup* as positive. Their difference is underlined in this scene.

We see her in the class room again telling students: 'I hope the reason that some of our friends are not amongst us today is of their own accord? ' – meaning that most of them could be imprisoned or killed. The rest of the lecture is a problem-solving session via western texts which are signs of the pressure and violence and function as nonverbal communication to share the era's pain. Meanwhile, the eager yuppie husband continues his wild approach to life by changing cars and apartments. He finds that having no regulations and rules is a rule itself. For him Turkey does not exist, 'he targets the world' he says. I think this expression summarizes the definition of globalization for a Turkish man of the era almost perfectly. Yet, the stock-market adventure of the husband ends in social and political disaster, taking down with it some ministers and a huge group of adventure-entrepreneurs. The woman loses the last ties with her 'identity'. The ship sinks as the man says: 'I know how to swim.' The film, overall, represents the immediate effects of the radical political and social changes in Turkey, at that time, on individuals' lives whilst focusing on a relationship between a man and a woman. The film has received several prizes in national and international film festivals. 'The Best Film', The Best Actress, 'The Best Actor' in the 6th Ankara Film Festival, the 3rd Best Film in the 14th Netherlands Film Festival, 'Best Film' prize of the Ministry of Culture, Turkey.

Deniz Bayrakdar

Notes

> Part of this analysis has been published in a broader article by Bayrakdar, D., 'Turkish Academics in Europe: An Autumn Tale' in Tomus, V. (ed) *Creating the European Area of Higher Education: in Voices from the Periphery*, Vol. 12, Springer Publications, 2006.

Bastards

O...Çocukları

Studio:
Energy Media & Productions

Director:
Murat Saraçoğlu

Producer:
Selay Tozkoparan

Screenwriter:
Sırrı Süreyya Önder

Cinematographer:
Cengiz Uzun

Art Directors:
Caner Gürlek
Rıza Doğan

Synopsis

After the military coup of 1980, a political prisoner Metin and his wife Meryem decide to flee the country after Meryem's brother Selim dies at the hands of the police during torture. Saffet, a friend of Meryem, makes the arrangements for their escape to Italy by boat. They leave their 7-year-old daughter Hazan with Mehtap, an ex-prostitute who has been babysitting the children of other prostitutes. Meryem gets sick during the trip. Employees of the refugee office help them to get Hazan back. According to the plan, an Italian couple would go to Turkey and bring Hazan to Italy – disguised as their daughter. To make the story convincing, a young Italian girl, Dona, starts teaching Hazan Italian at Mehtap's house. Saffet, who was also raised by Mehtap, falls in love with Dona. The story progresses with tragicomic twists and reaches a happy conclusion, with Dona managing to take all the children who are staying with Mehtap to Italy.

Critique

O...Çocukları (translated as Bastards) is Sırrı Süreyya Önder's second screenplay about the 1980 military coup and its effects on Turkish society. The name of the film and its posters created

Composer:

Tufan Kıraç

Editor:

Erkan Özekan

Duration:

120 Minutes

Cast:

Demet Akbağ
Özgü Namal
Sarp Apak
Altan Erkekli
İpek Tuzcuoğlu

Year:

2008

controversy, as it was the first time that a movie including offensive language in its title was shown at theatres. Despite its controversial name and interesting story, the movie did not do well at the box office. The rather rushed look of the film (from its cinematography to the editing) could be a key reason for its financial failure. Furthermore, rather unconvincing storytelling hampers the film. The story takes place during the early 1980s during the military coup period, but it fails to convincingly recreate the atmosphere of the period. Rather than offering insight into the harsh reality, its universe seems abstract. The film does not focus on the bloody side of the military junta, even though the trailer includes torture scenes. Other than the few short moments dedicated to these torture scenes, this is not the main concern of the movie. In approaching the military coup from a narrow perspective, the film helps to create the illusion that the physical and psychological damage of the military coup was limited to a small group of people, even though it transformed Turkish society as a whole.

References to the oppression are also almost completely missing from the movie. The reason why the cops are obsessed with locating Meryem and Hazan is never explained; the spectator leaves the theatre without knowing why Meryem was running away from the police. The neighbourhood where story is situated is pictured as a place with children playing in the street happily and a place where Dona spends two months without being noticed. According to the script, Dona plans to disguise Hazan as the daughter of an Italian family that comes to Turkey for the 23 April Children's Day celebrations. Her plan proves to be unrealistic and she fails to convince authorities. At the end of the film, Hazan and the other children from Mehtap's house come to say goodbye to Dona at the airport and they somehow manage to obtain passports as a group of Italian children. Dona manages to take all of the children to Italy, and this unconvincing ending is one of the weakest aspects of the film. What can be seen as somewhat excessive dialogue also dominates the film, and detracts from the visual power and appeal of the story.

Meltem Cemiloğlu Altunay

Bastards, 2008, Murat Saraçoğlu.

Cars of the Revolution

Devrim Arabaları

Studio:
Ekip Film

Director:
Tolga Örnek

Producers:
Tolga Örnek
Türker Korkmaz

Screenwriters:
Tolga Örnek
Murat Dişli

Cinematographer:
Hasan Gergin

Art Director:
Veli Kahraman

Composer:
Demir Demirkan

Editor:
İsmail 'Niko' Canlısoy

Duration:
115 Minutes

Cast:
Haluk Bilginer
Taner Birsel
Halit Ergenç

Year:
2008

Synopsis

Following the military takeover in 1960, the new President Cemal Gürsel offers a challenge to car-makers to build the first Turkish automobile, the Devrim. The project is undertaken by a consortium of engineers based at the State Railroad Directorate in Eskişehir in central Anatolia. At first the group of engineers are sceptical about the project's success but they are eventually won over by the group leader Gündüz, who relishes the challenge of being able to accomplish the task in the 130 days allocated by President Gürsel. However, the group becomes victim of its own success: many officials in government try their best to sabotage the project in the belief that it might disrupt the political *status quo*, in which bureaucrats thrive while actually doing nothing for the country's future. Despite their best efforts, the consortium manages to finish the project on time, and takes the completed automobile to the capital, Ankara, for a grand unveiling at the Parliament building. However, they are unaware of one final twist of fate that puts the entire project at risk.

Critique

Although set in the distant past, *Devrim Arabaları* comments directly on the present, focusing in particular on the ways in which bureaucrats consciously frustrate any attempts at innovation. Partly this is due to inertia, but there is also the element of fear: anything new might lead to reform, which would endanger the bureaucrats' position. Throughout the film they try to prevent the group of engineers from completing their project to create the first Turkish car, the *Devrim* (or Revolution). The official reason given is one of cost: over 1.4m Turkish lira ($500,000) has been spent in creating a prototype, at a time of economic crisis. In truth, however, the bureaucrats are riddled with jealousy, as their position as chief advisors to President Cemal Gürsel (Saît Genay) is put under threat. If the project proves successful – and thereby vindicates the President's dream of instilling a new sense of national pride among the people – the bureaucrats will no longer have the power to control the country's purse-strings (while simultaneously feathering their own nests). They employ several strategies, including cutting the budget allocated to the project by one third, and using the classic spoiling technique of persuading friendly journalists to print critical articles. As the grizzled old engineer Latif (Selçuk Yöntem) tells his idealistic junior colleague Necip (Onur Ünsal): 'Those who can't oppose him [the President] go around and attack us … Anyone who can't criticize his revolution is coming down on ours.' This is not the first time this has happened: Latif recalls a time in the not-so-distant past when the Republic had its own aircraft factory. Although very successful at the time, it was shut down by the bureaucrats who were reluctant to try anything new in case it affected their position within the social structure. Latif observes somewhat cynically: 'In Turkey no success goes unpunished, son.' In his view, history has a habit of repeating itself.

The engineers in *Devrim Arabaları* discover to their cost that their efforts are frustrated. The bureaucrats try every single strategy to stop them – quoting procedures, trying to prevent the supply of essential parts to complete the project, and persuading President Gürsel that the project as a whole is too much of a drain on the national finances. Stubborn to the last, the President continues to support the project, but finds that his own support is equally unwarranted. He goes for the first test-drive in the car outside the Parliament building in Ankara on October 29, 1961 (the anniversary of the foundation of the Republic), but finds to his cost that the Devrim car has run out of gas. From then on the project is doomed; the newspapers have a field-day with headlines like 'The Revolution Didn't Run,' referring both to the car and to the President's much-vaunted project to create a Turkish automobile industry.

Yet, Örnek makes us care for the group of idealists who have striven to create the car by showing the sacrifices they make: project leader Gündüz (Taner Birsel) sets aside personal difficulties in a childless marriage to his wife Suna (Vahide Gördüm), while Necip tries his best to juggle work commitments with looking after his pregnant wife Nilüfer (Seçil Mutlu). Necip's selflessness is well demonstrated in a sequence where he risks arrest during a curfew (imposed in the wake of the 1960 military takeover) to find apples for Nilüfer. At one point the President talks of the need to instigate a 'real revelation in [the Turkish] people's minds'; *Devrim Arabaları* suggests that this will only come about when ordinary people dedicate themselves to a cause, whether successful or not. Mr. Kline, a representative of the American Embassy (Charles Carroll) observes – in English – that, while the engineers might not be able to accomplish their project, 'they believe they'll do it, and that's more important.'

The film evokes the idealism of the early 1960s, a time when people genuinely believed they could achieve something, despite the best efforts of bureaucrats to stop them. They went to school during Kemal Atatürk's time (he died in 1938); a lot of them were sent abroad to study engineering, and on their return they wanted to pay back their debt to the state. They tried to pursue impossible projects, like making a car, and they just went ahead and pursued them. Just witnessing their idealism is wonderful to watch; they do not want to earn extra money, and they put their careers on the line, but they believe in what they are doing. Perhaps that kind of enthusiasm no longer survives in a world where business depends on money. Idealists still exist, but they have to come together once again, as they did in the early 1960s, and make opportunities for themselves.

Laurence Raw

Chainbreaker

Zincirbozan

Studio:
Türk Max TFT Production

Director:
Atıl İnanç

Producers:
Mehmet N. Karaca
Ayfer Özgürel
Avni Özgürel

Screenwriter:
Avni Özgürel

Cinematographer:
Gökhan Tiryaki

Art Directors:
Narin Deniz Erkan
Murat Aygan

Composer:
Emre Dündar

Editors:
Deniz Kayık
Bora Gökşingöl

Duration:
110 Minutes

Cast:
Bülent Emin Yarar
Suavi Eren
Orhan Aydın
Fatih Yıldız
Haldun Boysan

Year:
2007

Synopsis

Zincirbozan explores how Kenan Evren seized power in the chain of command and on the order of the Turkish Armed Forces, whist claiming that 'there is no other solution for our country in an atmosphere in which intellectual and physical malicious attacks continue to be directed to the existence, independency and regime of the Turkish Republic' on 12 September 1980, the date of the *coup d'état*. There are different political parties and groups that conflict with each other in the film, including the military, groups with opposing different political views, law enforcement officers of the government, and civil society. The story starts in July 1980, a period of martial law before the 12 September coup d'état. The American government is dissatisfied with Turkey's veto on NATO before the coup, and it cooperates with the Turkish Army to turn the tables. In the meantime, right and left conflict increases in the country. The National Security Council decides to seize power due to its dissatisfaction with both American pressure and the decisions of the President and the government. Evren and the National Security Council come to power with the coup, and the film ends with the new civil government founded after coup.

Critique

1980, in Turkey, is known as a year during which significant events in the political history of the Republic were experienced. There were a number of films made about the 1980 coup before the 2000s; stories about the period have significantly increased during the 2000s, with films focusing on the tragic stories experienced by individuals at the time. Zincirbozan is one such text that concentrates on this dark side of recent history through a story on revenge. The film is named after the Zincirbozan Military establishment in Çanakkale. This is also the place where politicians were subjected to compulsory residence after the coup. *Zincirbozan* seeks to highlight the profits behind the decisions and manners of the politicians and this radical political change. The film is factual, and one can easily sense the semi-documentary approach, looking at its narrative and aesthetic choices. The story offers a perspective that portrays the coup as totally 'American in origin', and the script was written by journalist/novelist Avni Özgürel. In this regard, the other political, military and civil powers behind the coup are ignored and America is foregrounded – laying the film open to criticism in terms of a shallow and simplistic portrayal. One of the elements of the movie that received much criticism is its representation of Kenan Evren and the National Security Council. In the film, Evren and the Council are presented as being obliged to stage a coup even if they had no desire to do so. Overall, the film reinforces the idea that it is of crucial importance to have films that focus on the period so that this period and the social and political repercussions of it are not forgotten.

Meltem Cemiloğlu Altunay

Clouds of May

Mayıs Sıkıntısı

Studio:
NBC Films

Director:
Nuri Bilge Ceylan

Producer:
Nuri Bilge Ceylan

Screenwriter:
Nuri Bilge Ceylan

Cinematographer:
Nuri Bilge Ceylan

Editors:
Ayhan Ergürsel
Nuri Bilge Ceylan.

Duration:
131 Minutes

Cast:
Mehmet Emin Ceylan
Muzaffer Özdemir
Fatma Ceylan
Mehmet Emin Toprak
Muhammet Zımbaoğlu
Sadık İncesu

Year:
1999

Synopsis

The film focuses on the problems and difficulties faced by Muzaffer and his close relatives: Emin, his father Saffet, his cousin and Ali, the younger nephew. On the eve of shooting his first film, the difficulty that faces the director Muzaffer is to find appropriate actors for his film and to persuade his close relatives to act in it. Emin, the father, is trying to catch up with the land surveyors, to persuade them that he should be the proprietor of the land that he has been foresting and working on for a long time. He keeps checking law books and writing petitions for this end. Saffet's challenge is to get out of town to 'save his life' and get a job in the city. Muzaffer promises Saffet that he will secure him a job in the city if he accepts acting in the film. Ali's problem is his yearning for a musical watch but, to achieve this, he needs to be able to keep an egg in his pocket without breaking it for forty days. Ali dutifully declines Muzaffer's suggestion of boiling the egg first on grounds of honesty, but then he gives in to cheating. Muzaffer begins his shooting, Emin keeps forgetting his lines, many scenes are shot over and over again. Emin finds out that the surveyors have expropriated the land he had been working on during his absence.

Critique

Mayıs Sıkıntısı/Clouds of May is about Nuri Bilge Ceylan's idealist father and also himself, the director, in the persona of Muzaffer, and his filming process. Emin, the father, is an idealist dedicated to work – planting new and different trees instead of cutting them down, like other villagers. Muzaffer's concerns with his own efforts of shooting the film within such limits leaves him ignorant of the problems of the crew. He can neither share the loneliness of the recently-widowed Uncle Pire in the trial shooting, nor the remarks of his parents upon time passing, when they watch the old videos together. Likewise, he weathers 'rebellious' Saffet's boredom, by promising him a job in İstanbul, if he agrees to appear in his film. When the film is finished, Muzaffer tries to persuade him to stay in the village, saying it will be difficult to get him a job.

The film is actually on the practice of film-making and implies a self-reflective style. Ceylan relates the process of film-making, by imposing himself or his alter-ego in the film. Art gives the permission to walk into people's lives, turn them into an object of art, order them about and get rid of them when it is done. An example of that is Muzaffer's secretly entering his parents' bedroom to place a sound receiver, thus invading their privacy; he makes Uncle Pire get up from his sick bed for trial shootings; he does not care about his loneliness and leaves grumpily when he finds him inappropriate for the role. He films Saffet without permission and causes him to quit his job so that he may act in his film, but he breaks his promise of finding him a job when the film is done. The film also testifies to the fact that art can be produced out of mundane life. In a Kracauerian sense, its minimalist narrative and visual aspects offering bare nature, as well as an unprofessional cast made up of relatives and a small production group, suggest a relation with Ceylan's *The Small Town* (1997). It ties itself to this former film by introducing familiar images with the sounds of cars, motorcycles, birds and conversations of the villagers passing by in the street. Shame and conscience surface in accordance with the director's motives behind film-making. In the first film, the turtle encodes the metaphor of conscience. In both films, school is the space of the feeling of shame. In the trial scenes shot at the primary school, Muzaffer records the shame of the student who misspells the teacher's word on the board. Both films imply a critical mood towards formal education. The answer 'nothing' from Ali in response to Muzaffer's inquiry about what he learnt at school questions the understanding of formal education. Ali's remark that they have not been taught about the turtle at school, even though it lives among them, suggests a critique of formal education, whereas the education in the village is totally down to earth. Its narrative, based on real-life incidents, gives the film a documentary style. Parents' comments on how they look older in the video or Emin's reaction to a sound in the video as if it were real bring to mind the question of the extent to which the film represents reality. This duality of truth and fiction also blurs the difference between performance and life. Emin, who cannot utter his lines properly and confuses the film-making with reality, gives an outstanding performance as an actor who cannot act. Inspired by his deeply admired playwright, Chekhov, the director juxtaposes the behavioural differences of town and city culture in a mild manner, refraining from turning his characters into extremely bad or good personas and expecting the audience to adapt a distanced perspective. This is a film worthy of the title of a minimalist, modernist 'art movie' with its emphasis on the cheating and detachment in art practices, its turning the experience of spectating into a conscious process and its fixing on the static instances.

Hasan Akbulut

Clouds of May/Mayis Sikintisi, 1999, Emin Ceylan/Muzaffer Özdemir, Nuri Bilge Ceylan © NBC Films.

Distant

Uzak

Studio:
NBC Films

Director:
Nuri Bilge Ceylan

Producer:
Nuri Bilge Ceylan

Screenwriter:
Nuri Bilge Ceylan

Cinematographer:
Nuri Bilge Ceylan

Art Director:
Ebru Ceylan

Editors:
Ayhan Ergürsel
Nuri Bilge Ceylan.

Duration:
110 Minutes

Cast:
Muzaffer Özdemir
Mehmet Emin Toprak
Zuhal Gencer Erkaya
Feridun Koç
Fatma Ceylan
Ebru Ceylan

Year:
2002

Synopsis

Having a gap between his ideals and his job as a commercial photographer, Mahmut has just got a divorce with his wife Nazan and lives alone. Yusuf, his distant relative from Çanakkale, comes to stay in his flat in İstanbul, where he is looking for a job. Mahmut does not like this uninvited guest and warns him to find a job soon. Yusuf, who really wants to be a seaman and go to faraway places and live a different life, cannot find a job despite his efforts. He accompanies and helps Muzaffer, during his trip to Anatolia, to take photographs for a small business, but they cannot develop a warm relationship. Muzaffer's mood fluctuates upon hearing that his ex-wife Nazan is preparing to go to Canada with her new husband. And when he cannot find the chain watch he needed for the shooting he blames it on Yusuf, who says he is not responsible. Next day Yusuf packs his things and leaves İstanbul.

Critique

Uzak (Distant) is the third film of Ceylan's 'provincial trilogy'. It takes place in İstanbul. The promise Muzaffer makes to Saffet on finding a job for him in *Mayıs Sıkıntısı* (1999) sets the basis of the relationship between Yusuf and Mahmut in *Uzak*. The film is about Yusuf's arrival in İstanbul and his stay with his relative Mahmut, the photographer, to find a job and about the tension between them. This tension is rooted in the discursive difference between urban and rural and eastern and western. Similar to Ceylan's earlier films, it is about the province and the spirit of the province. Yusuf is the Saffet of *Kasaba* (1997) and *Mayıs Sıkıntısı*, who wants to get away from the 'suffocating' life in the province. Mahmut, on the other hand, is both Nuri of Kasaba who is the knowledgeable person fond of intellectual discussions, and Muzaffer of Mayıs Sıkıntısı, who wants to shoot films. Mahmut is a nihilist, who claims that photography has come to an end, despite his previous wish to make films like those of Tarkovsky. He is now far from his ideals, life and people.

The film presents two differing lives: Yusuf watches box-office films and hangs the pop-star poster on the walls of his room, whereas Mahmut, in his study full of books, takes the side of 'high art'. This reinforces the split between low and high art, the rural and the cosmopolitan. However, Ceylan shows the audience that this split is not a genuine one by allowing them to peep when Mahmut watches porn after Yusuf goes to bed. Ceylan further emphasizes this difference by using a particular spatial configuration. In the city, Mahmut does not wander around in the open air because he is full of painful memories. Yusuf, however, wanders outdoors in order to reconnoitre, to gain some memories. There is no place called home for Yusuf, yet. He just takes refuge here. He chooses to break the rules; he smokes and drinks, although it is not allowed; he invades the home with the smell spreading from his wet socks; he threatens the modern urban host. All this reminds Mahmut of the past he abandoned, or wants to abandon, and the province he has within him.

Uzak/Distant, 2002, Emin Mehmet Toprak, Nuri Bilge Ceylan © NBC Films.

As the title of the film suggests, continuous snow becomes the sign of *distant* relationships when Ceylan keeps the distance between himself and the people or objects he is recording with his camera. The lighting choice which leaves Mahmut in the dark and Yusuf in the light most of the time seems to be related to Yusuf's accessibility, predictability, and Mahmut's inaccessibility and unpredictability. Ceylan implies that Mahmut is well aware of his indifference to people, his cynicism and that this awareness makes him suffer by portraying him continuously looking at the sea.

In *Uzak*, just as in his previous films, a sub-plot summarizes the theme of the film. The mouse Mahmut has been trying to catch for days is finally trapped and it falls on Yusuf's shoulders to clean up the mess. Trapped mouse symbolizes Yusuf and, just like the mouse he gets rid of, he will be cast aside from the city where he was unwelcome and will discover that it is really tough to survive. *Uzak* becomes the predecessor of the change in narrative in Ceylan's filmography by weaving a deeper psychological dimension of relationships between characters. Mahmut cannot find the chain watch he is going to use as an accessory for the filming and he blames it on Yusuf. Later on he finds it but he does not tell him, thereby reinforcing Yusuf's guilty conscience. Ceylan tries to make this feeling visible in the heart of his artistic production.

Hasan Akbulut

Don't Let them Shoot the Kite

Uçurtmayı Vurmasınlar

Studio:
Magnum Film

Director:
Tunç Başaran

Producers:
Tunç Başaran,
Jale Onanç

Screenwriter:
Feride Çiçekoğlu

Cinematographer:
Erdal Kahraman

Art Director:
Jale Başaran

Composer:
Özkan Turgay

Editors:
Müslim Ertuhi
Cem Gürbüzer

Duration:
100 Minutes

Cast:
Ozan Bilen
Nur Sürer
Füsun Demirel
Rozet Hubeş
Güzin Özipek
Güzin Özyağcılar
Meral Çetinkaya

Year:
1989

Synopsis

This film explores the idea of being a political prisoner and, as part of this, the prison conditions at the time of filming. It does this by focusing on the friendship between a political prisoner and a little boy called Barış, who lives with his mother in prison. İnci is a political prisoner who was convicted because of her thoughts, while Barış is the 5-year-old son, of a woman who was found guilty of drug use. As there is no one to look after him in the outside world, he entered prison as a boy and grew up there. Barış is a source of joy for all the prisoners. But his relationship with İnci is distinctive. Barış explores the concepts of the outer world, nature and love, through his interaction with İnci. The outer world for Barış is composed of a little piece of sky that is visible from the court. One morning he sees a kite, which excites him although he mistakes it for a huge, colourful bird. İnci promises that if she gets out of jail they would fly a kite together. Now freedom means for Barış 'to fly a kite with İnci'… When İnci's prison sentence ends Barış is very sad, and he protests that 'İnci forgot me'. At the end of the film, however, Barış sees a kite while he is looking at the sky and he believes that İnci has kept her promise (to come back in the form of a kite).

Critique

Uçurtmayı Vurmasınlar/Don't Let them Shoot the Kite is one of the films that sought to explore the 12 September 1980 military coup, and it sought to do so via socialist-realist criticism and understanding. The film was adapted from a novel of the same title (written by Feride Çiçekoğlu) and, directed by Tunç Başaran, it represents a historic moment in terms of Turkish cinema. The film narrates the story of the friendship between of 5-year-old Barış (Ozan Bilen) who had grown up in the prison during the oppression years (after 12 September), and İnci (Nur Sürer) who was one of the political prisoners. In the first scene, İnci is released but then starts to reflect on her time in prison. One of the striking aspects of Uçurtmayı Vurmasınlar is that it explores the impact of the coup from a child's perspective. Barış reflects on the meaning of his life, and we experience his sorrow at being incarcerated and suppressed. The kite that he glimpses in the sky in the court is a symbol that represents freedom in the film, and İnci draws a kite in the court to make Barış happy. Together they 'fly' the kites that they draw on the ground. The dialogue between Barış and İnci is significant in terms if the perspective that the film seeks to portray:

-It doesnt't fly here Barış, this court is a restricted place for it.
-So we fly a little kite.
-No way out. It's necessary to fly it on great meadows.
-What is a great meadow İnci?

Uçurtmayı Vurmasınlar is the story of children, like Barış, who do not know 'the great meadows' and political prisoners who know such places but are deprived of them (because their views contradict those expressed by the dominant political power). The meaning of the name of Barış (peace) is also significant as it is the atmosphere created by harmony and mutual tolerance. Barış tries to understand and perceive the adults' world through his childish mind. When he went to his mother's trial and was sitting in a park, he asks the soldier next to him: 'Is this outside?' Then he adds, 'My father is here.' One of the most significant scenes is when he shares his bagel with the soldier: he learnt to do this from İnci and the other political prisoners. Although the film has an atmosphere that is overly emotional from time to time, it foregrounds its humanistic perspective consistently throughout. The film also displays successful and convincing acting by the two lead characters.

Meltem Cemiloğlu Altunay

Dual Games
İkili Oyunlar

Studio:
Muhteşem Film

Director:
İrfan Tözüm

Producer:
İrfan Tözüm

Screenwriter:
Bilgesu Erenus

Cinematographer:
Ertunç Şenkay

Editor:
Mevlüt Koçak

Duration:
82 Minutes

Cast:
Tarık Akan
Zeliha Berksoy
Erol Demiröz

Year:
1989

Synopsis

The film is based on a couple who are experiencing changes in their lives and their relationship, during the period 1968-1988. In their youth, the socialist movement affects them both. They share the same ideals about making the world a better place. They get married and have a son. Soon after, the woman, who works in a bank and looks after the family, begins to get bored in this unrewarding and unproductive life. The man, on the other hand, unaware of the stress and depression his wife experiences, continues his daily routine. The man is a university lecturer who is able to improve himself intellectually and discuss world politics with his colleagues and students. Their traditional marriage ends when the woman's depression worsens. They both find new jobs and earn much more money, forgetting all their ideals they had when they were young.

Critique

İkili Oyunlar criticizes the corruption a group of people by focusing the narrative on a couple. The couple in this film represents degeneration in socialist politics and, in this regard, it is inspired by the changes within, and disappointment of, a generation. As the caption at the beginning of the film suggests: 'The characters in this film … are directly related to the youth of 1968 having given up their social expectations and the events in the film are not products of imagination.'

The woman character, Nur (Zeliha Berksoy) is a politically-conscious, critical, at times cynical, and outspoken woman. She seems to be more anxious about her corruption than the man, her husband, Erol (Tarık Akan). She is more honest with herself and towards her husband. The film starts in the year 1988, showing the woman at the hairdresser's looking stylish. Then there is a flashback to 1976. This time we see the same woman in a dressing gown sitting at a breakfast table and yawning. This part of the film depicts a traditional but bored married couple at home. Both the woman and the man cannot tolerate each other's behaviour anymore. The woman, Nur, complains about Erol's indifference to her situation. The main problem is that Nur labours both at home and at work whereas Erol works only at the university. In addition to the unequal working conditions, the couple do not communicate with each other much.

The other important year in the film is 1978, when the couple goes for a vacation in silent and peaceful countryside. The place and year are the main setting of the film: it is not only the longest part in the film, but it also the most critical in terms of its politics. They set up a tent and stay until they hear what they think may be a fascist group, and they quickly escape – which indicates their existing socialist sentiments. This episode in the film enables the couple to reflect on the changes and experiences they have undergone. The memories from the 1960s include the socialist students' burning of the automobile of the US ambassador in Turkey, Robert William Komer; the trials of socialist students in the court; and the protestations of the 6th US fleet. These are depicted as the most important events that Nur remembers about her generation. The scenes seem to be taken from news archives. Other than these scenes, this part of the film resembles a drama in that there are just two characters talking to each other. When it is considered that the film's script is based on Bilgesu Erenus's play, the resemblence to a theatre play is evident. Nur explains the basic reason of her depression as follows: 'Every word seemed filthy to me. It was as if I was the main cause of everything's becoming filthy. I stayed there and waited for them to take me together with the garbage.' She sat in front of the door of their apartment near the rubbish bins waiting for the cleaners to come. These sentences are indicative of her greater level of self-criticism. Erol seems more self-confident, intellectual, and he displays a greater tendency towards conformism. He accepts that the protestations of the 1960s were just the events of the past and that time has changed (and that this change may not unacceptable). He says to Nur that 'I can't play the role of a revolutionist anymore.' Moreover, he reads the beginning of an article that begins: 'God is dead. Marx is dead...' This indicates that he accepts the change and will adapt to the changes more easily. The scenes belonging to 1988 contradict the scenes from 1978. Both the physical appearance and character traits of Nur and Erol have changed. There is also a symbolic character in the film whom Nur meets everywhere and whose face resembles her son's toy Ibis. This character (Erol Demiröz) acts like the conscience of the couple, and especially of Nur. When he meets Nur at a bar, he says: 'Does this face belong to you?', indicating the change she has undergone or; in other words, her apparent corruption and insincerity.

While the film criticizes the degeneration of a group of socialist people, there is a little hope left with regard to the new generation. The younger generation, represented in the film by Ozan, Nur and Erol's son, and Erol's assistant, are totally different from their parents. Yet they are not portrayed in a solely negative fashion. Although they are unaware of their country's history, they seem more sincere than their parents. The dialogue in the film appear to be directly adapted from Erenus's drama. In short, it is a film that prefers to convey its theme overtly and in a theatrical fashion.

Funda Can Çuvalcı

Hazal

Hazal

Studio:
Umut Film

Director:
Ali Özgentürk

Producer:
Abdurrahman Keskiner

Screenwriters:
Onat Kutlar
Ali Özgentürk

Cinematographer:
Muzaffer Turan

Composers:
Zülfü Livaneli
Arif Sağ

Editor:
Özdemir Arıtan

Duration:
90 Minutes

Cast:
Türkan Şoray
Talat Bulut
Hüseyin Peyda
Keriman Ulusay

Year:
1979

Synopsis

In a remote village in Kurdish south-eastern Anatolia, the feudal order governs the life of the inhabitants. The village chief's daughter-in-law, Hazal, is forced to marry her husband's 9-year-old brother after the death of her husband on their wedding night. Hazal's sister-in-law, still unmarried, complains about the high dowry that her mother asks for her and eventually commits suicide after Hazal finds her in an intimate embrace with a man. However, the arrival of the civil engineers, who have come to construct the road that will connect the village to the heartland, positions the village for change. The landlord takes action against the engineers, arguing that the road is too dangerous for a community whose economy is based on smuggling. Emin, the mechanic, acts against the landlord and decides to work for the engineers and leaves the village with Hazal. Before they are able to escape, however, the landlord's militia kills them. The appearance of the construction machines on the horizon disrupts the villagers standing by the dead bodies of Hazal and Emin. The villagers run amok as the machines enter the village.

Critique

Hazal is Ali Özgentürk's first feature film after the short documentaries he made on the radical social movements of 1970s. He also worked as assistant to prominent directors like Yılmaz Güney and Şerif Gören. The film is a key example of the 'revolutionary' genre made by Socialist directors in the Kurdish south-east during the rise of the radical left in 1970s. The feudal social structure within the region was addressed as the main problem by the films in this category, and the tension between feudal and modern set the dramatic tone. Characters like the village chief and the landlord who resist modernization, a visionary villager who is a proponent of change, a woman who is forced to marry somebody other than her lover, and themes like feudal oppression, child mortality and unregulated violence, are all found in Hazal. However, partly due to his documentary background and partly to his close relationship with Güney, Özgentürk's main characters approximate reality more subtly as compared to the grotesque representations prevalent in the revolutionary genre. For example, the figure of the landlord, the personification of evil in other movies, in *Hazal* rationally warns the village committee against the danger of the road construction. During a meeting to discuss the possible repercussions of the road, he says, 'When the road comes, the state comes too. The state records your name, gives you an ID, gets to know about you, and intervenes in everything you do.' This rational attitude is matched by his charisma that the landlords in other films lack. Unlike many of the revolutionary films which depict the feudal order at its height, Hazal depicts the disintegration of the feudal system during the process of modernization. The visual representation of this process is quite remarkable. At the end of the film, the machines progress towards the village, carving the ground for the road as the villagers run helter skelter around the machines. The tremendous heft of the machines contrasts with human forms, which seem like ants from the bird's-eye view. However, considering oppressive state policy towards the region during the 1970s, the sympathetic attitude towards the idea of bringing the region closer to the state runs against the revolutionary ethic of the film.

Ali Fuat Şengül

Majority

Çoğunluk

Studio:
Özen Film

Director:
Seren Yüce

Producers:
Önder Çakar
Sevil Demirci
Seren Yüce
Özkan Yılmaz

Screenwriter:
Seren Yüce

Cinematographer:
Barış Özbiçer

Composer:
Gökçe Akçelik

Editor:
Mary Stephen

Cast:
Bartu Küçükçağlayan
Settar Tanrıöğen
Esme Madra
Erkan Can

Duration:
111 Minutes

Year:
2010

Synopsis

The film is about a middle class family living in Istanbul, in particular about their son Mertkan, who is in his early twenties. Mertkan and his dysfunctional, middle-class family together create a very familiar picture: an unhappy mother, a power-driven, ignorant, father and an aimless, disinterested son.

Critique

Çoğunluk (Majority) is director Seren Yüce's first feature film. In some respects, the film deals with a well-known story: a young man who falls in love with the 'wrong girl'. The girl, Gül (Esme Madra), with whom he falls in love, turns out to be Kurdish – an unthinkable match as far as his father is concerned. Unable to resist his father's authority, he gives in and breaks up with her. However, in many regards, this is only the side story, the story bordering the kernel of the film which stems from a daunting question: how do people become the ruthless, power-driven, selfish beings they are, oppressing and abusing whoever they can oppress and abuse and not always to advance their own interests but simply because they can.

The film opens with a few images that sum up the situation: Mertkan as a boy, no older than twelve at the time, is following his father in what appears to be a Sunday walk. He is behind, short of breath, hopelessly trying to keep up with his father but receiving no praise or recognition for his effort. However, this very moment, which asks the audience to momentarily sympathize with the boy, is turned upside down with the short sequence that follows: back at home Mertkan kicks the cleaning lady just because he can. Because there is no one else that he can kick but her. S/he who has power over another does exert his/her power (although usually 'his'). Mertkan's father pushes him to his absolute limit both physically and psychologically to be the man he wants Mertkan to be; in return Mertkan abuses the cleaning lady, who is, in his mind, the only person over whom he can exercise power.

Watching *Majority* at times becomes a painful experience, almost too familiar to be able to continue watching. Mertkan, who is an unsuccessful student, works (or rather hangs out) at his father's construction company. He spends his days playing computer games in the office, looking forward to getting out of it and, when he is out, he hangs out with his friends doing equally meaningless activities: watching people in shopping malls and driving aimlessly are some of his (and his friends') favourites. He is usually expected at home for dinner, as his father wants everyone around the table. However, the family meal consists of three people staring at a TV that we do not see and eating quietly, with tension ready to explode at any moment with any word. The feelings of dissatisfaction, resentment and entrapment are so well portrayed, both by the actors and the director (as he often leaves his audience staring at an open door when action is off frame), that at times it becomes almost tangible.

As the film develops, the small details reveal themselves to be the most important ones: the fact that you were not told off for kicking the cleaning lady; not taking any responsibility for crashing into a car while drink-driving and getting help from your father to forge the insurance documents; not paying the compensation owed to the victim of the crash and beating him up, to top it all, because he followed up on it; not standing up to your father when he calls your girlfriend 'god-knows-what-she-is-up-to' and 'not-your-equal'; not saying a word to your friends when they say 'you should screw her and leave her', are some of those small details that makes one not only ruthless and careless but also able to think that it is all right to be ruthless and careless. In this mindset it is mundanely 'normal' to think it is perfectly fine to empty your ashtray in the middle of the road; to discriminate against people based on where they come from; to talk passionately about serving the country, and even fighting for it, but having no issues with forging a document; and to praise a little child for holding a toy gun, letting him think it is an important part of becoming a grown-up man. These very insignificant instances, some of which may seem trivial when singled out, in accumulation make a person who s/he is, and who Mertkan is an emotionally retarded, abusive human being. Although there are brief moments of hope in his humanity, such as the moment when he tries to open up to his mother or in a sequence (likely to be a dream but not revealed for sure) where he cries when he hugs the taxi driver whose car he wrecked, these moments pass quickly.

A major truth in the film, and in real-life for that matter, is not that most people are like Mertkan in character but most people will, and do, exert power over another, when they have power. Director Yuce states in a number of different interviews that he wanted to criticize the Turkish society of which he is a member. His intention with the film was to look at the society through a family; to tell the majority's story and how discrimination is learned and normalized within the family. Hence Çoğunluk stands out as a brilliantly-executed film that poses very important questions for anyone who is concerned with rising inequality and discrimination among societies. However, all well-meaning social commentary runs the risk of being naive, and *Çoğunluk's* strength becomes its shortcoming as it lets everyone off the hook, particularly its audience, too easily.

The film received a number of awards at both national and international film festivals, including the prestigious Venice film Festival (Lion of the Future Award 2010) and the Antalya Film Festival (Best Film Award).

Özlem Köksal

Cogunluk/Majority, 2010, Esme Madra/Bartu Küçükçağlayan/Seren Yüce © Yeni Sinemacilar.

Mr Muhsin

Muhsin Bey

Studio:
Umut Film

Director:
Yavuz Turgul

Producer:
Abdurrahman Keskiner

Screenwriter:
Yavuz Turgul

Cinematographer:
Aytekin Çakmakçı

Synopsis

Muhsin Bey is a middle-aged man who enjoys Turkish classical music and is against arabesque music. Ali Nazik is a man with a passion for arabesque music, who moves from his village to the big city in the hope of becoming a singer. Muhsin Bey represents elitist values while Ali Nazik is representative of folk culture. Muhsin decides to finance the recording by the aspiring folk singer. Set in his ways, Muhsin is a conservative bachelor who delights in driving his car and listening to 78-RPM records, but he eventually falls in love with his neighbour and gives up his solitary lifestyle.

Critique

In 1980s' cinema, and in the context of depoliticization, film-makers focused on issues relating to individuality. This changed at the end of the 1990s, when civil society developed, freedom of opinion was strengthened, cinema started focusing on issues like urban life, and there was an increased interest in macro political issues as

Art Director:
Arzu Başaran

Composer:
Atilla Özdemiroğlu

Editor:
Demirhan Ersunar

Duration:
120 Minutes

Cast:
Şener Şen
Uğur Yücel
Sermin Hürmeriç

Year:
1987

well as economic and cultural conflicts as a result of urbanization. There were popular themes in films including rural-urban migration, people experiencing problems of urbanization, 'anomic urbanization', and the mundanity of city life. Cinema is a popular cultural domain which has represented aspects of all these issues. The most essential change affecting the relationship between the city, cinema and urbanization was the rapid development of a private sector, which is a consequence of Turkey's adoption of a liberal model. This development has resulted in the emergence of new social classes and the establishment of new values. Individualism has come to prominence, and the aims of individuals have been profit maximization in one's own interest, rather than demanding these advantages for others. The new perception of the aesthetics of the city has created new styles and sectors varying from music to fashion. In *Muhsin Bey*, the character Muhsin, portrayed with his admiration of classical Turkish music, reveals the temper of a modernized and elitist persona. At first, Muhsin rules over silent and humble Ali Nazik, who has just come to the city from a village. However, this is overturned and substituted by an inner expression 'I am coming out of my shell' as Ali Nazik experiences the sweet taste of money. The elitist Muhsin is left alone when his highly-cultured values are turned upside down. Muhsin's life style and cultural attitudes all go through a significant period of questioning and change with the arrival of Ali Nazik, who represents the patriarchal ideology and all that is not urban. Ali Nazik makes no effort to adapt to this urban life style. The film, in this way, problematizes the hierarchical relationship between the city and village; high culture and low culture, as well as the urban and uncivilised. These conflicts are neatly illustrated in a pivotal scene in the film, where Ali Nazik looks happy when getting a golden chain necklace and pink silk shirt, unable to resist the promises of consumer society and money, which becomes a code, a symbolic language to people like him. The film not only represents some of the crucial social and cultural changes that took place in the late 1980s, but also relays the message that those who cannot adjust to the modern urban life style, for whatever reason, refuse this urban life style by sheltering behind peasantry and creating their own sub-culture.

Aslı Kotaman

Mr Muhsin, 1987, Yavuz Turgul.

Seyyit Han: The Bride of the Soil

Seyyit Han: Toprağin Gelini

Studio:
Şeref Film

Director:
Yılmaz Güney

Producers:
Yaşar Tunalı
Abdurrahman Keskiner
Yılmaz Güney

Screenwriter:
Yılmaz Güney

Cinematographer:
Gani Turnalı

Composer:
Nedim Otyam

Editors:
Tahsin Demirand
Sezai Elmaskaya

Duration:
75 Minutes

Cast:
Yılmaz Güney
Hayati Hamzaoğlu
Nebahat Çehre

Year:
1968

Synopsis

Seyyit Han's friend Mursid refuses to let him marry his sister Keje, on the premise that Seyyit Han has too many enemies. He agrees to give him Keje's hand in marriage only if Seyyit Han can kill all his enemies. Seyyit Han sets out on a seven-year quest to finish them off. However, the day he victoriously returns to the village, he finds out that Keje is about to marry the landlord, Haydar. As it turns out, while he was away a rumour spread that Seyyit Han had been shot dead. Unable to resist the landlord's insistence, Mursid agrees to give Keje to the landlord against her will. In the hopes of putting a stop to the impending ceremonies, Seyyit Han visits Mursid, who claims that it is already too late to stop the wedding. Not dissuaded, Seyyit Han goes to talk to Keje directly. But before he has the opportunity, Mursid convinces Keje that cancelling the ceremonies would blight his honour. Keje sacrifices her love to uphold her brother's pride by telling Seyyit Han that marrying Haydar is her own will. On the wedding night, Haydar notices Keje's deep sorrow and decides to allow her to return to Seyyit Han, but not without evening the score. Haydar comes up with a plan, as a result of which he would not only save his reputation but also avenge Seyyit Han. On the morning of the wedding night, Haydar sends his servants to deliver the message that Keje wants to be with Seyyit Han. The servants catch Seyyit Han leaving the village. When he comes back he meets Haydar who says that he is indeed willing to give up Keje, but with one condition. There is an upside-down basket in the distance to which a camomile flower is attached. If Seyyit Han can shoot it in its yellow centre, he will earn Keje. Seyyit Han hits the target while Haydar rides away saying, 'You got Keje!' After a moment, Seyyit Han discovers that Keje is buried in the ground up to her neck. He hit the flower that was attached to the part of the basket directly in front of her head. In intolerable grief, Seyyit Han kills Haydar and his servants. In the end, Mursid, learning of Keje's death, fatally shoots Seyyit Han.

Critique

Seyyit Han is Güney's fourth film and the first one in which he demonstrated his own characteristic realist style. For Güney, the film is a manifesto against the Yeşilçam production system. *Seyyit Han* is difficult to categorize in any particular genre in Turkish cinema. Even though it takes place in a village, it uses innovative visual and narrative interventions to minimize the melodramatic elements prevalent in the melodramatic village genre. The film opens in front of a western-style saloon where Seyyit Han feeds his horse. Inside the saloon some shoot dice and one man is wearing a cowboy hat. This western saloon works successfully to differentiate Seyyit Han from various epic superhuman characters in the films against which Güney made this manifesto. The editing in the film also differentiates *Seyyit Han* from the other films of the period, in which the diegetic time unfolds in a linear fashion: here, the film starts in the middle of the story when Seyyit Han comes back from his seven-year quest. As the film progresses the pre-history of the quest is revealed little by little, and the beginning of the story superimposes the ending as voice-over. With its *verité* style, the wedding ceremony, which appears throughout the film, is somewhat detached from the main narrative. Throughout the wedding, depicted through a continuous long shot, Güney provides an authentic and ethnographically detailed account of a cultural process. Yet the process is integrated into the film through Seyyit Han's, Keje's and Haydar's subjective perceptions of the ceremony: Seyyit Han perceives the ceremony through its joyous music – as the music gets less audible, his sorrow grows deeper. Keje's extreme close-up, while she waits in the room for the groom, shows no emotion. The sound of the guns as part of the celebration make Haydar appear nervous as he prepares to meet Seyyit Han. On the excuse of the use of Kurdish names and ethnographic details from the Kurdish region, the film was banned by the board of censors and later passed on the condition that the film would not be shown outside Turkey.

Ali Fuat Şengül

The Angst

Endişe

Studio:
Güney Film

Directors:
Yılmaz Güney
Şerif Gören

Producers:
Yılmaz Güney
Süha Pelitözü

Screenwriter:
Yılmaz Güney

Cinematographer:
Kenan Ormanlar

Composers:
Şanar Yurdatapan
Atilla Özdemiroğlu

Duration:
85 Minutes

Cast:
Erkan Yücel

Synopsis

In order to earn enough to pay off a blood feud, Cevher goes to the cotton fields to work for the summer. If he works hard, by the end of the summer he will earn enough to cancel the blood feud and still have some left for the winter. While on the fields, Cevher's boss offers a substantial dowry to marry his daughter, Ayşe. Made distraught by the nightmares in which his blood enemies kill him, Cevher grows sympathetic to the offer. In the meantime, his hardship is complicated by the decision of the cotton workers to go on strike. When the boss refuses to pay the amount that he asks for, Cevher decides to break the strike, which positions him as an adversary among his workmates, who are unaware of his dilemma. At the end of the harvest season, the strike is still not resolved and Cevher fails to collect the amount to pay off the blood feud. His blood enemies arrive at the cotton field and claim his life in exchange for the debt.

Critique

Endişe was initially planned as a documentary account of cotton workers who migrate to the cotton fields in Adana every year for the entire summer and work under extreme conditions. The scenario is based on the three-month ethnographic research done by the assistant director Ali Özgentürk at Güney's request. By realistically representing the working conditions of the cotton workers, Güney aims to contribute to the intensifying workers' struggle of the period. However, at the very early stage of filming process, Güney was imprisoned and his assistant, Serif Goren, took

Kamran Usluer
Adem Tolay
Nizam Ergüden
Emel Mesci

Year:
1974

up the directing, which drastically changed the original premise of the film. Under Goren's direction, the film's focus changes from the workers' collective struggle to the personal struggle of Cevher who, having to pay the amount determined by the village council in exchange for his life in a blood feud, refuses to be a part of the workers' strike. However, despite this dramatic shift in the narrative, the documentary style remains an important aspect of the film. In order to sustain the documentary atmosphere, Goren successfully integrates the worker's mundane activities – fasting, praying, eating, and playing – to the narrative structure through a steady-cam wandering amongst the workers' tents. Another component of this documentary style is a radio set which stays on and audible throughout the film, informing the workers about the national and international events affecting their lives: the current crisis in the government, fluctuation in the international cotton ground prices, the Cyprus incident, etc.; all these embed the narrative into the socio-political conjuncture of the period. Radio, in the film, also functions as a link between diegetic space of the workers and the real space of the economy-politic of the cotton market. Perhaps sacrificing the initial class-based perspective on the conflict between workers and the employer, *Endişe* hints at another equally important conflict: the one between one's class position and tradition; Cevher's engagement in a blood feud prevents him from acting on his class position. *Endişe* received the 'best actor', 'the best original scenario', and 'the fest film' awards in that year's highly-controversial Antalya Film Festival, where the dissatisfied audience threw stones at the jury for their decision.

Ali Fuat Şengül

The Bus
Otobüs

Studios:
Pan Film
Hélios Films
Promete Film

Director:
Tunç Okan

Producers:
Tunç Okan
Jean-Louis Misar

Screenwriter:
Tunç Okan

Cinematographer:
Güneş Karabuda

Synopsis

A group of rural migrants leave the East of Turkey for Sweden in a bus, hoping for a better life. They have paid considerable amounts of money for the privilege. Leaving their Anatolian homeland for the first time, they discover that Stockholm is not quite the paradise they thought it might be. Left alone, unable to communicate with the outside world, and eventually abandoned by the bus-driver (who absconds with all their money), the illegal migrants undergo a series of humiliations. They see all the perversions of the western world – for example, a couple having sex in a phone booth. One of them is taken to a club, and picked up by a male prostitute. They are eventually forced to take refuge in their bus. As they sit frozen to death in an alien environment, one of them dreams of the life he left behind in the Anatolian fields.

Critique

Otobüs is very much a film of its time, depicting the experiences of many first-wave immigrants from Turkey to Europe. The significance of emigration for Okan's characters emerges early on in the

Composers:

Leon Françoli
Pierre Favre
Zülfü Livaneli

Duration:

91 Minutes
(Turkish release)

Cast:

Tunç Okan,
Tuncel Kartiz
Björn Gedda

Year:

1976

film, when the workers are still in Turkey and taking a break from their long bus journey. Okan cuts to a close-up of a bag of simple food – bread and cheese – and a disembodied hand taking it out of a paper bag and spreading it across a piece of newspaper. Okan subsequently cuts to the workers performing a folk dance by the fire, which is intercut with a shot of one of them squatting alone beside a lake. Both shots sum up the feelings of these migrants-to-be; they will try to hold on to their traditions, but at the same time they will experience feelings of great loneliness – or nostalgia for a past that can never be recovered.

It is a commonplace in film studies to identify the male gaze as symbolic of the unequal power relationships between men and women, as men seek to possess the object (particularly the female) they are looking at. *Otobüs* employs a similar logic by showing the workers gazing through shop windows in Stockholm at dummies modelling ladies' underwear. Okan also shows the Swedish citizens gazing at the Turks in similar fashion; clearly they would like to possess them – chiefly for sexual purposes. Having been bribed to come into a local club by the promise of food, one of the workers is treated as a sex object; the Swedish man tries to fondle him, while the other guests stare at him lasciviously, as if expecting him to perform a striptease. In such an environment it is not surprising that the Turk should react by leaping up off his chair and howling like a wild animal, a half-eaten chicken leg still in his right hand. The Swedes do not regard him as a person but as a plaything, providing as much sexual satisfaction for them as the sex film.

The migrants' sense of alienation from the host society is further emphasized in one of the film's most poignant sequences, as another Turkish worker gets lost in the Stockholm shopping centre and cannot find his way back to the bus (which in this film represents 'home' to the migrants, in the sense that it is the only thing symbolic of their homeland that they have left). In a series of hand-held camera shots, rendered deliberately jerky to emphasize the unnaturalness of the situation, we see the worker running round the deserted centre in an ever-more desperate attempt to find his friends. Okan cuts to an aerial shot, showing the worker as a black speck, resembling an ant desperately trying to crawl back into the wall. This is followed by a series of point-of-view shots of the camera swirling round the buildings; on the soundtrack his despairing cries for help can be heard. Suddenly a man walking a dog appears; in terror the Turkish man asks him where the bus is. The Swede, unable to understand what he says, picks up the dog and runs away into the rear of the frame. Okan repeats the sequence before dissolving to a shot of people's legs, as they walk to work. Clearly the Turk has had to stay out all night in a world where people take absolutely no notice of him; even when they do, they treat him as something to be feared, not as the pitiful wreck that he actually is.

Okan's film ends with a sequence that dramatizes the experiences of these unfortunate workers in a nutshell. It begins with a series of tracking shots, showing the bus being towed away from the square through the streets to the crusher. One shot, which shows the bus and the tow truck through the bars of an iron railing, perfectly sums up the Turks' pitiful existence; they are imprisoned in the bus, and about to be taken into custody by the Swedish police. The film's final shot shows the eyes of one of the Turks, looking to the right of the camera, which is followed by an aerial shot, held for some eight seconds or so, showing him being dragged away by the police. None of these unfortunate wretches have anything to look forward to, other than to be interrogated in an alien land, in an alien language, and subsequently face deportation. *Otobüs* was not filmed in Turkey at all, but in Sweden by Okan, who found that he could not raise the finance for the film at home. It is not just about Turks; it concerns anyone who feels ostracized for any reason within society.

Laurence Raw

The Law of the Borders

Hudutlarin Kanunu

Studio:
Dadaş Film

Director:
Ömer Lütfi Akad

Producer:
Kadir Kesman

Screenwriters:
L O Akad
Yılmaz Güney

Cinematographer:
Ali Uğur

Composers:
Nida Tüfekli
Mehmet Ali Karababa

Editor:
Ali Ün

Duration:
70 Minutes

Cast:
Yılmaz Güney
Pervin Par
Erol Taş

Synopsis

In an armed encounter with a gang of border smugglers, Lieutenant Sadri is murdered by a young smuggler, who, minutes later, falls prey to a soldier's bullet. This episode worsens the lot of the local merchants for whom smuggling is the primary source of livelihood. Zeki, the incoming lieutenant, increases border security, making smuggling even more dangerous for those who habitually transport goods across the heavily landmine-laden Syrian-Turkish border. After Ali Cello, one of the two main smugglers in town, refuses to transport his herd across the border, the rancher, Hasan Derviş, approaches Ali Cello's rival, Hıdır, the brother of the slain smuggler. Unlike Hıdır's companions, who want to immediately accept the offer, Hıdır rejects it after brief deliberation: Hasan has always worked with Ali Cello; this time he must have found the job too risky. There is one major difference between Hıdır and Ali Cello: Hıdır smuggles to escape poverty while, for Ali Cello, smuggling is a way to diversify his already lucrative business. This distinction affects their respective attitudes towards Lieutenant Zeki. Hıdır sides with the new lieutenant to counterbalance the pact between Ali Cello and the landlord Duran, who are trying to secure the economy of smuggling. Hıdır saves the Lieutenant's life when Ali Cello and Duran's men attempt to murder him. Appreciating Hıdır's help, the lieutenant engages himself in the betterment of the town, joining forces with an idealist primary school teacher, Ayşe. In an intimate conversation with Hıdır, Lieutenant Zeki promises him a job as a share-cropper on the uncultivated fields of the locality, and even succeeds in convincing Duran to let Hıdır and his family work on the fields. But Duran's motives are less than altruistic: having Hıdır and his siblings as sharecroppers, Duran now has the upper hand and forces them into smuggling. To ameliorate the dangers of smuggling, Hıdır hires a landmine remover, but the remover deceives Hıdır after receiving more money from Ali Cello. As Hıdır begins to transport the herd, the landmines explode one

Tuncel Kurtiz
Danyal Topatan
Osman Alyanak

Year:
1966

by one. After this ultimate betrayal, Hıdır kills both Ali Cello and Duran, and then escapes into the border ridden with landmines.

Critique

Based on a short story by Yılmaz Güney and directed by Lütfi Akad, *Hudutların Kanunu* is the first instalment of what later came to be known as the Anatolian Trilogy where the director set out to explore the socio-cultural life in different parts of rural Anatolia. The film takes place in Deliviran village located on the Turco-Syrian border and deals with some of the most debated issues of the period, like land reform, border smuggling, underdevelopment, and illiteracy. The film bears the mark of both Yılmaz Güney, who was intimately familiar with the socio-political realities of the region, and Akad who was a key figure in the 'social realist' movement of 1960s' Turkish cinema. With its realist representation of the region and the way it tackles the socio-economic problems, *Hudutların Kanunu* marks a turning point in the representation in the Turkish cinema of Kurdish South-East Anatolia, which had previously served only as an exotic background in the village melodramas, which gained popularity since 1950s. While the presence of a romantic relationship was fundamental to the village melodramatic genre, here the film develops and is resolved without romantic motivation. Due both to the censorship requirements and rising popularity of the state after the coup in 1960, in the films of this period, modernizing state representatives, like the army officer and the teacher, tended to be good natured and able to successfully solve the problems of rural Anatolia.. In contrast, representatives of the state, despite all good intentions, are proved powerless in *Hudutların Kanunu*. Like other films taking place in the region, feudal oppression plays a very important role in the narrative. In general, being oppressed becomes a psycho-social inclination of the people under oppression: the oppressed accepts his situation as the God's will. However, in *Hudutların Kanunu*, oppression results from social relations between the ruling class and the villagers and does not constitute a subject position.. The film was banned by the Censorship Board two times and finally passed on the condition that at the end of the film, Hıdır should tell his son that smuggling is a bad thing and he should return to school and avoid smuggling.

Ali Fuat Şengül

The Road

Yol

Studios:
Güney Film

Synopsis

Five prisoners, who are doing time for several reasons in İmralı Semi-Open Prison, are given a week's holiday. One of the prisoners, Seyit Ali, who has heard that his wife has been betraying him, takes the road to his village with the purpose of 'restoring his honour' for the sake of tradition. Upon arrival in his village, Seyit Ali finds out that his wife has been shut in a barn, so that he can

Cactus Film
Maran Film
Swiss Television

Director:

Şerif Gören

Producers:

Edi Hubschmid
Yılmaz Güney

Screenwriter:

Yılmaz Güney

Cinematographer:

Erdoğan Engin

Composers:

Sebastian Argol
Zülfü Livaneli

Editors:

Yılmaz Güney
Elisabeth Waelchli
Laura Montoya
Helene Arnal
Serge Guillemin

Duration:

108 Minutes

Cast:

Tarık Akan
Şerif Sezer
Halil Ergün
Meral Orhonsay

Year:

1982

kill her to 'cleanse' his 'honour'. He sets out on a journey with his wife on a cold and snowy day, with the hope that she freezes to death on the way. As Seyit Ali is not able to remain indifferent to his wife's suffering, he tries to help her but his efforts are fruitless. In the past, Mehmet Salih left his wounded brother-in-law behind during a robbery. His wife's family has not forgiven him, but he still loves her with passion. Despite her family's objections, the woman chooses to stay with her husband until she finally becomes the victim of the pressure of tradition; one day she and Mehmet Salih are both killed on a train. Mevlüt plans to spend the holiday with his fiancée; however, in the face of the heavy pressure and firm grip of the girl's family, he can never make his dreams come true. As Yusuf loses his permit, his journey ends before it begins and he cannot reunite with his wife, whom he misses very much. Ömer is determined not to return to jail. On the way back to his village, where people live off the fruits of smuggling, he is obliged to marry the widow of his brother who has lost his life in a mine field. A completely different life lies ahead of Ömer.

Critique

At the 1982 Cannes Film Festival, *Yol* (*The Way*) was granted the most prestigious award – the Golden Palm – and the panel was constituted of such names as Giorgio Strehler (Foreman), Gabriel Garcia Marquez, Geraldine Chaplin, Sidney Lumet, Mrinal Sen and Jean Jacques Annaud. The award was shared with *Missing* (Costa-Gavras). The film not only brought Turkey one of the most important awards of the history of cinema, but it also gained a special place in the history of cinema owing to the shooting process, which had been realized under difficult conditions, as well as the dispute between Yılmaz Güney and Şerif Gören with regards to the directing issues. In the literature, today, Şerif Gören's name is hardly mentioned and the film is widely referred to as a Yılmaz Güney film. Unfortunately, various screenwriters also fail to take into consideration the different professional approaches of the two directors during the shooting of the film, as well as the fact that Yılmaz Güney was in jail, and therefore was in no position to direct the film. Before Şerif Gören, Erdal Kıral started the shooting of *The Way*, which was written in prison by Yılmaz Güney under the title of 'Holiday'. The film, which was to be completed with a large cast and a big budget, would narrate the stories of eleven prisoners, who were on leave from a semi-open prison, through parallel editing. After seventeen days of shooting by Erden Kıral at Cunda Island, filming was stopped on the request of Yılmaz Güney and, from there on, the directing of the film was offered to Şerif Gören. Upon the completion of the shots, the reels were smuggled abroad and edited by a group of people under the leadership of Yılmaz Güney. Despite the award it received at the Cannes Film Festival, in Turkey the film did not come to the big screen for a considerable length of time. Finally, in 1999, it was presented to the Turkish audience. Permission was received for the release of the film only after the excision of the shots showing the Kurdistan border sign.

This film, which combines five different stories via dramatic parallel editing, is based on the idea that a person does not have to be in jail to be condemned – one can also be condemned outside the prison. The pressure of tradition, the despair arising from the socioeconomic conditions and the cruelty of life transform the outside world to a prison that is even more difficult than the real one. Within this concept, both freedom and captivity emerge as 'relative' issues, which take on a meaning on a spatial basis in line with the historical, social and psychological determinations. Especially when the production conditions are taken into consideration, we can see that one does not have to be closed in a cell to feel a captivate: the repressive, dark environment of the country can be felt in every frame of the film, as arising from the oppressive presence of the military government which came to power right after the 1980 coup d'état. The main factor which imprisons a society both within and outside the walls is the loss of the faith in freedom and trivialization of the freedom concept.

As a joint product of the film director Şerif Gören and the screenwriter Yılmaz Güney, and by virtue of both its cinematography and narrative structure, *The Way* must be considered as an important juncture in Şerif Gören's career. *The Way* bears various characteristics of Şerif Görren's cinematography; yet the director has treated the theme of social divisions in a manner that is rarely seen in the Turkish cinema. As Roy Armes (1981) has pointed out, *The Way* follows a tradition in Yılmaz Güney's scenarios written for *Sürü* (The Herd) and *Düşman* (The Enemy). Güney does not try to find solutions to the existing problems; his goal is to examine the paradoxes which lie within social structures. He unfolds the terrible disruptions created by the military government following the 1980 coup d'état in the daily life of the community, and in a social environment which aims at modernization, on one hand, but which is overwhelmed by feudality on the other.

The paradoxical nature of the characters is reflective of the paradoxes within the social structure. For this reason, the people encounter impassable 'ways' at every step they make. Gören planned to finish the film with a scene showing a train emerging into the daylight from the obscurity of fog to emphasize that, despite all obstructions, there is a hope. However, Güney did not use this scene; instead the image of the train disappearing on the screen is preferred. In fact, this is a more realistic ending for the last Güney film depicting Turkey's situation in those years. The film narrates how the oppression created by the military and the new rules implemented by the coup d'état added immense heavy pressure to the existing feudal rules and traditions. It also explores the difficulty of finding a way out. In 1982, at the Cannes Film Festival, the film received the Ecumenic Jury Award together with the Golden Palm and, in 1983, it received the Best Foreign Film Award of the French Syndicate of Cinema Critics.

Ali Karadoğan

Yol, 1982, Tarik Akan/Şerif Sezer/Yılmaz Güney © Güney Film/Cactus Film.

The Small Town

Kasaba

Studio:
NBC Films

Director:
Nuri Bilge Ceylan

Producer:
Nuri Bilge Ceylan Films

Screenwriters:
Nuri Bilge Ceylan
Emine Ceylan

Cinematographer:
Nuri Bilge Ceylan

Synopsis

Focusing on the relationships between the three generations of a family living in Western Turkey, *Kasaba* (*The Small Town*) consists of three parts. The first part is an ordinary snowy winter day in a primary school. In a classroom where students of different grades study in the same room, the day starts with a poem that students recite everyday. The teacher comes in and calls the roll and makes one of the students read the subject of that day's lesson from the book. Ismail, late for school, comes in and hangs his wet socks on the line attached on the stove in the class. A smell the teacher senses makes him check the students' lunch-boxes while they are carrying on reading and he sees that the food in 11-year-old Asiye's lunch-box is rotten. The second part is about an excursion Asiye and her brother Ali make in nature on the way back from school. Asiye and Ali walk in the forest, eat fruit, come across with a turtle and a donkey, and they can hear that the hunters are busy hunting nearby. The third part is about a night that Ali and Asiye spend with their parents, grandma, grandpa and their elder cousin Saffet in the field. Family members tell each other what they have been

Editors:

Ayhan Ergürsel
Nuri Bilge Ceylan

Duration:

82 Minutes

Cast:

Mehmet Emin Toprak
Havva Sağlam
Cihat Bütün
Fatma Ceylan
Mehmet Emin Ceylan

Year:

1997

through, what they witnessed, their experiences and sorrows in the recent and distant past; sometimes they have a row, shout and accuse each other. Ali and Asiye fall asleep and have dreams.

Critique

Kasaba is Ceylan's first film, mostly starring his family members. It is regarded as a minimalist film, looking at the nature and the world of grown-ups from a child's point of view. The film opens with some keywords associated with the phrase 'small town' (kasaba) including monotony, boredom, oppression, oppressive ethical codes, peace, quiet, nostalgia, childhood, serenity, past, loneliness, close encounters, small business owners, sincerity, market place, scorching heat in the afternoon, motorbikes spoiling the quiet – thus introducing the audience to the small town's universe of meaning. The film uses a non-linear narrative structure. This is as result of an attempt to represent the sense of being a child and, therefore, offering a perception of time and space through the perspective of a child. The concept of time looks different from that of the capitalist western world; the time of life is so dependant on nature that even the days of the week are not differentiated.

The story of the small town, which has a deep impact and special place for the director's real life, is told in three parts. In the first part, we get a sense of a place which is 'routine' and yet bizarrely 'peaceful' at the same time: a sense of indefinite time. The school sequence demonstrates the clash between a child's innocence and imagination and formal education. Ceylan builds up his narration by focusing on the details within a monotonous time cycle. A good example of this can be seen in the camera movement focusing on the sounds and images of water dripping from the socks of İsmail who is late for school. The scene is shot in real time and we are expected to take in images and sounds offered at a slow pace.

In the second part, the focus is on nature and relationships between people and nature, but, again, from the children's point of view. The director implies that the passage from childhood to adulthood is made through domination over nature. The director promotes an ecological viewpoint through the shots from a donkey's perspective and an upside-down turtle's gaze. The third part consists of the conversations between the family members gathered around the fire about life, work and knowledge. *Kasaba* is returning-home story that questions the sense of belonging but does not give a clear answer concerning the question of where the home is. The turtle found by the kids in the forest, carrying its home on its back – therefore being a homeless traveller – is used as a metaphor of home and belonging throughout the film. 'The turtle is both Nuri the local, who goes back to his home town despite having been abroad for studying, and Saffet, the homeless traveller, who does not want to spend his youth in the town and yet cannot help feeling a belonging to it; the turtle is a sign where the themes of leaving and staying intersect (Akbulut 2006: 70-1). The turtle turned upside down by Ali and put down on its feet by Asiye again is also related to the concept of conscience. Ali's dream, in which his mother falls from the window like the turtle, points at the feeling of guilt in the development of conscience.

Individuality, simplicity and clarity defining Ceylan's cinema is, in this film, related to childhood intertwined with nature. In fact, the film can be described as pastoral because of its narration and structure. Its three sub-divisions all convey the purity and naivety of Ceylan's perception of his hometown and the comparison between culture and nature. Overall, the film has a philosophical and anthropological look on life: human beings, knowledge, culture and death.

Hasan Akbulut

Three Monkeys

Üç Maymun

Studios:
Zeynofilm
NBC Film

Director:
Nuri Bilge Ceylan

Producer:
Zeynep Özbatur

Screenwriters:
Ebru Ceylan
Ercan Kesal
Nuri Bilge Ceylan

Cinematographer:
Gökhan Tiryaki

Art Director:
Ebru Ceylan

Editors:
Ayhan Ergüsel
Bora Göksingol
Nuri Bilge Ceylan

Duration:
109 Minutes

Cast:
Yavuz Bingöl
Hatice Aslan
Ahmet Rifat Şungar
Ercan Kesal

Year:
2008

Synopsis

Driving home late one night on a deserted road, an aspiring politician hits a man. Leaving the body in the middle of the road, he drives on. Elections are approaching and, desperate to advance his career, he enlists his driver, a quiet family man, to take the blame for the accident and go to prison on his behalf. Servet promises Eyüp a pay-out on release but, while he is incarcerated, Eyüp's wife and son take the payment as an advance, triggering a series of incidents with devastating consequences. A stark depiction of class divides and personal dissatisfaction, Three Monkeys presents us with an image of İstanbul that is neither picturesque nor easy to live in. While Eyüp is literally imprisoned, his wife and son are trapped by the frustration of being unable to envisage a more comfortable future. Their lives follow a rhythm of monotonous, unceasing desperation, marked by moments of violence that do little to alleviate the oppressive sadness. Small pockets of exhilaration – a party, the beginning of an affair – are quickly erased by the grinding reality of a world without opportunity. There is no release in sight, and the film closes with a thunderstorm that mirrors the internal explosion that will surely come.

Critique

Winning Ceylan the award for best director at the 2008 Cannes Film Festival, Three Monkeys divided its critics. For some it was a masterpiece, while others dismissed it as a slick and superficial digital extravaganza. It is certainly a flawed work, building on Ceylan's previous films visually and thematically, but stumbling backwards over its clunky, moralistic plot. The overt religious and historical allusions are heavy handed, cutting out the subtle humour that made Distant (2002) and Climates (2006) so watchable. The storyline of Three Monkeys plays like a television melodrama – infidelity, vengeance and class dynamics all get a look in. A kinder critic might read this as a nod to Yeşilçam's hyper-real plotlines but, here, they are mashed together so forcefully that even Ceylan's bold editing cannot hide the clumsy construction of the film's framework. When Eyüp imitates Servet, and asks a poor

Armenian waiter to take the punishment for his son's crime, the mirroring feels contrived. For viewers who loved the open endings – or are they beginnings? – of Climates and Distant, the denouement of Three Monkeys is disappointing. Ceylan tries to recapture a sense of possibility in the last long shot of Eyüp standing on the terrace engulfed in rain, but by then it is too late – the feeling of anything goes has already been lost. But beyond its plot the film is a remarkable one. Ceylan's ability to express whole worlds in a single image results in a set of shots as complete as photographs. Like its predecessor, Climates, Three Monkeys is a digital film but, while the former maintained a naturalistic aesthetic, in Three Monkeys Ceylan embraces the possibilities of digital post-production, adjusting the colour and lighting for expressionistic effect. White walls turn a sallow yellow and reds pop like blood bursts. Seen from the window of Eyüp's modest apartment, the water is a glittering azure. Not only does the stark colour put the characters in an uncomfortable physical space that reflects their emotional nausea, it also gestures toward the awkward position the family occupies in Turkey's shifting class structure. Neither desperately poor nor comfortably rich, they struggle to find satisfaction. Ismail (Ahmet Rifat Şungar) finds a job, but has no car to do it, Hacer's (Hatice Aslan) work in a large commercial kitchen contrasts with the life of Servet's stay at home wife. At times the characters seem almost swallowed up by the act of commuting – the family lives a long way from the city hub – disappearing into the densely latticed shadow as they march daily under the train overpass. In all of his films Ceylan has played with structure and in Three Monkeys the experimental editing emphasizes the unease. At times the sounds overlap, and the sound of one shot bleeds into the next. A phone rings unanswered in Eyüp's apartment for an uncomfortably long time, only to be picked up in the next shot in Servet's office. Servet and Hacer take a car ride that seems to be taking place both in the past and the future, the present time conversation punctuated by moments of voice-over that might be thoughts, or might be snippets from future conversations. Furthermore, the image shifts fluidly in and out of normal speed and slow motion.

There are more temporal shocks when a long-dead son makes an appearance. Wet, blue and wide-eyed, this ghost child punctuates the film with a force that is stunningly affective. Ceylan has brought the strangeness of the otherworldly into his films before, often cutting dream sequences into the course of the action so swiftly that it takes a while to catch up. In Three Monkeys the ghost joins the family as if alive, but Ceylan sets up the cuts so that his appearances come as a shock. The first time, he is seen as a blurry shadow creeping forwards through a patch of light. Later, his arm flops over Eyüp's shoulder in an eerie and strangely heartbreaking gesture of comfort. Here, Ceylan succeeds where so many horror films do not – he elicits a moment of genuine hair-raising surprise from the audience, and the tension that builds in between these scenes adds to the sense of alarm. The success of these ghostly apparitions is Three Monkey's triumph, and the sadness that the dead child evokes in his living family affirms that, beneath the dazzling surface, it is film with real heart.

Sarinah Masukor

To Go: My Marlon and Brando

Gitmek

Studio:
Asi Film

Director:
Hüseyin Karabey

Producer:
Hüseyin Karabey

Screenwriter:
Ayça Damgacı
Hüseyin Karabey

Cinematographer:
Emre Tanyıldız

Art Director:
Alper Yanar

Composers:
Kemal Sahir Gürel
Erdal Güney
Hüseyin Yıldız

Editor:
Mary Stephan

Duration:
93 Minutes

Cast:
Ayça Damgacı
Hama Ali Khan
Volga Sorgu

Year:
2008

Synopsis

Gitmek (To Go: My Marlon and Brando) is Hüseyin Karabey's first feature film after a number of short films and political documentaries. The film is based on the true story of a young Turkish woman, Ayça Damgacı, who fell in love with an Iraqi Kurd, Hama Ali. They meet during a film shoot in İstanbul and fall in love. Both Ayça and Hama Ali were working as actors at the time and are acting as themselves in Karabey's film as well. When his time in İstanbul comes to an end, Hama Ali goes back to Iraq and their relationship continues over the phone, as well as in letters they send to each other. Although Hama Ali promises to come back to İstanbul for her, a year later, in 2003, Iraq is invaded by The United States of America, making it impossible to travel to and from the region. As the situation in Iraq deteriorates (even to have a basic telephone conversation becomes impossible), Ayça runs out of patience and starts looking for ways to go to Northern Iraq herself. The film follows her journey as she travels from border to border, trying to find a way to meet her lover.

Critique

Shot on location, *Gitmek* is an unconventional love story in many ways, not only because a journey from west to east takes place voluntarily but also because the journey is undertaken by a woman. The film crosses physical borders and also formal borders, combining documentary techniques with fiction. The opening sequence, for instance, is from the making of the film, shot by a hand-held camera in an open field. The director's voice is audible at the background giving orders to the film crew, while Ayça is getting ready for the scene. The scene creates complex temporal and spatial relations as three different temporalities are intertwined together: the time of the initial event (the journey that was taken by Ayca herself prior to the film), the representation of it (making of the film) and the represented event, the work itself. By opening his film with this footage, Karabey twists the distinction between these different chronotopes (per Bakhtin). He opens the film by making these different temporalities visible to the audience, rather than rendering them invisible.

However, this is not only an aesthetic choice but also a choice that is determined by the social and political conditions in the region, particularly with regards to the scenes in Eastern Turkey, an area which is predominantly populated by Kurds. Karabey explains that he combines documentary and fiction in order to be as explicit as possible about the reality of the region. When Ayça arrives at a Kurdish village, in which the bus she is travelling in stops for a few hours, she joins in a wedding celebration that is later disrupted by security forces who ask that it ends. Karabey, instead of creating the scene, filmed a real wedding as it happened as well as its disruption by security forces. Similarly Ayça's encounter with the Turkish border police (as Ayça enquires about the possibility of crossing the border) and the evacuated village (a grim fact of life in the region, mainly due to the clashes between the Turkish armed forces and Kurdish militants) were filmed on location, with no manipulation, without 'enhancing' the reality or changing its 'look'. Karabey says that he could have reconstructed these scenes, rather than waiting for them to 'really' happen, as it would not change the fact that they do happen. But, he did not 'want to allow a space for arguing that it does not happen and that [he was] misleading the audience.'

However, perhaps the most noteworthy aspect of the film is how it deals with narrative time. Karabey relies predominantly on epistolary form to tell its story, using video letters and telephone conversations to narrate the story. Throughout the film we watch Hama Ali's video letters to Ayça, and hear Ayça's letters to Hama Ali in her voice as diary entries. Even though we never see the couple in the same frame, and indeed in the same temporality, Karabey creates a simultaneous dialogue between the two characters using letters and telephone conversations. As the video letters are played, the director cuts to Ayça who is speaking on the phone or writing a letter, as if these acts (the time of the video letter and the time of the telephone conversation) are in the same temporality: an illusion of conversation is created through editing as the director arranges Ayça's answers in a way to form a meaningful conversation with Hama Ali's video letters. Such use of letters not only creates an illusion of presence, the epistolary narrative problematizes geography and territory, creating a certain time-lag between the characters and, therefore, within the narrative.

There are five video letters in the film and each one, with the exception of the very last letter, contains excerpts from the, somewhat absurd, films in which Hama Ali had acted in Iraq, giving the text a self-reflexive quality. Although the letters help Karabey capture the story, they do not solely function to serve the flow of the plot. The director, playing with the belated nature of letters and hence with the notion of linear time, challenges the language of progressive time by means of dislocating it. In his very last video letter, Hama Ali records his attempt to cross the Iraqi border to Iran to meet Ayça, who is waiting for him there. As he is speaking to the camera, an unknown source fires a shot and kills him. This last letter forms the last scene of the film and, within the diegetic time, takes place while Ayça is waiting for Hama Ali. However, this time, we 'read' the letter before Ayça does. The problem of the belated nature of the letters becomes most visible with this scene, as Hama Ali haunts the narrative with his video letter. His camera, functioning as an extension of his vision, continues recording even after he is shot dead.

Gitmek, although acknowledging the confined geographical and discursive space, focuses on the possibility of action, of going away and breaking away. This is due to the discursive space that is created as a result of the political changes that took (and continue to take) place in political, social and economic life in Turkey. However, it should also be noted here that films such as *Gitmek* are also the result of changing technological conditions that make the access to the industry relatively easy. *Gitmek* was shot digitally, making the production process considerably cheaper than 35mm film. With an ethical use of camera (never going too close to a scene of pain or intimacy), its non-judgemental approach towards its characters (never dismissing Ayça even when she displays the utmost ignorance about how the other half lives, exemplified by her reaction to the conditions under which the illegal immigrant Soran has to live), *Gitmek*, was one of the most refreshing first films made within the last decade in Turkey and one of the best, if not the best, films made in 2008 in the country.

Özlem Köksal

To Go: My Marlon and Brando, 2008, Hüseyin Karabey.

TRANSNATIONAL
CINEMA

'I come from this European auteur thing … I'm producing the stuff I'm doing, I'm writing the stuff I'm doing, I'm directing the stuff I'm doing. In the end it's me on the front line …' (Fatih Akın 2008)

Transnational cinema has proved itself to be a contentious term that is relatively fluid in definition. Often used as an antithesis to the concept of national cinema, it has proven equally, if not more, difficult a term to conceptualize. Transnationalism is a term bandied about when discussing contemporary cosmopolitan films, particularly those from European countries, which often include international casts and/or directors. Turkish cinema, as with that of most countries, has reflected an awareness of the lucrative global market by moving away from the insular films of yesteryear. It could be considered that Turkey, as a country, faces themes of transnationalism within in its culture: as a country it borders Europe and the Middle East and herein is a cause of the belonging and identity themes that are woven throughout the films; the country's reconciliation between modern European attitudes with generations of Islamic traditions is one of the interesting and unique causes of these themes.

Fatih Akın is a Turkish-German (for want of a better term). Born to Turkish parents in Germany, his heritage has been influential on his works, which are considered as examples of transnational cinema. Akın's works fits within the concept of cosmopolitan transnationalism in that he obtains a unique perspective from his knowledge of the Turkish culture, but viewed objectively from afar with the experience of growing up in another culture. His films such as *Head-On/Gegen die Wand* (2004), In *July/Im Juli* (2000) and most recently *Soul Kitchen* (2009) include casts of German, Turkish and Greek nationalities, or at least parentage, and the funding is often obtained from more than one country. Often the characters' heritage serves as an integral facet of the plot which adds depth to the character through an empathy brought on by the anticipated problematic adjustment of adapting to an exilic life.

Ferzan Özpetek left Turkey to study film in Italy and has made almost all of his films in Italy. He has written and directed all of his films, starting with *Hamam: The Turkish Bath* in 1997. Özpetek's body of work is an example of transnational cinema, with actors of different nationalities, and the storylines, while distinctly European, could be transferred

Left image: *Auf Der Anderen Seite*, 2007, Nurgul Yesilcay/Patrycia Ziolkowska, Fatih Akin © Anka Film/ Dorje Film.

to any country. His films certainly sit within Hamid Naficy's well-known phrase 'accented cinema', a reworking of transnational cinema, defined as work that 'cuts across previously defined geographic, national, cultural, cinematic and metacinematic boundaries' (Naficy 2006: 363). Certainly, in his more recent films, even the Turkish characters speak Italian and are unburdened by issues that are common in characters from Turkish films, or other nationalities for that matter. Many of Özpetek's recent works have been successfully released in America despite their Italian language and depictions of overt homosexuality. It is difficult to consider theories around transnationalism, particularly when discussing directors, without relying on authorship as a key central point of analysis. As Asuman Suner points out when a director in exile uses their exilic experience within their films that this is an extension of authorship theory in that it provides an identifiable 'fingerprint' on their work (Suner 2006: 365). This idea is easily applicable to Özpetek's work in that a recurring theme in his work is that of the extended family. Certainly the plots of *The Ignorant Fairies/Le Fate Ignoranti* (2001) and *Saturn in Opposition/Saturno Contro* (2007) are centred on groups of disparate characters whose familial links are broken and choose to surround themselves with unrelated people who act as family. As with *Sacred Heart/Cuore Sacro* (2005), The *Facing Window/La Finestra di Fronte* (2003), *The Ignorant Fairies* and *Saturn in Opposition*, the death of a pivotal character is explored and the reverberations within this substitute familial circle are played out. The exilic theme is further highlighted with the casting of Turkish actress Serra Yılmaz in most of his films. Her character often assumes the role of the Turk living in Italy, drawing inevitable comparisons with the personal experiences of Özpetek.

Some of Özpetek's and Akın's films have similarities in that they deal with the issues of identity and revealing it. Both consider the culturally-different divides that are apparent in people, often family members, from different generations. Both directors have experience of Turkey as well as the country that they are living in and in many ways this feeds into their works. Özpetek draws upon the familial similarities from the Italian culture to the Turkish culture in tackling the issues of identity, through re-establishing it, or being open with it in terms of sexuality. Akın takes a different stance in that his characters are made all the richer for having diverse backgrounds. Rather than resorting to the idea and status of a foreigner abroad, his films deal, not always overtly, with the deeper emotional impact that comes from cultural merging. Whatever definition is used, both Akın and Özpetek's films make interesting examples of transnational cinema. Their unique cultural backgrounds, combined with the integration within another culture, have provided a truly fascinating 'fingerprint' on their works. It is therefore the aim of this section to look in detail to some of their films.

Robert Manning

Notes

1 Nacify, H. cited in Suner, A., 'Outside in: "accented cinema" at large', *Inter-Asia Cultural Studies*, Vol. 7, No. 3, 2006.

Edge of Heaven

Cennetin Kıyısında

Studio:

Corazón International

Director:

Fatih Akın

Producers:

Fatih Akın
Klaus Maeck
Andreas Thiel

Screenwriter:

Fatih Akın

Cinematographer:

Rainer Klausmann

Art Director:

Seth Turner

Composer:

Shantel

Editor:

Andrew Bird

Duration:

122 Minutes

Cast:

Nurgül Yeşilçay
Baki Davrak
Tuncel Kurtiz
Hanna Schygulla
Patrycia Ziolkowska

Year:

2007

Synopsis

Ali is a retired widower who lives in Germany. He meets a fellow Turkish native, Yeter, and proposes that she lives with him in exchange for a monthly stipend. Yeter, who has worked as a prosti-tute until then, gives up her job. Ali's son Nejat, who is a lecturer at a German university, does not approve of his father's choice, until he finds out more about Yeter and discovers that her hard-earned money is sent home to Turkey for her daughter's university studies. Yeter dies after being hit by Ali. Seeing the violence caused by his father and in an attempt to search for Yeter's daughter, Ayten, Nejat travels to İstanbul. He decides to stay in Turkey until he finds her and takes over the management of a bookstore. Nejat does not know that Ayten is a young political activist who has already gone to Germany to find her mother and to run away from the Turkish police. Ayten is befriended by German student Lotte, who invites Ayten to stay in her home. Lotte's mother Susanne does not warm to Ayten; she particularly does not agree with her daughter having a relationship with another woman. Ayten gets arrested and is confined for months while awaiting political asylum. When her plea is denied, she is deported and imprisoned in Turkey. Lotte fol-lows her and goes to Turkey to help and, by chance, meets Nejat in the bookstore. Walking in one of the back streets in İstanbul, she is robbed. As she is running after the robbers, she is shot to death. Finding out about the loss of her daughter, Susanne travels to Turkey and helps fulfil her daughter's mission – to save Ayten. Witnessing all this, Nejat is inspired to seek out his father, now residing in a village in the Black Sea coast in northern Turkey.

Critique

Fatih Akın's *Edge of Heaven* provides substantial material for defining the parameters of diasporic cinema within an evolv-ing cross-cultural context. It is transnational in terms of its mode of production as a film produced by Germany, co-produced by Turkey; and in association with Italy. The film also carries all the traits necessary to be considered under the concept of accented cinema. There are different accents and different languages in the literal sense. There are different journeys and characters are almost constantly in transit, either physically or emotionally. The thematic content of *Edge of Heaven* particularly invites consideration for the contours of national and cultural production that takes shape in confrontation with various forms of identity. Spread between four different towns in two countries, the film focuses on the ten-sion between Germany and Turkey, cultural division between two cultures, and the tension between the first- and second-generation Turkish-Germans, conflicted about their identity and belonging. The film has the capacity to represent different positions – German, Turkish and bicultural, bilingual – in relation to the ultimately discur-sive and therefore continually contested nature of identity (includ-ing sexual, political, ethnic and religious transgressions). *Edge of*

Heaven calls for an exploration of the conflicts and relationship between representation and the represented; cultural production and the world in which such production takes place. In representing identity politics, the film reveals aspects of the moral, cultural, political and ethnic fabric of the German-Turkish connection. The film, indeed, proves significant as a text that offers the miniaturized version of subcultures in German (and Turkish) society.

Eylem Atakav

Head-On

Gegen die Wand

Studio:

Arte Bavaria Film International
Corazón International
Norddeutscher Rundfunk
Panfilm
Wüste Filmproduktion

Director:

Fatih Akın

Producers:

Stefan Schubert
Ralph Schwingel

Screenwriter:

Fatih Akın

Cinematographer:

Rainer Klausmann

Art Directors:

Sırma Bradley
Nergis Çalışkan

Composers:

Alexander Hacke
Maceo Parker

Editor:

Andrew Bird

Duration:

121 Minutes

Cast:

Birol Ünel
Sibel Kekilli

Synopsis

Widowed and suicidal, Cahit enters into a marriage of convenience with Sibel, a woman he meets at a rehabilitation clinic. Sibel had tried to kill herself to escape her overbearing family. What starts out as an arrangement soon becomes something more when Cahit starts to fall in love with Sibel. Sibel enters into a number of relationships, one being with Niko. In a rage, Cahit accidentally kills Niko and begins a prison term, with Sibel realizing her feelings too and agreeing to wait for him. Having been disowned by her family after news of her promiscuity and Cahit's prison sentence hits the headlines, Sibel goes to live with her cousin in Turkey. Soon Sibel begins a trail of self destruction. She transforms her image and abuses drugs and alcohol; on one such binge she is raped and then picks a fight with a group of men and is left for dead. Upon his release from prison Cahit goes to İstanbul to find Sibel, who now has a boyfriend and child. Sibel agrees to flee to Mersin, Cahit's hometown, with him, but finds herself unable to leave her new family.

Critique

Head-On is the fourth feature by director Fatih Akın. *Head-On* interestingly portrays the issues surrounding second generation immigrants and the crisis of identity faced with living in a culturally-different society from one where familial ideals are thrust upon them. Cahit is an immigrant who has unremorsefully lost touch with Turkish culture. At one point Sibel's brother says to him 'Your Turkish sucks. What did you do with it?' Cahit responds 'I threw it away'; showing his lack of respect for the language and the country. However, after his journey from being suicidal and desperate and leaving prison to find Sibel, the place he wants to return to is his home town of Mersin. These sentiments are reflected in Sibel's journey too: Sibel would rather die than lead the life chosen for her by her parents. Interestingly she exploits the cultural difference: in one instance she rejects the advances of a man she has led on by saying that her husband will kill him if he does not leave her alone. Without a direct reference to 'honour' killings, it does show the lawlessness of some family ties. Sibel, in Germany can use her Turkishness to advantage over men. In Turkey, however, she finds a

Catrin Striebeck
Meltem Cumbul

Year:

2004

different scenario. She is raped and also beaten and stabbed with no punishment appearing (on screen at least) for the perpetrators (all men).

Turkish men are portrayed particularly negatively in *Head-On*. Cahit himself is portrayed as unpredictable and prone to violence. Sibel's male family members are shown to be traditional to the extreme where they disown her because of an affair, and they will not let her leave the family home unless married, driving her to a suicide attempt; and her brother beats her for holding hands with another man. In İstanbul the aforementioned rape and stabbing happens at the hands of Turkish men. The film, as found in many examples of transnational cinema, presents the problems arising from a clash of cultures caused by a duality of nationalities. Many of the main characters are Turkish yet, at the same time, German and, in a way, this leads to them being neither, This creates a great deal of hostility throughout the films in terms of expectations based on culture. In fact, the female characters other than Sibel are shown to be less problematic than their male counterparts. Both Cahit's lover and Sibel's cousin are independent women with decent careers; her cousin is divorced and the other uses Cahit when she want sex. Both are shown to be independent without the need for a permanent man in their lives.

Ironically, considering Sibel's rebellion against the Turkish expectations and Cahit's neglect of his Turkish roots, the film ends with Sibel and Cahit in Turkey. The freedom provided by Germany caused more problems than the culture that they escaped from and, although the film is open-ended, they both seem to have found peace by embracing their roots. Sibel's struggle with finding her identity takes her through a complex transition: from using her femininity and ethnicity to trying to hide it when she cuts her hair into a less-feminine style. In Germany she is unique and exotic. In Turkey she is not. Sibel and Cahit make an unlikely pairing and their chance meeting spins their lives off in totally different directions, but ultimately for the better. Sibel has escaped her familial ties, and Cahit, who had found freedom in Germany – perhaps too much freedom that he was unprepared for – seemed calmer back in Turkey after his years away.

Overall, the film evokes a kind of urgency for the characters to find themselves and happiness, and shows the impact of people who enter their lives for a short time and the hypocrisy of cultural facades that people adhere to. In some ways it is critical of the façade provided by the expectations of a 'good' Muslim. In one particularly resonant scene the husbands show respect for their wives, yet at the same time talk about visiting brothels. To their families they are the dutiful husband, yet to their friends they expose the reality. This pretence is mirrored in Sibel's marriage: Sibel marries Cahit to please her family and the subsequent consequences reinforce that those who marry for the wrong reasons find themselves in something much worse.

Robert Manning

Head-On, 2004, Fatih Akın © NDR/Panfilm.

Loose Cannons

Mine Vaganti

Studio:
Fandango and Rai Cinema

Director:
Ferzan Özpetek

Producer:
Domenico Procacci

Screenwriters:
Ivan Cotroneo
Ferzan Özpetek

Cinematographer:
Maurizio Calvesi

Art Director:
Carlo Rescigno

Composer:
Pasquale Catalano

Synopsis

Tommaso Cantone has returned to his family home to reveal his sexuality to his family over dinner and, thus, using it to separate his life from theirs. He intends to return to his male lover in Rome to pursue his desire to become a writer rather than taking over the family pasta business. Sharing his intentions with his brother Antonio before the dinner, Antonio pre-empts his announcement by dropping his own bombshell at the family dinner, causing his father to have a heart attack. Tommaso, to protect his father from further stress, decides to remain in the family business and continue to hide his sexuality. Keen to see Tommaso, his boyfriend Marco visits with his flamboyant gay friends, which sets into motion many re-evaluations which culminate in Tammaso's grandmother, the titular 'loose cannon' taking the ultimate action to lead to happiness for the family.

Critique

Ferzan Özpetek's *Loose Cannons* plays like a soap opera with its melodramatic twists in the plot and the uncomfortable dysfunctional familial dinners, which Özpetek stages so well, bringing tensions to a head with a neatly-formed resolution. In the film, Özpetek highlights the generational divides created through

Editor:

Patrizio Marone

Duration:

110 Minutes

Cast:

Riccardo Scamarcio
Carmine Recano
Alessandro Preziosi
Ennio Fantastichini
Lunetta Savino

Year:

2010

expectations and personal fulfilment. Tommaso sees his hidden homosexuality as big an issue, as his hidden career choice; both, he feel will disappoint his family and alienate him from them. This particular plotline is mirrored by his grandmother's own choice to follow her head rather than her heart on her wedding day decades earlier. In spite of the soap-opera style resolution, there are enough minor characters with their own agendas to raise the film to one of Özpetek's best. The burgeoning relationship between Tommaso and Alba certainly raises the question of how far he is prepared to go to keep his family happy. Following Özpetek's films, it is apparent that they have become slicker as time progresses.

Özpetek alternates between comedies and the deeper dramas and his latest film fits nicely as a trilogy with The Ignorant Fairies/ Le Fate Ignoranti (2001) and Saturn in Opposition/Saturno Contro (2007), which both have a similar assortment of misfit characters with problematic lives. In all three, it takes the death of a loved one to bring the people together to realize that there is so much more to people than the paths they take in life and how priorities can be lost in leading a duty-bound life. The distinct Mediterranean setting, characters and sentiments take a light-hearted look at the family ties and the issues that pass from generation to generation. Indeed, all of the characters in the Cantone family are keeping up appearances to conceal a façade to present to their family; the father's main concern is what other people will think of his son being gay, rather than his own personal thoughts; the aunt is hiding a secret lover; the mother is in denial of what is happening; and the grandmother has a secret from years before. The two sons conceal their sexuality and lack of interest in taking over the family business. Tommaso's adulterous father is the character who has least to hide, but buckles under the secrets of others. Yet, he is the least sympathetic of all the characters. He symbolizes the values of a bygone era, perhaps less bygone in southern Europe and Turkey but still a vestige of the past, where family and societal expectations are adhered to. The clash that the younger generation causes by daring to be their own person are played out beautifully in Özpetek's film. By maintaining the comedic tone, the actions can be exaggerated and perhaps the boundaries pushed further than an equivalent dramatic film might be allowed to. Özpetek's Almodovar-esque style enables the film to remain in the mainstream without being banished to the unnecessary 'gay film' label and, with this positioning, the theme of 'concealment of the true self' can be applied to all members of a highly-conservative society whatever their orientation.

The arrival of Tommaso's friends from Rome signifies a crossroads in the protagonist's journey. Once wanting to escape at all costs, Tommaso had settled quite easily into his new life of pretence and this is unsettled by his being faced with his immediate past in the same way that his father was unsettled by being faced with the future. This is reflected perfectly in the dream-like sequence following the grandmother's funeral in which past and present unite in a harmonious party. In his more recent films Özpetek has moved away from depictions of Turkey. Notably the stories and cast are very Italian and *Loose Cannons* was his first film to not feature the Turkish actress Serra Yılmaz; yet the film shows the possibility of European films becoming transnational when raising pan-global issues of themes such as familial expectations.

Robert Manning

Soul Kitchen

Studios:

Corazon International
Dorje Film
Norddeutscher Rundfunk (NDR)
Pyramide Productions

Director:

Fatih Akın

Producers:

Fatih Akın
Ann-Kristin Homann
Klaus Maeck

Screenwriters:

Fatih Akın
Adam Bousdoukos

Cinematographer:

Rainer Klausmann

Art Director:

Seth Turner

Composer:

Pia Hoffmann

Editor:

Andrew Bird

Duration:

99 Minutes

Cast:

Adam Bousdoukos
Moritz Bleibtreu
Birol Ünel
Anna Bederke

Year:

2009

Synopsis

Zinos runs a restaurant called Soul Kitchen. His girlfriend Nadine is going to work in China and Zinos has the intention of joining her there at a later date. When Zinos' brother Illias is released from prison he gives him a job at his restaurant. An old school friend, Thomas Neumann, hopes to buy the restaurant from Zinos and reports him to environmental health in a bid to get a better deal. Zinos hires a new chef and the restaurant's popularity grows. After hurting his back, and running into difficulties with the tax office, Zinos decides to go to China leaving his brother in charge of the restaurant, but at the airport he meets Nadine with a new boyfriend; she has returned to Germany after the death of her grandmother. Abandoning his plans to go to China, Zinos returns to the restaurant to find that Illias has lost the restaurant to Thomas during a game of poker. Attempting to steal back the deeds before they are registered with the land registry, Zinos and Illias are arrested and Illias returns to prison. After Neumann is put in prison for tax evasion, Zinos borrows the money from Nadine to buy back his restaurant and spends Christmas there with his physiotherapist.

Critique

Soul Kitchen is a marked change of genre for director Fatih Akın. There are similarities, in that many actors from his previous works appear – Adam Bousdoukos (*Head-On* [2004], *Solino* [2002]); Moritz Bleibtreu (*Solino*, *In July* [2000]; Birol Ünel (*Head-On*, *In July*) – and that the film portrays characters of other nationalities living in Germany. But the change here is that being of Turkish or Greek descent is not an issue. Comparing the issue raised in Akın's more dramatic works, it could be expected that the 'foreigner' abroad could provide many farcical or slapstick elements in a comedy, but the foreigner issue is relatively irrelevant in a comedy about Zinos, who tries his best but life and other peoples actions get in the way. What could so easily be a film about stereotypical foreign characters turns into something much more thoughtful. The nationalities of the characters is incidental and it is indeed a very modern look at Europe where national borders are frequently merged to produce a land populated by people with the same dreams, aspirations and problems, rendering the nationality a non-issue yet, at the same time, appealing to all cultures.

Interestingly, Akın's works highlight the muddled identity of second-generation immigrants and while the second-generation theme is continued within *Soul Kitchen*, this is just treated as an aside rather than an issue. The film is about the life events that befall the well-meaning protagonist at a key period in his life when everything changes but, in the end, returns to how it began. During the first act he is preparing to join his girlfriend in a foreign land, but he endures a back problem, a break up with his girlfriend, and his brother's unexpected release from prison, and the loss of his restaurant. At the end of the film, his back problem is sorted, his brother is once more in prison, he gets his restaurant back and he has a new girlfriend. His efforts to salvage the relationship go awry with farcical results (the cybersex scene is as funny as it is unforgettable). The moral of the tale could be easily borrowed from the Wizard of Oz: 'If I ever go looking for my heart's desire I won't look further than my own backyard' as the audience is carried toward a happy, if somewhat conventional, ending.

Akın co-wrote the script with lead Adam Bousdoukos, who has claimed that the idea is based on his own experiences of running a restaurant. Bousdoukos is of Greek parentage and raised in Germany, indicating that he would have had similar experiences to Akın of the split identity promoted from growing up in a culturally-different country from one's parents'. The script benefits from this unique pairing in that, comedy aside, the love- and life story portrayed is effective and raises it to the standard of Akın's more dramatic and perhaps pessimistic films. Perhaps the writing partnership has also resulted in the pared-down ending; fans of Akın's previous works may be left unsatisfied by the ending, which is tied up perhaps too neatly for all of the characters, but this is more than likely a result of the genre in which the film is placed. Also of note is that the female characters in the film, whilst acting as catalysts for many of the situations within the film, are relegated to smaller roles with less substance; following the strong female leads in *Head-On* and *Edge of Heaven* (2007); their absence is noticeable, but without reducing the effect of the film, especially in a completely different genre. Considering *Soul Kitchen* in relation to Akın's other works, in one respect it makes a refreshing change for the nationality to be less of an issue, rather than being the central axis of the narrative. Yet the depth of character of the protagonists in, for example *Head-On* is missing in *Soul Kitchen*. However, these minor criticisms are negligible in a work that shows another side to a director that interestingly shows how his Turkish-German heritage has contributed to films populated by characters that deftly portray identity, and loss of it, in an excellent manner.

Robert Manning

Soul Kitchen, 2009, Adam Bousdoukos/Birol Ünel, Fatih Akın © Corazon International.

The Turkish Bath

Hamam

Studios:

Sorpasso Films
Promete Film
Asbrell Productions

Director:

Ferzan Özpetek

Producers:

Marco Risi
Maurizio Tedesco

Screenwriters:

Ferzan Özpetek
Stefano Tummolini
Aldo Sambrell

Synopsis

Franceso lives in Italy with his wife. When his aunt dies in Turkey he goes to sort out her estate. Upon arriving he finds that she owned a Turkish bath or Hamam and he decides to stay on to restore and re-open it, antagonizing a developer in so doing. He moves in with the family that cared for his aunt, and a friendship with their son Mehmet develops into something more. Francesco's wife Marta comes to stay and catches Francesco kissing Mehmet. During the subsequent meal she reveals that she has been having an affair with their friend Paolo for two years. Marta stays in İstanbul but moves out of Francesco's home. Reading the letters returned from Francesco's Mother to his aunt, Marta begins to piece together why his aunt left Italy for İstanbul and understands the love she felt for the city. Francesco is fatally stabbed on the steps to the bath. Finding herself repeating the transition that happened to Francesco's aunt, Marta decides to stay on in İstanbul.

Critique

Hamam is Ferzan Özpetek's first feature and portrays perfectly the merging of two cultures. In fact, the film spoon-feeds the culture to a global audience. In his latter films he would move away from

Cinematographer:
Pasquale Mari

Art Directors:
Ziya Ulkenciler
Virginia Vianello

Composers:
Aldo De Scalzi
Pivio

Editor:
Mauro Bonanni

Duration:
94 Minutes

Cast:
Alessandro Gassman
Mehmet Günsür
Francesca d'Aloja

Year:
1997

depictions of Turkey, yet many of the sensibilities of the characters are distinctly Turkish. It shows the integration of the Italians into the Turkish culture and is also a prime example of transnational cinema in that it is co-funded by two different European countries. It also has a distinct Turkish identity, yet the film itself is about the blurring of national identities. The film is actually Özpetek's life in reverse in that he moved from İstanbul to Italy to pursue his chosen career. Francesco, in the film, moves to Turkey to carry out business, but then finds that he is more fulfilled in Turkey and chooses to stay there. In fact, many of the Özpetek traits that would be recurring themes in his later works are to be found in *Hamam*: the fluidity of sexuality is dealt with in Fransesco's relationship with Mehmet; the 'revelation at the dinner table' is a key scene in the film; and the recurring theme of belonging, often written about when considering Turkish cinema, but particularly prevalent in Özpetek's work. The absent family provokes the protagonist to find a substitute family, provoking a quasi-incestuous relationship with Mehmet. Ironically the family is so oblivious to this potential homosexual relationship that, when Francesco's wife wants to separate from Francesco, Mehmet's mother innocently suggests that if they need some space then Francesco can share Mehmet's bedroom. Interestingly, this is the heart of *Hamam*: like his aunt before him, Francesco moves from the, perhaps, more liberal Europe, where he is constrained by the life he has created, yet he feels more able to explore his sexuality in the less-liberal Turkey. The family Francesco lives with are highlighted as being traditional when they want their 20-year-old daughter to marry so as not to miss her chance. Yet these cultural constraints provide the freedom for Francesco and Mehmet to conduct their affair without suspicion. In the eyes of their family, and perhaps local society, it seems out of the question that they could be homosexual. The everyday homo-social bonds that blur the borders of homoeroticism of the overly-masculine cultures provide the perfect disguise for the homosexual relationship to flourish.

Through Francesco, the film appears to be about finding yourself, and somewhere you can be happy spiritually, and is about taking a break from your life to find out what really matters. Like many of Özpetek's films, not least *Loose Cannons* (2010), the death of a pivotal character provides the catalyst for self discovery and freedom for others. This is explored in detail in *Sacred Heart/Cuore Sacro* (2005), *The Ignorant Fairies/Le Fate Ignoranti* (2001) and in *Opposition/Saturno Contro* (2007), as in *Hamam*. The underlying theme is that people in your life can make it a richer experience, but also they can act as shackles that inhibit a full life. Before dying Francesco found this. However, most interesting is the story of Marta. In the first half of the film her role is very small but, when she arrives in İstanbul, her journey is as interesting as Francesco's. She has more to return to in Italy: a good career, Paolo her lover and a luxury apartment and comfortable lifestyle. Her journey in Turkey makes her realize that the superficial gains have not made her as happy as a rich cultural experience. Although this journey is only explored in the final act through her reading Francesco's aunt's letters and her own experiences, it is this aspect of the film which leaves a lasting impact. Francesco had many reasons for not wanting to return to Italy in that he had a business and lover. Marta's reasons to return to Italy are the same as Francesco's to remain in Turkey, yet the audience is left expecting her to stay after being seduced by the delights of Turkey.

Robert Manning

RECOMMEND

READING AN

Abisel, N (1994) *Türk Sineması Üzerine Yazılar*. Ankara: İmge Yayınevi.

Adanır, O (1994) *Sinemada Anlam ve Anlatım*. İzmir: Kitle Yayınları.

Akbal Süalp, Z T (2010) 'Geniş zamanlı tarihin şiiri', in A Doğan Topçu (ed.) *Derviş Zaim Sineması: Toplumsalın Eleştirisinden Geleneğin Estetiğine Yolculuk*. Ankara: De Ki Yayınları, pp. 10-25.

Akbulut, H (2005) *Nuri Bilge Ceylan Sinemasını Okumak: Anlatı, Zaman, Mekân*. İstanbul: Bağla,.

Akser, M (2010) *Green Pine Resurrected: Film Genre, Parody and Intertextuality in Turkish Cinema*. Lampert Publishing.

Algan, N (1996) '80 Sonrasında Türk Sinemasında Estetik ve İdeoloji', 25.*Kare*, 16: 5-8.

Altınsay, İ (1984) 'Sinemamızın Son Dönemi Üzerine Notlar I', *Yeni Olgu*, vol. 3 (9): 21-48.

And, M (2001) 'Tiyatro Karikatürler Geleneği,' *Popüler Tarih*, no: 10, March:98-99.

Armes, R (1981) 'Yilmaz Guney: The Limits of Individual Action', *Framework*, Summer.

Arslan, S (2011) *Cinema in Turkey: A New Critical History*, Oxford and New York: Oxford University Press.

Atakav. E (2012) *Women and Turkish Cinema: Gender Politics, Cultural Identity and Representation*. London and New York: Routledge.

Atakav, E (2011) '"There are ghosts in these houses!" On New Turkish Cinema: Belonging, Identity and Memory', *Inter-Asia Cultural Studies*, Vol. 12, No. 1: 139-144.

Atakav. E (2011) 'Cinema in Turkey: a New Critical History', *Screen*, Vol. 52, No.4: 535-537.

Avcı, Z (1984) 'Türk Sineması Kadına Bakıyor mu?', *Videosinema*, vol. 5: 65-66.

Balan, C (2008) 'Wondrous Pictures in İstanbul: From Cosmopolitanism to Nationalism', in Richard Abel, Giorgio Bertellini & Rob King (eds), *Early Cinema and the 'National'*. New Barnet: John Libbey Publishing, pp. 172-185.

Bayrakdar, D (1996) 'Mother-Daughter Relationship in the Family Melodrama', in N Dakovic, D Derman & K Ross (eds) *Gender and Media*. Ankara: Med-Campus Publications.

Bayrakdar, D (ed) (2003) *Türk Film Araştırmalarında Yeni Yönelimler 3. Karşılaşmalar*. İstanbul: Bağlam Yayıncılık.

Bayrakdar, D (ed) (2004) *Türk Film Araştırmalarında Yeni Yönelimler 4. Türk Sineması Hayali Vatanımız*. İstanbul: Bağlam Yayıncılık.

Bayrakdar, D (ed) (2006) *Türk Film Araştırmalarında Yeni Yönelimler 5. Sinema ve Tarih*. İstanbul: Bağlam Yayıncılık.

ED

RESOURCES

Bayrakdar, D (ed) (2009) *Cinema and Politics: Turkish Cinema and The New Europe*, Newcastle: Cambridge Scholars Publishing.
Bilgiç, F (1998) *Türk Sinemasında 1980 Sonrası Üslup Arayışları*. Dokuz Eylül Üniversitesi, Sosyal Bilimler Enstitüsü, Sinema, Televizyon ve Fotoğrafçılık Anasanat Dalı, İzmir, (PhD thesis).
Çeliktemel-Thomen, Ö (2010) 'Osmanlı İmparatorluğu'nda Sinema ve Propaganda, 1908-1922', *Kurgu Online International Journal of Communication Studies*, June 2010, vol: 2:1-17, Eskişehir: Anadolu University.
Christodolou, C K (1997) *The Manakis Brothers, The Greek Pionneers of the Balkanic Cinema*, Thessaloniki: Organization for the Cultural Capital of Europe.
Derman, D (1996) 'Mother and Daughter Relationship in the Family Melodrama: *Teyzem*' in N Dakovic, D Derman & K Ross (eds) *Gender and Media*. Ankara: Med-Campus Publications.
Dönmez-Colin, G (2008) *Turkish Cinema: Identity, Distance and Belonging*. London: Reaktion Books.
Dorsay A and Ayça, E (1973) 'Bedia Muvahhit ile Konuşma', *Yedinci Sanat*, No: 9: 90.
Dorsay, A (1984) 'Sinemamızda Yeni Cinsellik ve Özgür Kadın Tipi', Gösteri, No: 49: 58-60.
Eleftheriotis, D (2006) 'Turkish National Cinema', in Dimitris Eleftheriotis & Gary Needham (eds) *Asian Cinemas: A Reader & Guide*. Edinburgh: Edinburgh University Press, pp. 220-28.
Erdoğan, N (2006) 'Narratives of Resistance: national identity and ambivalence in the Turkish melodrama between 1965 and 1975', in C Grant, & A Kuhn, (eds) *Screening World Cinema*. Oxon and New York: Routledge.
Erdoğan, N (1998) 'Narratives of Resistance: National Identity and Ambivalence in the Turkish Melodrama between 1965 and 1975', *Screen*, vol. 39, no. 3: 259-71.
Erdoğan, N (2003) 'Powerless Signs: Hybridity and the Logic of Excess of Turkish Trash' in Karen Ross, Brenda Dervin & Deniz Derman (eds) *Mapping the Margins: Identity Politics and the Media*, Creskil: Hampton Press , pp.163-76.
Erdoğan, N (2004) 'The Making of Our America: Hollywood in a Turkish Context', in Melvyn Stokes & Richard Maltby (eds) *Hollywood Abroad*. London: BFI, pp. 121-32.
Erdoğan, N and Göktürk, D (2011) 'Turkish Cinema', in Oliver Leaman (ed) *Companion Encyclopaedia of Middle Eastern and North African Film*. London: Routledge, pp. 533-73.
Erdoğan, N and Kaya, D (2002) 'Institutional Intervention in the Distribution and Exhibition of Hollywood Films in Turkey', *Historical Journal of Film, Radio and Television*, vol. 22, no.1, pp. 47-59.

Esen, Ş (2000) *80'ler Türkiye'sinde Sinema*. İstanbul: Beta.

Evren, B (1998) *Türk sinemasında Yeni Konumlar*. İstanbul: Broy Yayınları.

Gibbons, F (2004) 'We know we can live together', *The Guardian*, 1 May, Available at http://www.guardian.co.uk/film/2004/may/01/books.featuresreviews/, accessed 3 Oct 2011.

Girelli, E (2007) 'Transnational Orientalism: Ferzan Özpetek's Turkish Dream in Hamam (1997)', *New Cinemas: Journal of Contemporary Film* Vol. 5 No. 1: 23-28.

Güçlü, Ö (2010) 'Silent Representations of Women in the New Cinema of Turkey', *Sine/Cine: Journal of Film Studies*, vol. 1, No. 2, Autumn: 71-85.

Gürata, A (2006) 'Translating Modernity: Remakes in Turkish Cinema', in Dimitris Eleftheoritis & Gary Needham (eds) *Asian Cinemas: A Reader and Guide*, Edinburgh: Edinburgh University Press, pp. 242-54.

Güvemli, Z (1960) *Sinema Tarihi Başlangıcından Günümüze Türk ve Dünya Sineması*, İstanbul: Varlık Yayınevi.

İ G [İ Galip Arcan] (1919) 'Mürebbiye Filmi', *Temaşa* 17, 1 June: 1-2.

Işın E F (2010) 'The Soul of a City: Hüzün, Keyif, Longing', in D Göktürk, L Soysal, & İ Türeli, *Orienting İstanbul. Cultural Capital of Europe?* (eds) London and New York: Routledge, pp. 35-51.

Jaafar, A (2007) 'Snow Better Blues', *Sight and Sound*, February: 25.

Kalkan F and Taranç R (1988) *1980 Sonrası Türk Sinemasında Kadın*. İzmir: Ajans Tümer Yayınları.

Kayalı, K (2006) Yönetmenler Çerçevesinde Türk Sineması. Ankara: Deniz Yayınları.

Kır, S (2010) *İstanbul'un 100 Filmi. İstanbul'un Yüzleri Serisi- 8*. İstanbul: İstanbul Büyükşehir Belediyesi Kültür A.Ş. Yayınları.

Köksal, Ö (2012) *World Film Locations: İstanbul*. Bristol: Intellect.

Maktav, H (2000) 'Türk Sinemasında 12 Eylül', *Birikim*, No: 138: 79-84.

Margulies, R (ed) (1997) *Manastır'da İlân-ı Hürriyet*. İstanbul: Yapı Kredi Yayınları.

Onaran, O (1994) 'Türk Sinemasında Anlatı Üstüne Bir Deneme', 25. Kare. 8: 30-34.

Özen, S (2012) 'Balkanların'ın İlk Sinemacıları mı? Manaki Biraderler', *Toplumsal Tarih 219*, March: 60-67.

Özen, S (2012) 'Manakilerin Objektifinden Hürriyet', *Toplumsal Tarih 220*, April: 50-57.

Özön, N (1962) *Türk Sineması Tarihi (Dünden Bugüne) 1896-1960*. İstanbul: Artist Sinema Ortaklığı Yayınları.

Özön, N (1970) *İlk Türk Sinemacısı Fuat Uzkınay*. Türk Sinematek Yayınları,.

Özgüç, A (1993) *100 Filmde Başlangıcından Günümüze Türk Sineması*. İstanbul and Ankara: Bilgi Yayınevi.

Özgüç, A (1990) *Başlangıcından Bugüne Türk Sinemasında İlk'ler*. İstanbul: Yılmaz Yayınları.

Özgüç, A (1998a) *Türk Filmleri Sözlüğü: 1914-1973*. İstanbul: Sesam.

Özgüç, A (1988b) *Türk Sinemasında Cinselliğin Tarihi*. İstanbul: Broy Yayınları.

Özkaracalar, K (2003) 'Between Appropriation and Innovation: Turkish Horror Cinema', in Steven J Schneider (ed) *Fear Without Frontiers: Horror Cinema Across the Globe*. Guildford: FABPress, pp. 205-17.

Özön, N (1970) *İlk Türk Sinemacısı: Fuat Uzkınay*. İstanbul: TSD Yayınları.

Öztürk, S R (2004) *Sinemanın Dişil Yüzü: Türkiye'de Kadın Yönetmenler*. İstanbul: Om Yayınevi.

Prime Ministry Ottoman Archives (1919) DH.EUM.AYŞ, 2/2, 21 C 1337.

Robins, K and Aksoy, A (2000) 'Deep Nation: The National Question and Turkish Cinema Culture', in Mette Hjort & Scott Mackenzie (eds) *Cinema and Nation.* London: Routledge, pp. 203-21.

Scognamillo, G (1990) *Türk Sinema Tarihi*, Birinci Cilt, 1896-1959, İstanbul: Metis Yayınları.

Scognamillo, G (2003) *Türk Sinema Tarihi.* İstanbul: Kabalcı Yayınevi.

Scognamillo, G and Demirhan, M (1999) *Fantastik Turk Sinemas.* İstanbul: Kabalcı Yaynevi.

Şener, E (1970) *Kurtuluş Savaşı ve Sinemamız.* İstanbul: Ahmet Sarı Matbaası.

Simpson, C (2006) 'Turkish Cinema's Resurgence: The "Deep Nation" Unravels', *Senses of Cinema*, vol. 39.

Smith, I R (2008a) 'Beam me up, Ömer: Transnational media flow and the cultural politics of the Turkish Star Trek remake', *Velvet Light Trap* vol. 61: 3-13.

Smith, I R (2008b) 'The Exorcist in İstanbul: Processes of transcultural appropriation within Turkish Popular Cinema', *Portal: Journal of Multidisciplinary International Studies* vol. 5 no.1.

Stardelov, I (2003) *Manaki.* Skopje: Kinoteka na Makedonija.

Suner, A (2007) 'Cinema without Frontiers: Transnational Women's Filmmaking in Iran and Turkey', in K Marciniak, A Imre & Á O'Healy (eds) *Transnational Feminism in Film and Media.* New York & Basingstoke: Palgrave Macmillan.

Suner, A (2006) *Hayalet Ev: Yeni Türk Sinemasında Aidiyet, Kimlik ve Bellek.* İstanbul: Metis Yayınları.

Suner, A (2010) *New Turkish Cinema: Belonging, Identity and Memory.* London: I B Tauris.

Taş, A (2001) *1960'lardan 1990'lara Türk Siyasal Sineması.* Marmara Üniversitesi, Sosyal Bilimler Enstitüsü, Radyo, Televizyon ve Sinema Anabilim Dalı, İstanbul, (PhD thesis).

Teksoy, R (2008) *Turkish Cinema* (translated by Martin Thomen and Özde Çeliktemel). İstanbul: Oğlak Yayınları.

Tombs, P and Scognamillo, G (1998) 'Dracula in İstanbul: Turkey' in Pete Tombs (ed) *Mondo Macabro: Weird and Wonderful Cinema Around the World.* New York: St Martin's Press, pp. 102-15.

Tunalı, D (2005) *Batıdan Doğuya, Hollywood'dan Yeşilçam'a Melodram* (Melodrama from West to East, Hollywood to Yeşilçam). Ankara: Asina Books.

Tutui, M (2011) *Orient Express: The Romanian and Balkan Cinema.* Bucharest: Noi Media Print.

Woodhead, C (ed) (1989) *Turkish Cinema: An Introduction.* London: SOAS.

Yalçınkaya, C (2011) 'Never my soul: Adaptations, Re-makes and Re-imaginings of Yeşilçam Cinema', *Refractory: A Journal of Entertainment Media*, vol. 18.

Zaim, D, Sönmez, R and Tutumluer, S (2007) 'Sinema sanatının seyirciyle barışık olması gerektiğine inanıyorum', in B D Özdoğan & A Oğuz (eds) *Sinema Söyleşileri: Boğaziçi Üniversitesi Mithat Alam Film Merkezi Söyleşi, Panel ve Sunum Yıllığı, 2006.* İstanbul: Boğaziçi Üniversitesi Yayınevi, pp. 71-88.

TURKISH CINEMA ONLINE

Altyazı
http://www.altyazi.net
The website for the prestigious film journal. The website provides a range of reviews, blog entries in addition to discussion forums, a film archive and interviews with film-makers.

Association of Documentary Film-makers in Turkey
http://www.bsb.org.tr/english.html
Established in 1997 the Association includes freelance film-makers, private production companies, documentary makers at Turkish Radio and Television, university professors, and film students throughout Turkey.

Cine Shadow
http://cineshadow.wordpress.com/
This blog features Turkish films, directors, festivals, actors, statistics, film criticism, audience and media reception, film history, and all other aspects of Turkish cinema; it is led by graduate students of the Faculty of Art, Design and Architecture at Bilkent University in Ankara.

Directory of World Cinema
http://worldcinemadirectory.co.uk/
The website for the Directory of World Cinema series featuring film reviews and biographies of directors.

General Directorate of Cinema
http://www.sinema.gov.tr
Supported by the Ministry of Culture and Tourism, the General Directorate of Cinema in Turkey supports film production, archiving of films and collaborates with other national and international

Internet Movie Database
http://www.imdb.com

Source of information for cinema and industry news which provides the reader with detailed information of films, film-makers, actors and actresses.

Nuri Bilge Ceylan
http://www.nuribilgeceylan.com/
This is the official website of the director that provides detailed information on his films, biography and news about his films.

Öteki Sinema
http://www.otekisinema.com/
An online platform that is dedicated to the 'lovers of bad films'. Literally meaning 'the other cinema', this website provides the reader with reviews and posters of B-films, Yeşilçam films as well as the exploitation films of the 1970s.

Sine/Cine: Journal of Film Studies
http://www.sinecine.org/
This is the website for the peer-reviewed journal of film studies that publishes articles in Turkish and English on a range of topics.

Sinematürk
http://www.sinematurk.com/
An archive of Turkish cinema online. This website provides reviews as well as production details of films. It can be regarded as the Turkish version of Internet Movie Database. The website also provides the readers with an opportunity to comment on and create a discussion environment about films.

Turkish Cinema Newsletter
http://turkfilm.blogspot.co.uk/
The website is a useful resource providing a detailed list of production companies in Turkey. It

Turkish Cult
http://turkishcult.net/site/
The website was established in 2009 by a group of cult film fans, with the aim of introducing Turkish cult movies to audiences from around the world.

Turkish Film Channel
http://turkishfilmchannel.com/blog/
The blog provides news about recent Turkish films. It also provides reviews of films.

Turkish Film Council
http://www.turkishfilmcouncil.com/
The Turkish Film Council's aims are to connect Turkish film professionals with their counterparts abroad; to present Istanbul in particular and Turkey in general as a film shooting location to visiting film-makers; and to increase film production in Turkey. The website offers news and reviews as well as a list of production companies film-makers may work with.

Yeşim Ustaoğlu
http://www.ustaoglufilm.com

This is the official website of the director that provides detailed information on her films, biography and news about his films.

Zeki Demirkubuz
http://zekidemirkubuz.com/
This is the official website of the director that provides detailed information on her films, biography and news about his films.

Festivals

Amsterdam Turkish film festival
http://atff.nl/
In its third year, the festival is proving to be popular. It reached more than 6000 spectators during the years of 2010 and 2011.

Ankara International Film Festival
http://www.filmfestankara.org.tr
In its twenty-fourth year, the festival showcases and awards the works of film-makers from around the world.

Boston Turkish Film Festival
http://www.bostonturkishfilmfestival.org/
The website dedicated to the festival which is on its eleventh year as of 2012. Turkish films have indeed been screened under the Boston Turkish Arts and Culture Festival for the last seventeen years.

Flying Broom International Women's Film Festival
http://festival.ucansupurge.org
The website for the festival, which has been running for the last fifteen years in Ankara, celebrating the work of women film-makers from around the world.

International Antalya Golden Orange Film Festival
http://www.altinportakal.org.tr/en/index.html
The Antalya Golden Orange Film Festival is one of the oldest and the longest running film festivals in Turkey, running since the mid-1950s.

Istanbul International Film Festival
http://film.iksv.org/
The website for the festival, on its 32 years, which aims to encourage the development of cinema in Turkey; to promote films of quality in the Turkish market; and to introduce international film institutions to the Turkish cinema industry.

Izmir International Short Film Festival
http://www.izmirkisafilm.org/
The website for the festival, which has been running successfully since 2000. Along with the competition programme, the short film programme presents carefully-selected films from around the world and screenings are supported by Q&A sessions, panel discussions and workshops to the benefit of artists and audience, creating an important meeting point between film-makers and the audience.

London Turkish Film Festival
http://www.ltff.co.uk/
Since 1993 the festival brings together the work of Turkish film-makers every year. It offers a variety of awards and a prestigious competition. The festival enables those in the United Kingdom to watch films from Turkey. It also offers Q&A sessions with directors, actors and actresses as well as the crew members of films.

Los Angeles Turkish Film Festival
http://www.latff.org/
The website for the festival. The purpose of LATFF is to promote awareness of Turkish Cinema on the West Coast of the US and to provide networking opportunities among film-makers. The festival showcases the work of Turkish film-makers in Los Angeles.

Miami Turkish Film Festival
http://miamiturkishfilmfestival.com/
Running for the last two years, the festival is proving to be already well known for its exhibition in Miami of popular Turkish films.

New York Turkish Film Festival
http://www.newyorkturkishfilmfestival.com/
The website for the festival which has been running in New York since 2006.

TEST YOUR KNOWLEDGE

1. What is Yeşilçam?
2. What is the name of the long running international women's film festival in Turkey?
3. What is the name of the Turkish actress widely known as 'Sultan'?
4. In which film does Nuri Bilge Ceylan co-stars with his wife Ebru Ceylan?
5. Who, in the Turkish film industry, is known as the director of women's films?
6. What is the name of the actor who often collaborated with director Yavuz Turgul?
7. In Turkish films, where does Bosporus refer to?
8. Name three recent films that take the 1980 coup as central to their narrative.
9. Who is the famous stand-up comedian who also made the sci-fi film GORA?
10. What is the name of the comedian who also starred in Nuri Bilge Ceylan's *Once Upon a Time in Anatolia*?
11. What was the title of Nuri Bilge Ceylan's first feature film?
12. What is the title of the film to which Orhan Pamuk dedicates a chapter in his *Black Book*?
13. What is the name of the director who made the cult film *Time to Love*?
14. What is the title of the film in which Fatih Akin explores the music scene in Istanbul?
15. The film *The Bandit* is considered to be the pioneer of a series of films considered as 'new Turkish cinema'. Who is the director of this film?
16. Which film has won the prestigious Lion of the Future Award in 2010 at Venice Film Festival?
17. Which film refers to Marlon Brando in its title?
18. Which Yeşim Ustaoğlu film won the 49th Berlin International Film Festival's Blue Angel Award?
19. Who is the well-known theatre actress who stars in *Vizontele, Eyvah Eyvah, Eyvah Eyvah 2, Bastards and Kurtuluş Last Stop*?
20. Which film tells the story of the little boy Barış, who lives with his mother in prison?

21. Who is the screenwriter of *Don't Let them Shoot the Kite*?
22. Which film is Ferzan Özpetek's first feature film?
23. Which film tells the story of the arrival of television in Eastern Turkey?
24. Which documentary film by Eylem Kaftan focuses on 'honour crimes' in Turkey?
25. Which 1980s' film, starring Müjde Ar, focuses on the lives of prostitutes?
26. In which Atıf Yılmaz film does Türkan Şoray star as Mine?
27. What genre of films is Cüneyt Arkın known for?
28. Which actor is known for his Ömer the Tourist character?
29. In which film does Zuhal Olcay plays the documentary film-maker who gives up her marriage to pursue her career?
30. Which film won the 2011 Grand Prix Award at the Cannes Film Festival?
31. Which film starts with a scene of the suicide of a comedian in a Superman costume?
32. Who won the Palme D'Or at the 1982 Cannes Film Festival with his film *The Road*?
33. Which comedy film adopts a Western style to tell the fake story of two Ottoman agents' journey to America?
34. Which film, starring Özgü Namal as the Meryem character, focuses on 'honour' crimes?
35. In 2008, at the Cannes Film Festival, who won the Best Director award and with which film?
36. Who directed the 2009 film *Soul Kitchen*?
37. Which film won the 1964 Golden Bear award at the Berlin Film Festival?
38. Which fantasy film is a reworking of *Captain America*?
39. Which 2004 sci-fi film stars Cem Yılmaz as Arif?
40. Which company is the distributor for Yavuz Turgul's 2010 film *The Hunting Season*?
41. Who directed *After Yesterday Before Tomorrow*?
42. Which is the most popular city in Turkish cinema?
43. When was Ankara International Film Festival founded?
44. In which city does the Flying Broom International Women's Film Festival take place?
45. What is the title of the 2008 blockbuster film that tells the story of a macho man who tries to win the heart of his childhood love?
46. *Bliss* is adapted from a novel. Who is the author of the novel of the same title?
47. Which production company made *Vizontele* and *Vizontele Tuuba*?
48. Name three concepts that new Turkish cinema focuses on, particularly since the 1990s.
49. What is the title of the short documentary by Yeşim Ustaoğlu that focuses on the lives of women and the seasonal migration that takes place in the Black Sea region?
50. Which film was Derviş Zaim's feature debut?

Answers

1. A metonym similar to Hollywood, which is used by the film industry in Turkey, to refer to popular cinema
2. Flying Broom
3. Türkan Şoray
4. *Climates*
5. Atıf Yılmaz
6. Şener Şen
7. Istanbul
8. *My Father and My Son, Bastards, The International*
9. Cem Yılmaz
10. Yılmaz Erdoğan
11. *The Small Town*
12. *My Licensed Beloved*
13. Metin Erksan
14. *Crossing the Bridge*
15. Yavuz Turgul
16. *Majority*
17. *To Go: My Marlon and Brando*
18. *Journey to the Sun*
19. Demet Akbağ
20. *Don't Let them Shoot the Kite*
21. Feride Çiçekoğlu
22. *The Turkish Bath*
23. *Vizontele*
24. *Vendetta Song*
25. *How can Asiye Survive?*
26. *Mine*
27. Fantasy
28. Ayhan Işık
29. *After Yesterday Before Tomorrow*
30. *Once Upon a Time in Anatolia*
31. *Magic Carpet Ride*
32. Yılmaz Güney
33. *The Mild West*
34. *Bliss*
35. Nuri Bilge Ceylan – *Three Monkeys*
36. Fatih Akın
37. *Dry Summer*
38. *Three Mighty Men*
39. *GORA: A Space Story*
40. Warner Bros
41. Nisan Akman
42. Istanbul
43. 1988
44. Ankara
45. Recep Ivedik
46. Zülfü Livaneli
47. BKM
48. Identity, memory, trauma
49. *Life on their Shoulders*
50. *Somersault in a Coffin*

NOTES ON CONTRIBUTORS

The Editor

Eylem Atakav is a Lecturer in Film and Television Studies at the University of East Anglia, where she teaches courses on world cinemas; women and film; women, Islam and the media. She is the author of *Women and Turkish Cinema: Gender Politics, Cultural Identity and Representation* (2012). She is currently working on two edited collections: *Women and Contemporary World Cinema* (with Karen Randell) and *From Smut to Softcore: Sex and the 1970s World Cinema* (with Andy Willis).

Contributors

Hasan Akbulut is an Associate Professor and the Chair of the Department of Radio, Television and Cinema at Kocaeli University. He teaches film theories, film analysis, dramaturgy, visual culture and media literacy. His articles on Turkish cinema, melodrama, representation and women, 'art' cinema and film reviews like *Persona, Far From Heaven* and *Ararat* have appeared in journals and anthologies. He is member of editorial board of *sinecine: journal of film studies*. His books include Nuri *Bilge Ceylan Sinemasını Okumak: Anlatı, Zaman, Mekân* (*Reading Nuri Bilge Ceylan's Cinema*, 2005), *Kadına Melodram Yakışır* (*Melodram suitable for Women*, 2008) which received the best cinema book prize (Anadolu Üniversitesi, 2008) and *Yumurta: Ruha Yolculuk* (*Egg: Journey to Soul*, 2009) with Seçil Büker.

Murat Akser is an Assistant Professor of Media Studies in Department of Film and Television at Kadir Has University İstanbul, Turkey. His MA is in Film and his PhD in Communication and Culture from York University, Toronto, Canada. He has published articles on film parody and political film in various publications including *Canadian Journal of Film Studies* and has a recent chapter in an edited volume *Film and Politics*. He is the author of *Green Pine Resurrected: Film Genre, Parody and Intertextuality in Turkish Cinema* (2010).

Cihat Arınç is a writer and academic researcher based in London. He is currently a PhD candidate in the Department of Visual Cultures at Goldsmiths College, University of London. He has studied film at İstanbul University and received a master's degree in the philosophy of film at Boğaziçi University. His research focuses on the spectral medium of cinema as a time-based technology of memory revealing self-reflexive processes in documentation. His research interests include focusing on the mnemopolitics of film around the themes of displacement, narration and haunting: contemporary film theory, documentary, biopic, video oral history, experimental video essay, auto-ethnographic film, historical narrative cinema, and contemporary film cultures in Turkey.

Savaş Arslan is Associate Professor of Film and Television Studies at Bahçeşehir University in İstanbul. He is the author of *Cinema in Turkey: A New Critical History* (2011) and the co-editor of *Media, Culture and Identity in Europe* and the author of *Melodrama* (in Turkish).

Canan Balan is an assistant professor in the Film and Television department at İstanbul Şehir University. She received her PhD degree from the University of St Andrews with a dissertation on early cinema spectatorship in İstanbul. She has published articles on early cinema, shadow-play and the cinematic representations of İstanbul.

Deniz Bayrakdar is the dean of the Communication Faculty, Kadir Has University, İstanbul, Turkey and chair of the Film and TV and New Media MA programmes. She teaches European Cinemas and Cities and Cinema at the Department of Radio, Film and Television. She was the coordinator of the local organization committee of the IAMCR 2011 in İstanbul. She has organized the Turkish Film Studies Conference since 1998 and published eight edited volumes of the series. Her publications include *Cinema and Politics* (2009); *Mapping the Margins: Identity Politics and the Media* (2006) with Karen Ross.

Funda Can Çuvalcı graduated from the department of American Culture and Literature at Hacettepe University in 2002. She completed an MA degree at Anadolu University in the Department of Cinema and TV in 2007. Currently, she is teaching English and English Literature in a Language School in Eskişehir and continuing her PhD in the Department of Cinema and Television in Anadolu University.

Meltem Cemiloğlu Altunay is an instructor in the Cinema and Television Department at Faculty of Communication Sciences in Anadolu University (Turkey). She graduated from the Department of Cinema and Television at the same university and obtained her MA degree from Anadolu University Graduate School of Social Sciences, where she is working for her doctorate. She is a member of International Eskişehir Film Festival and Communication in the Millenium (CIM) International Symposium organization committee.

Özde Çeliktemel-Thomen received a BA degree in History from Boğaziçi University in 2006 and an MA degree with merit in History at Central European University in 2009. She is currently a PhD candidate at University College London. Her research areas include cinema history, late Ottoman cultural and visual history.

Özlem Güçlü is a PhD candidate in Media and Film Studies at the University of London (SOAS) with a thesis entitled 'Silent Female Characters in the New Cinema of Turkey: Gender, Nation and the Past'. Currently, she works as a research associate in the Sociology Department of Mimar Sinan Fine Arts University in Turkey. She has published articles on the new cinema of Turkey, and recently finished co-editing a special issue on 'Queer' for *Toplumbilim* (2012).

Ali Karadoğan is a Lecturer in the Faculty of Communications at Ankara University, where is doing his PhD, and where he lectures on scriptwriting, Turkish cinema and film history. Karadoğan is the author of three edited collections: *Bir Sinemanın ve Sinemacının Serüveni: Halit Refiğ* (2003), *Bir Yüzün İki Hali: Tarık Akan* (2005) and *Yoksul: Zeki Ökten* (2007). He also contributed to volumes entitled: *Çok Tuhaf Çok Tanıdık:*

Vesikalı Yarim Üzerine; Film Çeviriyorum Abi: Şerif Gören Sinemasında Öykü, Söylem ve Tematik Yapı (2005) and Sinemada Son Adam: Makinist-Ankara Sinemaları Tarihi (2008) with Burçak Evren.

Özlem Köksal received her PhD degree from University of London, Birkbeck College with a thesis on the relationship between memory, history and cinema in Turkey. She is the editor of *World Film Locations: İstanbul* (2012) and currently teaches film and television studies at Bilgi University in İstanbul.

Ayman Kole studied at the University of Sydney, completing a Bachelor of Arts degree with a triple major: English, Performance Studies, and Studies in Religion. He also completed an MA in English in 2006 and wrote the short story *The Mirror*, which was a Phoenix Journal finalist, published by Sydney University Press. He has worked as a writer for various publications and DVD releases concerning Turkish genre films and as a Film & Creative Writing lecturer at Qantm/SAE Institute. He currently is doing a PhD at Charles Sturt University.

Aslı Kotaman is vice manager at Plato School of Media, Art and Design, İstanbul and an Assistant Professor at Plato Meslek Yüksekokulu. She graduated from Marmara University. Her dissertation was entitled: 'Mental Collections: From Yeşilçam to contemporary Tele-novelas'. For much of her academic career, Kotaman has focused on Turkish cinema and Turkish television serials, melodrama and cultural memory. She is the author of several articles on the subjects of Turkish cinema, cultural memory, cinema and the city. Her current academic work addresses the question of religion and how it influences Turkish cinema.

Robert Manning is a PhD student at the University of East Anglia. He is researching the political backdrop to the 'genre' of film noir. His research interests are on Turkish Cinema, representation of gender in film and television as well as the horror genre. He is also an Associate Tutor in the School of Film, Television and Media Studies at the same university.

Sarinah Masukor is a PhD candidate at Monash University in Melbourne, writing on the films of Nuri Bilge Ceylan. She loves slow open takes and shots that look like photographs, and Ceylan's work fuels both of these obsessions. But it is the way he uses editing to surprise that she likes best, finding the leaps in time and space startling every time.

E Nezih Orhon is Professor in the Cinema and Television Department and the dean of School of Communication Sciences at Anadolu University in Eskisehir, Turkey. He regularly produces and publishes research articles on national and international cinemas, as well as taking part in conferences. He teaches film production and directing courses in Turkey and Germany. He is one of the board members of the Eskisehir International Film Festival and co-director of Dialog: Greek-Turkish Short Film Festival.

Saadet Özen is a PhD student at Boğaziçi University, İstanbul. She received her MA at Boğaziçi University, Department of History with her study on the Manaki Brothers' still and moving images during the Young Turk Revolution. She has co-written and co-directed two documentary films, Ankara (2011) and The Last Caliph (2012). Her main area of research is the political use of visuality in the late Ottoman period. She has published a book on the history of the French school Notre Dame de Sion, several translations from French into Turkish and articles both on literature and history.

S Ruken Öztürk is Professor in the Department of Radio, TV & Cinema at Ankara University. She is the author of *Postmodernizm ve Sinema* (co-translated & coauthored, *Postmodernism and Cinema*, 1997), *Sinemada Kadın Olmak* (*Being a Woman in the Cinema*, 2000), *Sinemanın Dişil Yüzü* (*Female Side of the Cinema*, 2004), *Çok Tuhaf Çok Tanıdık* (co-authored, *The Strangely Familiar, The Familiar Estranged*, 2005), and *Zeki Demirkubuz* (2006). She has also written two articles: 'Uzak/Distant' in *The Cinema of North Africa and the Middle East* (ed: G D Colin, 2007), and 'Hard to Bear' in Flavia Laviosa's edited collection entitled *Visions of Struggle in Women's Film-making in the Mediterranean* (2010).

Laurence Raw teaches in the Department of English at Başkent University, Ankara, Turkey. His recent publications include *Exploring Turkish Cultures* (2011), *Adaptation, Translation and Transformation* (2012), and *Merchant-Ivory Interviews* (edited collection, 2012). He is currently working on a book entitled *Six Turkish Film-makers*, to be published by the University of Wisconsin Press.

Iain Robert Smith is a Lecturer in Film Studies at the University of Roehampton, London. He is author of the forthcoming monograph *The Hollywood Meme: Global Adaptations of American Film and Television* (2013) and editor of *Cultural Borrowings: Appropriation, Reworking, Transformation* (2009). He has published articles in a range of journals including *Velvet Light Trap* and *Portal*, and he is currently a co-investigator on the Arts and Humanities Research Council funded research network 'Media Across Borders'.

Todd Stadtman is a regular contributor to the website Teleport City. He also writes about international cult cinema on his blog *Die Danger Die Die Kill!* and for *The Lucha Diaries*, a website that he authored dealing with Mexican luchadore cinema.

Ali Fuat Şengül is a doctoral candidate in the Department of Radio-TV-Film at the University of Texas at Austin where he is currently working on a thesis entitled 'Cinema and the Production of Nation-Space in Turkey'. During his doctoral study Şengül organized and taught social documentary workshops in Turkey. His research interests include theories of cinema, social documentary, experimental film, visual anthropology, and modernization and its visual cultures in the Middle East.

Dilek Tunalı graduated from the Department of Cinema-TV, Faculty of Fine Arts, Dokuz Eylül University. She completed an MA with a thesis entitled 'Researching Historical, Social and Cultural Structuring through Adaptations of Aziz Nesin' in 1996. Her PhD thesis (2005) was entitled 'Impacts of Cultural and Intellectual Structuring on Turkish Melodramatic Cinema'. She has since written *Batıdan Doğuya, Hollywood'dan Yeşilçam'a Melodram* (*Melodrama from West to East, Melodrama from Hollywood to Yeşilçam*, 2006).

David Lee White is a playwright and novelist currently living in New Jersey. His plays include *Blood: a Comedy and Slippery as Sin* and his novel Fantomas in America is available from Black Coat Press. He has also contributed writing to Video Watchdog, including the first full-length article on film-maker Yılmaz Atadeniz in English, co-written with Kaya Özkaracalar. His website is www.davidleewhite.net.

FILMOGRAPHY